Summer Camp, Oshima Island

In 1981, Arthur Meek, aged twenty one, took himself away from the familiarity of his Somerset home to live in the suburbs of Tokyo to train at Nihon University Karate Club.

"Nichi Dai" had a reputation; severe training methods that turned out great fighters.

Could Arthur handle the heat?

Nihon University
Tokyo

Spring 1981

One

The journey had ended as we pulled up outside the grey aged building that sat right on the expressway. It looked bleak, like a disused factory, and at midnight there was no hint to what lay behind the many rows of black windows of the three-story complex. From here on another a kind of journey would begin. This was the dormitory where I was hoping to spend the rest of the year living, training, and 'enjoying' the hospitality of Nihon University Wado Ryu Karate Club.

Kobayashi Sensei helped me with my cases but stopped me at the open doorway,

"Shoes!" he said, the first sign that I had now entered a different culture. I removed mine and copied Kobayashi by putting on a pair of pale blue plastic slippers from the pile scattered around the bottom step. We climbed the three flights of stairs to the second floor and were greeted in the corridor by one or two bleary eyed students in tracksuit bottoms and t-shirts who seemed to be making a real fuss over seeing one of their senior instructors present, bowing, shouting almost, and doing everything at the double. I'm pretty sure it wasn't for my benefit.

We were ushered into a small dining room that had a distinct smell, not unpleasant, a mixture of old furniture with that of Japanese tea and other spices. There was another doorway in the far corner that led to a small kitchen. At this point I felt nervous as Kobayashi barked at the two or three students and they responded on the double by preparing two places at a table. The students eyed me on occasion as if I were to blame for their insomnia, a sort of 'I'll have you later' kind of look. Great start! However, we sat around the table as Kobayashi introduced me to my fellow students. I amused them with my poor Japanese which I had taken time out to study from a phrase book. I amused them further when I produced my Karate licence and showed them who had passed me my first grading five years earlier, none other than Kobayashi who sat a little bemused, struggling to remember when and where etc. I was then served a little food, and whisky, which was hardly welcome, unlike the hot shower that followed.

I had a quick look around the facilities of our abode and primitive would be a fair description. There were three toilet cubicles apart from the urinals and I hadn't seen toilets like that since a school trip to France when I was thirteen. There was no bowl to sit on, just a ceramic hole in the floor. I didn't know which way to face when I was in France and I had no better idea now. I just made sure my feet were well out of the way.

Around one o'clock we turned in, Tanabe Sensei was away so Kobayashi Sensei and myself took his room for the night. I was reminded that running was at six that morning!

For a spring morning it was wet, so much so that early morning training was to be in the dojo rather than the nearby park. Even though it was early after an excited late night I was filled with even more excitement and a little nervousness as I was able to view the opposition so to speak. I followed Kobayashi down the stairs, donned my trainers and stepped out on to the street where the rest had all lined up to greet us with a loud,

"Ohayo gozaimasu!" (Good morning). Kobayashi led us into a gateway around the side of our dormitory block into a small car park where we had parked the car the previous night. What I hadn't noticed the night before was the Karate dojo that was set back some twenty metres from the roadside. Unlike the old dormitory building it had a newness in its wooden construction and as we were led barefoot inside the immaculate wooden floor glimmered with our reflections as we limbered up. We wore only our tracksuits for the early training so there was quite a mixture of colour and design and I tried to size up the extent of abilities I would be mixing with.

As we jogged around the dojo, I studied the instructor who was now conducting this morning's procedures. Although not much taller than me Kobayashi Katsumi Sensei's build was wiry and he stood very upright with a hint of authority that made him seem ten foot tall. I had vivid recollections of training with this respected instructor in the February of 1976 when he visited my home town to conduct a training and grading session. Up until then I had witnessed the likes of Hamaguchi and Kubo brandish their powerful style of Karate but Kobayashi was quite different, smooth, lithe, very quick, and athletic. As a complete novice I remember peering through the window of the local school gymnasium trying to catch a glimpse of this thirty-year-old Japanese man at the peak of fitness as he sparred with the senior students of my club. He was flamboyant with his legs and would kick high then suddenly stoop low to sweep away the opponent's legs before jumping up to punch an unguarded face. Demonstrations of this nature would often be his specialty at the National Championships at Crystal Palace. Moon face was a nickname he had unknowingly adopted among the members of my club; his face was rather oval and he often wore a stern expression but it would light up with a glow when a smile of some magnitude would spread across its surface if anything remotely funny should attract his attention.

Kobayashi's hair was still as long as I had remembered it in the seventies, almost as if he were holding on to something of a reminder of his days in fashionable London Town. Returning to Japan in 1979 Kobayashi continued to teach for a living by opening dojos in and around Tokyo as well as assisting at the university from which he had graduated.

Nihon University had for years carried the reputation as the fighting man's source of development in Wado Ryu Karate. Tatsuo Suzuki had graduated from here, as well as Masafumi Shiomitsu, Fuji, Maeda, Murase, an endless list of international instructors and fighters. So, was this the right place for me or one step too far? I pondered much during this first introductory session.

Before embarking on this intrepid trip, I had sought the permission and advice of my instructor back home, Shiomitsu Sensei, who agreed to contact the relevant authorities once he was satisfied that I was serious enough in my intentions. There had been one or two previous foreign visitors to the club who had unfortunately left an unsavoury reputation so it was decided that I could go once Shiomitsu was happy, after all his reputation was also at stake. Over a period of several months, I trained on many courses where Shiomitsu could look at me and be convinced in his own mind. Finally, he agreed to endorse my visit with one proviso; "if you let me down" ...he then put his fist to my face. Enough said!

So here I was then, under the full scrutiny of over twenty pairs of eyes, there were one or two familiar faces from the night before but there was no emotion of recognition as I nervously loosened up next to Kobayashi, almost as if he were my guardian. The only sound was the creaking of the sprung wooden floor beneath our bare feet.

A shout broke the silence and a circle was formed around the edge of the dojo. In the centre a student led the exercises; ' ichi, ni, san, shi, go, roku, shichi, hachi, ku, ju. Ichi, ni, san, shi, go roku, shichi, hachi, ku, ju' and so the mantra continued as we all followed the stretching intently. We then broke our inertia to begin our run around the dojo perimeter. As we jogged, I took in the full extent of the finery of its construction; narrow sliding windows were set into the walls just above floor level, larger frosted windows above head height let in most of the light, the sills of which were the resting place for little hand towels. The wall opposite the entrance was adorned with a solitary Japanese flag and as I jogged in pace with the rest of the club, I noticed that the large mirror along from the doorway was in fact a sliding door that was partly opened to reveal a small room. Above this mirrored door was the 'kamidana', a shelf that held a small shrine typical of any dojo. Makiwara punching posts 'grew' in one or two places around the edge of the dojo from the floor like little wooden trees as if to decorate the sparsity of an already completely wooden house with even more wood.

We ran around the dojo which measured about twelve metres long by ten wide for about twenty minutes, working up a little sweat in the spring warmth. Despite the rain that fell outside, the humidity was still evident even though it was early on an April morning. Kobayashi finally called 'yame' and paired everybody off to practice a little randori (light sparring) and the emphasis was on light; as in no contact. That suited me fine on my first day's training, for I was barely off the plane and felt, mentally, a little in two places. I changed with several partners with the customary bow and I was a bit taken aback at the loud 'onegai shimasu!' and 'arigato gozaimashita!' before and after each exchange. Tall, short, stocky, wiry they were all different except for one thing; their hair was cropped short, almost army-like, and that was the noticeable thing that struck me already that day; they were like one unit. Despite their different dress code that morning there was uniform in their motion, and even in their style of fighting; with good control they loved to attack the face. Moreover, in the presence of a senior instructor there was the utmost discipline. Nobody spoke unless spoken to. 'Best fall in line' was the reminder to myself.

Morning training was over at seven by the clock on the wall and we filed back quietly to our concrete abode next door. There was a sudden rush of activity as some students started to sweep the corridors and dining room. Some were cleaning the toilets and showers and another small group became busy in the kitchen preparing breakfast.

After showering and changing, Kobayashi and I were summoned to the dining room where already all students were sat at their places awaiting our arrival. There was a curt command which must have meant something like 'backs straight!' because they all stiffened in their seats and then something was said in unison before they began to eat. I watched carefully to see if they ate their food in time, but no, they scoffed quite heartily without any extra help.

I looked warily at the bowl of a sticky substance in front of me and then at the other bowl next to it. Now up to this point I had never eaten anything Japanese in my life. I had enjoyed a Chinese from the local take-away but I can assure you that is no preparation for this culinary challenge of the Land of the Rising Sun, especially when prepared by young knuckleheads. Now, if there were ever a dish to serve someone to put them off Japanese food for life it would be 'natto'.

"Eat!" said Kobayashi, "good for health".

Quite whose health he was referring I wasn't sure. I dutifully copied my revered instructor and wound the orange sticky goo around my chopsticks and took a mouthful. It was awful. I couldn't take it out again but I didn't want to continue either! I tried to listen as Sensei explained about the fermented bean curd, but that only made the taste worsen. Finally, I swallowed and grabbed the bowl of what I was told was soup next in line in front of me. I took a mouthful. I think somebody had forgotten to rinse this bowl of its previous contents after washing up. There were bits of cabbage, potato, onion, and all sorts floating around.

"Ah miso soup!" someone said. I didn't care, it was marginally better than the previous dish and it washed away the sticky remnants. I was of course cause for amusement among the lads around me, which kind of broke the ice so I continued with the soup and a little boiled rice before drinking the green tea served me. One of the boys switched on the little portable TV that was perched on a table at the far end of the cluttered dining room and we all quietly watched a Japanese version of The Big Breakfast.

Fortunately, a hungry student robbed me of the remaining unwanted natto that was in a small bowl in front of me and although I had eaten most of the rice that was in another bowl Kobayashi told me not to leave anything. There was but a small mouthful that I had left but he urged me to polish it off. I looked at the bowls in front of the students around me and there was not a morsel left in front of anyone, not even a grain of rice.

After another 'back straight' command there was another loud after meal exclamation from everyone. I tried to pick out what was said but any sense was lost in the speed and colloquialism. To me it sounded like "go sauce the chestnuts!" Despite my advanced purchase of my phrase book, I wondered how on earth I was going to pick up the language. Anyway 'go sauce the chestnuts' would do for the time being.

My first day on Nichi Dai territory was a Sunday, which meant no afternoon training. It also meant that students could go off for the day so the dormitory quickly became deserted. It was an ideal time for me to do a little recce of my new home. The peace was soon broken when I heard Karate type shouting coming from the bottom floor of our block. I went out onto the pavement where I could see an open window from where the shouts could be heard. Through the window I saw a group of students working hard at various weight lifting apparatus. They were training in small groups shouting and encouraging those pressing or lifting the barbells. They eyed me suspiciously before turning back to their training.

I continued to wander further around the concrete

construction and realized this was a dormitory of some considerable size. I could make out room after room containing personal belongings hanging on the walls, various sports clothing trying to dry in the damp spring air. Behind this huge building was a sports field where I could see several individuals pitching a baseball to bat wielding comrades and these too were emitting sporting shouts at the tops of their voices. Beyond this sandy grassy field were yet more pitches separated by high mesh fences containing other groups of athletes playing soccer, rugby, American football, all shouting to their hearts content in the mid-morning drizzle.

Returning to the dormitory of the Karate club I was greeted by two students who invited me to lunch. Was this to be another sojourn into 'gastroandromeda?" I wondered. They told me Kobayashi was sleeping so we walked a few hundred yards along the busy dual carriageway introducing ourselves as we went. One lad introduced himself as Kikuta. He spoke good English and was curious to why I had come. He told me every one had presumed I was an American for they had had a few visitors from the States recently at championship time.

We stopped outside a restaurant called Denny's. My mouth was already chewing in anticipation of the hamburger that was on display in the window. Inside we sat and enjoyed a large coke and the grilled meat that sat between two slices of sesame bun with mayonnaise. The thought crossed my mind whether I could buy a few burgers to stock up with for later. To say it went down well is an understatement of magnitude. We shared some more conversation and I particularly remember asking about the nightlife in the area. After all, at twenty-one I considered life to be a balance of work and play. The response was a bit mute so I left it at that hoping to glean more later. The boys paid the bill and welcomed me to Japan. A good omen I had hoped.

In the afternoon an extremely important visitor stopped by our digs, so important it seemed that even Kobayashi was on his toes. There were shouts of "chop, chop" coming from all the way up the stairway. Students who had been secretly dozing their Sundays away were all at it, jumping into the corridor standing bolt upright "chop! chop!" they all bellowed. What the hell were they shouting? If the man who appeared was so important why were they dare telling him to hurry up I wondered?

"Konnichiwa" Kobayashi said to this man who appeared rather frail but only seemed in his fifties. I realized ' konnichiwa' was the word they had all uttered in their colloquial tongues shortening the word to just 'chawa'. I bowed deeply to his eminence along with the rest.

"This is Tanabe, kantoku coach," said Kobayashi and we followed Tanabe into the room in which we had slept the night earlier.

"Aasa Meek" said Tanabe Sensei.

"Hai" was my response, the only word I knew to say at the right time without offending anyone. Kobayashi explained that this was the elder brother to Hideo Tanabe the club coach and was responsible for the recruitment and overall running of the club from its headquarters. He had stopped by to give me an impromptu interview. Through Kobayashi, as interpreter, I answered a few questions and then he asked me to perform Pinan Shodan kata in front of him. Now, bearing in mind we were in a room that could barely sleep two people, and which was cluttered with trophies, not to mention my unpacked bags, I thought this a little odd but my response was quicker than you could say, "chop chop!" I went through the kata as best as possible without kicking anything valuable, which I thought was a result.

Fumihiro Tanabe pondered for a moment and then gave me a choice; I could stay at a nearby flat or bed sit and come training at the allotted daily session four until seven in the evening, or I could stay at the dormitory for a modest monthly fee and live alongside the rest of the students. I chose the latter because it made sense financially, but it was also the best way to get a true insight into this frugal way of life. He made it clear that I should learn some Japanese and live by the house rules.

"Hai" I said. He smiled.

The monthly fee worked out at around forty pounds, which meant I could budget for the rest of my needs. My fee would cover breakfast and evening dinner plus training.

The rest of that evening was uneventful as one by one students could be heard returning from their day off. There were more shouts of, "chop, chop" as I realized some were older boys being greeted by their juniors. There was an evening meal of some fried food in batter which was ok, after which I returned to my little room alone to reflect on my first day.

Kobayashi had left to teach Karate elsewhere so I was able to relax a little before I was told to switch out my light by one of the lads next door. It was ten o'clock.

My mind drifted to the familiar world I had left behind only twenty-four hours earlier; my family, girlfriend, my mates, and the Karate club back home in Bridgwater.

Tomorrow, I guess it all starts for real in the dojo.

TWO

I was roused at five forty the next morning by one of the students and I quickly donned my tracksuit bottoms and t-shirt and filed down the stairs with the rest of the lads and was told to just put on some old flip-flops that were scattered around in the entrance of our block. It was raining so we sauntered to the dojo leaving one lad behind; he couldn't find his flip-flops!

The training that followed was much the same as the day earlier except there was no real urgency as I had first seen and I guessed it was because Kobayashi was absent. The same guy as before led the warm up and I figured he was the most senior. We ran around almost slovenly as we shook off our sleep and this continued for more like half an hour after which we paired off again. We practised 'one-two' punches to the face; front hand followed by reverse punch. All the students seemed to carry the same demeanour in that they were extremely relaxed in their fighting stances before suddenly shooting forward at high speed with two punches that almost seemed as one. Kiai shouts accompanied every attack and I couldn't help thinking if you were outside listening in you would assume there were a hundred or so Karateka within these four walls, rather than the twenty something, such was the din. Morning training finished prompt at seven.

After training we sauntered back to our dormitory and Kikuta asked if I knew where Kobayashi Sensei was and what time he could be expected. As if on cue, as we slipped off our sandals a familiar mustard coloured Toyota drew up alongside the kerb and every student who hadn't already entered the building was standing to attention doing their routine bowing and 'nice day sensei' performance. Kobayashi told me to be ready quickly and that I would have to miss breakfast. 'Shame' I thought.

Within ten minutes I was sat dozing in the passenger seat alongside my sensei enroute to the airport to meet Hideo Tanabe who was returning from a former student's wedding. At the airport I was treated to a more regular meal of coffee and toast, a proper breakfast! After a wait of some two hours, it became apparent that our expected traveller was not coming, so we endured another hour journey back across town. While listening to an American radio station play the likes of The Carpenters and The Doobie Brothers, I took in the city sights I had missed during my nighttime arrival. Traffic was often at a standstill for no apparent reason and maximum speed was only ever about fifty miles per hour as we followed the expressway. It weaved precariously between high rise tower blocks of offices, banks, hotels, and department stores that seemed stacked so close together that one push of a giant hand could start the inevitable collapsing of the dominoes trick. There was still a constant drizzle which, added to the spray off the road along with the humidity, gave a steamy sheen under the low cloud cover. Much of the expressways in Japan are built well above ground level so the journey gave me the impression of some futuristic travel in a sci-fi film as we flew past windows eight or nine storeys high.

We returned to the university dormitory just after lunchtime so we both relaxed in the small guest room and as I stretched out on the straw tatami beneath me, I could only think of the first three-hour training session that awaited me at four o'clock.

I was roused at three thirty and told to bring my Karate gi. My previous nervous anticipation was unfounded as once more I was back in the Toyota to travel in another direction across Tokyo to a small district of almost rural characteristic. We drove down quiet narrow streets that followed the course of a riverbank until I could pick out the unmistakable shape of a classic looking dojo. A large wooden construction, with huge sliding doors and windows, sat regally in a clearing among the houses.

The early evening was still warm, drying the rain that had welcomed me for the first two days.

For one hour I watched as Kobayashi taught a class of just four children. Then I trained along with two adult novices for an hour and a half going through the customary basic techniques of our Wado Ryu style. Kata then followed, the five Pinan Katas to be precise, every move punctuated by my instructor's interjections of "too slow" or "once more."

Kobayashi's fluency of movement reminded me of that time back home. Only this time there were only three of us so the intensity was greater especially as this was my first class under scrutiny. I took every command to heart and persevered to go faster and stronger. The two novices ended their class and I continued to train, this time with the pre-arranged fighting techniques with my instructor as my partner. By now the sweat was running freely but I lapped up the personal tuition offered to me.

"Ichi, ni, ichi, ni;" (one, two, one, two), Kobayashi repeated, encouraging me to keep in time. I moved as quickly as I could and as correctly as possible. We then broke into some free sparring and by now I was flagging slightly as the heat was finally taking its toll. Yet this was what I had come for and so this was the time to get down to business. We sparred for several minutes at a fast but well controlled pace trying to impress each other with as much versatility as possible. Kobayashi's movement was as slick as I had remembered and often his speed of punch and good timing caught my unguarded face. When he moved forward, I couldn't stop him; as light as he was, it was like trying to stop a racehorse.

"Hai, owarimasu" he uttered to call time. I only noticed the soreness of my feet as we walked to the small changing room in the corner. Before we left, we laid out some tatami mats over the polished wooden floor. The dojo was shared with an Aikido club so it was customary to prepare their mats for them for the following day. We also brushed the dojo out before departing.

I slept soundly in the car for the duration of our return to the university dormitory and once inside welcomed a cool shower before a bit of supper. One of the junior students had found an old toaster in one of the cupboards in the kitchen and after shaking out its old contents had prepared the finest supper for our benefit; cucumber on toast!! A luxury that could only be matched by the level of training I had earlier received. I commissioned the toaster and decided that breakfast time from now on would at least be Continental if not Full English. Not accustomed to the sultry weather my throat was craving liquid of any description; I downed some green tea and then later drank cold water from the tap.

After supper Kobayashi decided that I should move into a room shared with other students. It belonged to the younger first year boys. Already six futons were laid out across the floor adjacent to one another from the doorway to the far end by the window. As I stepped inside, I remember thinking it a bit intimate for my liking. A tall youngster quickly took my case and put it in one of the cupboards behind the sliding doors that ran along the full length of the room on the left. Typically, the floor was tatami and opposite the wall of cupboard on the right was a shelf at no more than knee height that was adorned with various personal belongings and a TV, which the rest of the occupants were sat watching. From the cupboard my helper pulled out a spare futon, much to my relief, and stretched it out near the doorway next to the wastebasket, then all the rest of my roommates shifted their 'beds' a bit further towards the window. That was that, I had moved in. My eager helper introduced himself as Enomoto and with that, the other five youngsters moved forward to join the conversation. Enomoto spoke remarkably good English all but one slight speech flaw, "why have you come to this pwison?" he asked. Obviously Enomoto was not impressed with the hospitality of Nichi

Dai. Furthermore "I don't like Tanabe Sensei" just about made my welcome complete.

We sat in a group and excitedly exchanged conversation, comparing cultures, and discussing young men's topics. They asked if I knew Sheena Easton, who apparently was on tour of Japan at the time, and whether I liked Japanese girls, which was a dumb question because all I had seen up to this point was the inside of a Toyota and two dojos. However, I answered both questions in the affirmative and that went down well so I made a friend or two that night. Enomoto explained the system of the establishment to me; each room housed its own year from first to fourth, the youngest were eighteen progressing to the twenty-two-year-olds. They were the fourth years or 'senpais' consisting of the captain, who, I had noticed, took lead of the morning training. There was also a vice-captain and manager. There was one other, and I don't know to this day if he had a position of any sort except a general pain in the neck, but that will become apparent later. However, higher rank was to be respected or trouble would ensue.

One of the lads switched over the TV to 'Soul Train', which was an improvement to the period drama that was showing and being a soul fan myself we enthusiastically rocked along to Earth Wind and Fire's 'Boogie Wonderland'. Suddenly all my roommates jumped to attention as my other friend Kikuta, a third year, entered our room. He wandered around to each of the boys asking them questions and they systematically replied with fervent 'hais' and 'iiees' (yes and no) as they did their best not to offend their higher grade. This then was a point I had to ponder in that small space of time; I was twenty-one, not as young as Enomoto and company, but I was also not in any way a senior grade. Should I jump up and act accordingly or stay sat as if nothing was of any importance? Diplomatically I sat up on my knees, a sort of halfway gesture. Kikuta mocked me a little as he teased me about my interest in soul music as he had probably done with the others. "If you like disco" he said, "then we will go one night". Then he looked at the others as if to impress upon them that he was already my mate. "Great" I thought, I could be an object of desire in an all-male environment!! Now perhaps I understood Enomoto's opening statement about being in prison. Kikuta ordered lights out as it was just after ten and I settled under my covers next to the wastebasket near the door only a foot from Enomoto. I drifted off with one eye open.

I was awoken suddenly with Kikuta shaking my shoulder, "Get up Aasa, Tanabe Sensei wants to see you". There was a general rush of noise outside our room as students hurried about slamming doors, switching lights on then off again. I hurriedly put on a tee shirt and tracksuit bottoms and followed Kikuta next door to the small room

I had already been acquainted with the previous nights.

Hideo Tanabe sat cross-legged on his tatami in front of a low table and gestured for me to enter and be seated opposite. Kikuta sat to one side of us and poured some red wine for the resident coach then a glass for me. Some peanuts and other crisp-like snacks were scattered across the remainder of the table. Tanabe mockingly scolded Kikuta and so Kikuta, with an embarrassed smile, quickly jumped up to put the assorted delicacies on a plate. No need for the interpreter to sum that little exchange of "where's your manners?" They spoke about me for a minute or two, which made me feel a little uneasy. I wondered if my first two days here had somehow not gone down too well. Shiomitsu's parting words were already haunting me and I hadn't even completed a proper training session. Perhaps that was it, last night I was off with Kobayashi and not in the dojo as expected!

"Meek" said Tanabe "you are Shiomitsu student?"

"Hai" I replied.

"I am Tanabe," he said sternly.

Hideo Tanabe was resident coach of Nihon University. Unlike Kobayashi, he was a short stout figure of almost boxer like features with a broad nose that could have borne the signs of the odd altercation and a hairstyle that with its parting was hanging on to a generation a bit younger than his thirty something years. In fact, he pointed to his nose and asked me "how old?" For that split second, I had to think whether his nose was in any way different in age to its owner but I quickly guessed and stuck a nice round thirty in the answer to which he smugly and proudly responded "thirty-six".

Although this revered instructor in front of me exuded vanity, much of it was very tongue in cheek and he seemed to delight in creating a joke or two even if it was at the expense of others.
With the introduction over we had a pleasant couple of hours exchanging Karate talk, cultural differences, and Japanese girls. My new Sensei was jovial but with a sharp intuition despite his lack of good English. Kikuta interpreted much of the conversation enjoying his position and the chitchat.

Tanabe was proud, of his position, of the club, its reputation, and the history he shared with the many infamous graduates that had since left its four-year period of hospitality. He drew my attention to the trophies that surrounded us, polished, and well positioned; I knew all about these prizes for I had come close to clattering one or two during my impromptu demonstration the day before. I looked at the memorabilia I was shown of the many different countries Tanabe had visited in his years as competitor and coach. Photos of him and other senior instructors during their younger days filled albums and he would often mention Shiomitsu Sensei with a fondness and respect that was not simply for my benefit.

He also asked if I knew certain English instructors, some of whom had visited his dojo. Some he mocked, some he praised. This man didn't suffer fools. However, he then proceeded to name a few celebrities that had 'trained' with him, Englebert Humperdink was one, as well a member of the rock band Emerson Lake and Palmer. There were others but I began to get weary and struggled to take in so much so late, apart from which, the red wine was starting to have its effect on my jet lagged brain. Sensing this, Tanabe waved me off to get my head down.

I finally returned to my futon sometime after midnight. I juggled the day's events around in my mind thinking and wondering about the time ahead that waited.

I woke with a start when the sound of a beeping alarm clock found its way into my brain. 'I hadn't slept' I thought. Yes, I had for my eyes were struggling to open and focus. No sooner than the alarm had stopped then another went off, then another. Had I got drunk last night and crashed out in the doorway of a clock shop? Bare feet were now stepping over me and stepping into plastic slippers lined up outside the room.

"Aasa, get up" Enomoto urged, "We must be first!" I jumped up, suddenly remembering where I was and followed my roommates along the corridor down the stairs. "I'm not dressed," I thought. I then realized I hadn't bothered to undress the previous night. The red wine I had consumed clouded my thoughts, so I now had a hangover to greet me for this early start. As I stepped outside my eyes were not ready for the glare of sunlight that even at six o'clock on a spring morning pierced my delicate eyes causing me to squint.

I lined up along the pavement with the rest of my roommates and faced the doorway from which we had just emerged. A moment or two later other guys shuffled out of their slippers into their training shoes squinting in the sun. "Ohayo gozaimasu!" "Ohayo gozaimasu!" my room mates shouted to everyone who joined us. I joined in these morning greetings that were sometimes stifled by the noise of the traffic that flashed by us on the busy expressway, yet not one reply came from the recipients of all those polite morning greetings.

The captain took his position in front of our line and proceeded with the already familiar stretching routine to the tune of 'ichi, ni, san shi' etc. I was already thirsty as we set off on our jog along the roadside, up over a footbridge to the opposite side, then into a park that was well hidden from the road by its surrounding trees. I ran with the pack following the path that meandered left and right past various children's climbing apparatus, park benches, public toilets, until I realized we had done a full circuit. We then continued for a further three circuits, probably a couple of miles altogether.

I stopped when the others had gathered at our original starting point and now, without Kobayashi for company, I felt quite isolated as all eyes were studying the new addition. We paired off and began some shadow boxing while facing our partners in a simulated sparring match.

"No touch" I was reminded by my partner. We continued for ten minutes or so changing partners but each time keeping good control in our distanced sparring.

"Yame!" was called and we did a short warm down. Then there was further discussion between the captain and his comrades before I was approached by one of the seniors.

"Today we run six times," he said. I was confused. "Six times" he repeated this time gesturing with his hands circling around the park.

"No, I think it was three or maybe four laps" I replied.

"No, six!" he said. Once more I said I was sure it was four or five at the most. He became annoyed and once more said "six times" in a firm voice. Then I suddenly realized that all other eyes were on me and that something was happening here. I then worked out our little problem; if anybody should ask, we ran six laps of the park. The moment of realization spread across my face in the form of a smile as if to translate that their little secret was safe. The others too smiled and relaxed. We then all sauntered back to our digs. On the way I asked Enomoto where Tanabe was. "Sleeping" he said. I wished I had done the same. However, apart from a raging thirst I felt quite refreshed and fully recovered from the previous night.

The minute we returned our floor became a hive of activity and I joined my first-year friends in mopping the corridor and the stairs while the other gangs were doing their chores before breakfast. We then all stood in a row along a trough-like steel sink as we washed and cleaned our teeth under the cold-water taps that sprouted out of the wall.

I sat with Enomoto at the breakfast table and he kindly prepared some toast for me while the others lined up with bowls in hand to fetch their fill of rice from the large cauldron in one corner. After the customary back straight command, we waited until Tanabe appeared and sat at his place that was already prepared. He then quickly stood up, walked to where I was sat, looked at my two pieces of dry toast and said something to which all occupants of the dining room roared with laughter. I blushed and laughed along without any idea of the joke. He sat and we then ate. I looked out the corner of eye and watched as the various strange dishes were shared and quickly consumed. I was more than happy with my toast and the green tea which I found very refreshing and surprisingly thirst quenching.

After breakfast all my roommates quickly changed into smart uniforms and packed little rucksacks before departing for college; so, before long the whole third floor that housed the Karate club fell silent. I packed away my futon stretched out on the tatami and began writing a diary as well as swotting up on a bit of Japanese.

I knew I had some time to kill before the afternoon training session so I took time out to wander a little further afield away from our dormitory and found a few small shops plus a post office so I returned and wrote a few postcards. The anticipation of the first training session proper in the dojo that stood ominously next-door was in the back of my mind.

THREE

I wrote out the address of my home back in the UK and began to write of the few details of my new home to my parents. My decision to pack in my job and come to Japan wasn't the best news they had heard in recent years especially as I had sounded so excited, but as always, they were prepared to support me wherever possible. I had to cash in my ten-year savings plan after only a couple of years since I had started it and that with my bit of holiday pay gave me about seven hundred quid to live on. I think secretly my parents had hoped my sojourn wouldn't last five minutes especially in view of my spending habits. Naturally they were worried and they found it hard to understand why I needed to do this, and I guess I failed to fully understand their concern. The previous two years I had decided to do a little boxing along with my twin brother so my Mother had had her fair share of letting things go, but suffering a few sleepless nights along the way. However, the other side of the world was drastic and my parting moments at Gatwick airport were not for the faint hearted. My Dad on the other hand was always the pragmatist, worrying about the finance, my future, he didn't really understand why I wanted to do Karate in the first place let alone travel six thousand miles to do so. Perhaps he thought I was really trying to piss him off.

The fact that I started Karate at all came down to relentless persistence on my part. At thirteen when the world of martial arts caught my attention and the rest of the world for that matter through the passing of Bruce Lee and the release of Enter the Dragon, I first sounded out my Dad to join the local Karate club. “It’s a mug’s game” he responded, relating tales he had heard in work of the dangerous activities that took place in THAT club. So, at thirteen I was dismissed as a non-starter. Or so my parents thought. Undeterred I trained from books; big books, little books, Shotokan, Kung Fu, Bruce Tegner, these were the sources to satisfy my thirst as I followed the text and pictures and worked out in my ten by eight bedroom. I sparred with mates in the local park. I walked to school like Kwai Chan Cain wearing ankle weights hidden under my trousers and an unusually heavy bag on my back.

In 1975 approaching my sixteenth birthday my Dad finally relented so I shot down to the Wado club, whose members all knew me by name for I had sat and watched so many of their training sessions.

It was a decent club too, hard training, lots of scrapping, regular visits from the Japanese instructors that resided in the UK. I was soon in my element; training four days a week plus all the running I was able in between classes. The fighting I loved, basics and kata I enjoyed but the fighting was the inspiration for my training. By the age of twenty I had joined the United Kingdom Wado Kai squad. This was a step up in class with the likes of Jeoff Thompson, Nieman Prince, Mel Parry, Jerome Atkinson, John Moreton; the list is endless of the well-known fist and foot pugilists of that generation.

I guess in many ways, my Dad holding me back only served to strengthen my resolve. Like the master to a potential pupil who is kept outside the gates of the Shaolin Temple for days on end in all weathers to prove his worth. Only in my case it was a couple of years. Thanks dad. Oddly enough when I boxed, he was always front row getting close to the action, shouting for all his worth. As they say, "The fight game is a funny old thing".

So, my first correspondence home had to be well worded to give peace of mind to the folks at home so they could share with the neighbours their exciting news compared to the mundane chat that usually took place. I smiled as I imagined my Mum listening to, "did you know the price of bread went up two pence?" and then responding with "in Tokyo...." to top all the news that was worth listening to. My Mum was sad at my absence, but I imagined gushed with pride whenever my situation was discussed. Bless her.

Around three o'clock students started to drift back to their respected rooms and I watched as the lads in my room prepared various Karate gis before getting changed into their own. I noticed that every gi worn had a large motif stitched on the left breast, two characters to denote Nichi Dai, short for Nihon Daigaku. I noticed also most of them wrapping what seemed surgical tape around their toes. I silently changed and watched as senior senpais came in and collected their gis from the junior kohais who had washed and dried them in time for training. I duly followed when my colleagues left for training. When entering the dojo each of the guys not only bowed, which as a tradition I was already accustomed, but loudly uttered what sounded like "sejimasu!" This was repeated every time they came in or went out. The seven of us then grabbed some old cloths and wrung them out in a bucket of water in order to wash the floor. No wonder the floor was in such good nick. After we had wiped the floor, I noticed each of my first-year compatriots kneel, do a little rei (bow) in seiza before relaxing on their backsides, cross-legged, so I also followed suit and sat on the end of their little line, just inside the door. We had hung our little hand towels on the windowsill above our heads, and now we waited. After a few minutes I saw another group of seven or eight karateka approach the dojo in the sunlight. The first years jumped up and welcomed them and they in turn bowed on entry with the customary "sejimasu" and took up their position further along the wall from us and sat quietly. Another minute the third years came in and sat opposite the second years after everybody had once again jumped up to "konnichiwa" them in. Finally, the most senior group at five minutes to four entered and after the same salutations from all present they sat in their spot opposite us. What a carry on, up and down several times, I was already sweating. This was no exaggeration. I think I inherited the profuse sweating from my dad. It never took much for my forehead to run. However, it was never in any way an indication of my fitness level, I could sweat for England but still keep up with the rest of them. Just one of my over enthusiastic bodily functions, I guess. I won't elaborate on any of the others.

I looked at the two groups opposite and they looked at me. I tried to read their thoughts by their expressions. It didn't look good, but then again, they might be thinking the same thing so keep on looking; I've been here before I reminded myself. Of course, at fifteen, I had joined a Karate club of some repute armed only with tracksuit and tee shirt but soon made progress to earn a little respect. Then at seventeen joined a boxing club with experienced seniors and one or two of them were keen to test out the Karate man. But I would always hold my own. That was the key in my mind, not to prove anything to anyone except to be able to hold my own until it really mattered. When I stepped into the boxing ring opposite my opponent I searched for the same clues, and often came up with the same answer; I'd rather be at home in front of the telly, but let's do it anyway.

A shout and we were up and doing the already familiar warm up followed by a new routine where we would pair off and do some partner assisted stretch with massage. We then lined up without an instructor in front of us and I wondered if Tanabe Sensei ever did anything. We did a formal kneel in response to the captain uttering the commands then I saw one of the senior groups walk to one corner of the dojo.

“Jun zuki hidari gamae!” and we were away, up, and down the full length of the dojo covering the basic techniques. I noticed there was one guy in the corner just stood in shoulder width stance simply punching in time with our movements. Odd I thought.

Every now and again the captain would shout someone's name and they would reply with a firm “hai!” then “so!” yet the captain did not break his position but continued with the ‘one two’ as we trained in time. I noticed Enomoto's reply was louder than anyone else as he trained alongside me. For someone who didn't like it here he sure was enthusiastic. After a while 'Yame!' was called then 'kyukei!' for a break so we returned to our original seated position. Four fifty said the clock on the wall. I wondered what was to be in store after the first session.

Five o'clock and we gathered some heavy ankle weights strapped them to our ankles and formed two lines opposite one another. Again, to the rhythmic count of the captain, we stood in fighting stance and began to front kick on the spot. The kicks were not performed fast but half speed. At forty repetitions we discarded the leg weight and continued with another twenty, changed stance then repeated the same on the other leg. Back to left stance and another forty roundhouse kicks, without the weights this time, and again on the other leg. The front of my thighs from the hip to the knee began to burn as we then lined up to begin a series of kicking combinations up and down the full length of the dojo; front kick and roundhouse; front kick with side kick; roundhouse and side kick and so on. The soreness on my feet from the previous night began to return so now my legs were suffering from the top to the very bottom.

We then lined up closely to the back of the dojo and in relay form started another series of kicks up and down, this time at high speed. I struggled to keep up with the boys either side of me as they seemed to glide with little effort and my burning feet were worsening.

Five fifty said the clock as we rested once more. I wondered how many hundreds of kicks we had performed in those fifty minutes. I followed suit as the other members wiped the sweat from their faces.

Hideo Tanabe entered and we quickly lined up in two rows opposite one another. We adopted left fighting stance and performed left right punches surging forward between two people opposite as they performed the same at speed passing us. We would then turn and repeat the same moves in right stance. This continued in sets of ten of maybe five sets in as many combinations with kicks as were possible. Tanabe reappeared from the door behind the mirror fully donned in his immaculate white gi and began barking at individuals. They would automatically break from their fighting stance and stand to attention with a loud "hai! so!" as they responded to the instruction given them before resuming their position.

I knew without looking I had blisters. Not just little ones but big, squishy, bloody ones. As training continued, I tried to stay off the sore spots, which only hampered my movement, so that Tanabe barked at me, at my strange gait. Still, the more he shouts I thought the more I can stand up straight and ease my pain for a few seconds while I give him my fervent response. I felt like a saddle-sore cowboy with bowlegs as I tried to stay off the big toes and the balls of my feet. I looked enviously at the tape lashed around the feet of my fellow karate mates and inwardly cursed them for not letting me know. As I went across the dojo, I noticed my little blood spots were mixing in with my sweat giving it a smeared raspberry ripple effect. I was in a bad way, sore thighs from the kicks and a wreck from the ankles down. I even looked for a bit of sympathy in the faces of the odd familiar face but that was like finding the pint of lager I was dreaming about tucked away under my hand towel. My mind drifted to my local pub, The White Hart, where I used to sup my pint listening to the likes of The Moody Blues and their Nights in White Satin. That just made things worse so I imagined punching the captain in the head; marginally better.

'Yame' was called, but before I celebrated out came striking shields and focus pads. We lined up in front of these and took turns to attack. At least we had a chance to hold the equipment, which served to rest us for a while. This training too seemed endless and I'm sure my kiai shouts were more like cries of anguish. The clock boasted ten past seven and I felt mocked by its display of hands, for I was sure we should have finished by now. Makiwara training then followed and we took it in turns to punch the straw padded wooden post, thirty solid punches on each hand. Now my hands will be disfigured along with my feet I thought. To finish off the day's proceedings we did various exercises from handstand press-ups to pulley rope punching. My whole body ached. 'Yame' was called and we formed a circle in which another senior jumped into the middle and led us through twenty or so punches in a deep wide legged stance as if to just get shot of the last bit of energy that may have been left hiding in our bodies.

We lined up and I caught a brief glimpse of my tired beetroot red face in the mirror. Pretty good I thought compared to how I felt inside. We proudly repeated some dojo maxims after the captain's lead. There was a quick word from Tanabe to all students but my limited Japanese failed to pick up any idea of what was said. Then we broke from our positions to head back to our rooms. The lad from the corner joined us as we left.

In all the excitement of the last three and a half hours I hadn't noticed the fall of darkness outside and in fact the coolness of the evening was like a refreshing wash after the stifling atmosphere of the Karate dojo. As I gingerly donned my flip-flops Kikuta and his mate Fujimoto hurriedly approached and asked how I was after the session. "Ok" I lied, "just a little thirsty". So, they led me to a vending machine that sat on the roadside and kindly slotted in a few yen for me and I hastily pressed any button because all the cans inside on display looked so inviting. I took all the liquid I could before actually swallowing, and then the taste of ice-cold tea hit my taste buds. Anything but cold tea! I wasn't even keen on the stuff served piping hot from the teapot let alone after it had been left to stand for three years.

We had supper, curry, and rice, or rather 'karee rice' so with that further insight into the Japanese language I ate and it was delicious. All through the mealtime I drank copious amounts of water plus the green tea. Yet, I remained thirsty.

I showered and then shared the big tub in the corner of the shower room with Oshima who seemed quite jovial enough although very limited in his English. He was a little taller than the average student in the club and I had noticed earlier in training that he seemed one of the stronger lads of the third-year group.

Returning to my room all the first years gathered round me to ask how I was and what I thought of the training. After assuring them I was fine I hung my gi, which was soaked through, on the cupboard and I pulled out the futon from within to stretch out and inspect my damaged feet. Not much to be done here I thought just a good night's sleep ready for the next day. However, Kikuta and Fujimoto came in and decided to take me to Denny's again. A trip to Denny's with its westernized layout and air conditioning was a real tonic, none surpassing this night as we ordered a beer, my first. I was a bit miffed when they served up only small glasses, but the refreshing liquid was an oasis on this arid evening and I downed the stuff without reserve.

We returned to our rooms by the compulsory time for lights out at ten and I slipped into my futon and fell sleep in one move.

The various alarm sounds roused me once more from the deepest of sleeps and I sat up quickly to realize I was far from the world I had visited during the night, a pleasant familiar world of familiar friends and familiar places. However, before I had time to think of where I had been in my dreams I was pulling on my socks, jogging bottoms, and t-shirt to make my way down the corridor and stairs. The sudden pain from my feet slowed my panic to keep up with the rest and so my morning run became a lazy jaunt in the park. I didn't stop, for that would have been throwing my hand in, so I just did what I had to in order get around, which was probably no more than most of the others were doing anyway. But I like running and I wanted to make the most of the opportunity to stretch my legs a bit, but the soreness of the feet told me to save it for another day.

As I ran slowly that morning I took in the full picture of the park, as well as its occupants. What I hadn't noticed the previous day was now partially visible in the morning sunshine. Almost hidden among the bushes or behind the trees that lined either side was the occasional, large cardboard box. I saw tramps stirring from their sleep and peering out in the early morning sun as they were disturbed by the pitter-patter of tiny feet in trainers. The cardboard box was their home and within it all their possessions. They looked at me with sorrowful empty expressions as I stared at them in surprise.

However, these homeless people were not entirely alone living in this park, for it was also home of some of the biggest crows I had ever seen. They were like dogs, and noisy with it. I once saw a girl cycling along the path stop and get off her bike because one of these beasts was stood stubbornly in her way. It didn't move so she turned around and cycled the other way. If there are any film directors out there looking to do a remake of Alfred Hitchcock's The Birds then come to Japan, in particular this park. They say Japan is one of the safest countries in the world but I wouldn't mind betting the odd tramp has come to grief from one or two mean and hungry crows. There were no senior instructors present this morning so a few laps were followed by some stretching then the saunter back.

I had bought a small jar of jam on my previous day's walkabout so I enjoyed my toast with a generous helping of the strawberry stuff and, if the truth were known, some of the other guys were a little envious. I even had some boiled rice to go with it. Very cosmopolitan, I thought. I must say the rice that was cooked in that kitchen was the best I had tasted so at least I was getting the staple diet inside of me. I just wasn't quite ready for the other stuff. I like fish but not whole ones for breakfast covered in soy sauce with various pickles. However, at around a pound for a small jar of jam and remember this was 1981, which would make it about four times that by now, I knew I couldn't be this extravagant forever.

Tanabe said very little this morning as he joined us to eat so I guess the novelty of the foreigner had worn off. This suited me in a way because I felt more at ease talking to the lads of my room and I thought this would be a better way of learning the ropes here, and the language. However, like the previous day after breakfast everybody cleaned, washed, swept up and then departed, to leave me alone with only my thoughts for company.

I was tempted to rest up my feet for the rest of the day before training but the curiosity got the better of me. I ventured farther afield along the main road that passed by our establishment. I reached a crossroads over which a flyover blocked out the morning sun so I turned right and continued until I came across a little shopping district and a station. Here I hoped to find something written in English I could buy to maybe study or even simply find of interest, but Hachimanyama is a rather remote district of Tokyo and my search was fruitless. This was only my fourth day here and I was already missing conversing or reading something in my native tongue.

I returned from my little excursion and tended to my damaged feet. I knew this was going to be a problem for the rest of the week so

I had to find a way of protecting the affected areas as much as possible. One of the boys of my room, Tanaka, entered and straight away came to my aid. He was a quiet lad who wore what seemed UK National Health glasses on the end of his nose so on inspecting my feet he appeared to be the doctor I was hoping for. Out came some tape, scissors, and a bit of gauze and in no time my feet were patched up ready for action.

The boys of my room all donned white belts for training. I asked Enomoto about this and he explained that although they were all first dan black belt grades from school they could only wear white belts until they had completed their first term or so in university. They would then progress to brown for another period until finally their black belts could be worn after which they would continue to grade on to second dan etc. It was therefore a kind of probation period within Nihon University.

I duly changed at three twenty and was in the dojo for half past.

I sat on the end of the first-year line crossed legged and knew I was to be in for a torrid time because of the condition of my feet. Blistered feet were nothing new to me, as I'm sure thousands of martial artists would also have gone through this dilemma. I remember squad training with the stars of the seventies in Coventry or London or somewhere and after an hour of bouncing around on our toes some of the top fighters having to don trainers to alleviate the pain for the remainder of the session. I thought back then how sensible that was. I'm thinking in this situation how stupid if I should suggest such a thing. I smiled at the irony of my predicament.

The warm up and the basics I endured ok but off we went with the leg weights and the constant repetition of all the kicks we did the previous day and then it all came back again, the stinging pain; the squishing of my blood finding little exits of my blisters; and my constant effort of trying to stay off the sorest of places. An hour seemed like a lifetime, and I could have cried at the situation I was in. I was probably as fit as any of these lads, but I was forced to take it easy every chance I had and that was not my way. For the two seasons I had boxed Wednesday nights were a full night's training at the community centre for me. The Karate club shared the same gym, so from six forty-five until eight I trained with the boxing club, got changed and trained with the Karate club until ten o'clock. So, three hours of training was well within my capability even though that was only once a week, not six. I guess the intensity of this training was bound to have its effect on my body somewhere, but by now I wish it were somewhere else other than my feet. It was like rampant toothache, there was simply nothing to do but put up with it.

The guy in the corner was still at it and I was curious to ask about his predicament. Was he being punished for something and unable to enjoy the training alongside the rest of us? I remember thinking I'd like to find out what he did so I too could have some quality time standing still.

Tanabe entered around five thirty and so the intensity of training rose further. This time we did some counter punch training. Five students lined up at the back of the dojo while the rest lined up in teams to attack with any kick. The five at the front had to defend with a counter punch by either stepping in to the attacker or side stepping the kick and punching. On no account was there to be any backward step, which was difficult anyway considering our backs were virtually against the wall. However, there was on occasion the odd step in retreat and Tanabe went mad stopping the class and demonstrating the futility of such a move because there is no chance to counter the kick. He then took the unfortunate guilty individual to task by kicking towards his body and then giving him a hearty slap around the face as he stepped back. This then was their general work ethic, which I was about to embrace in my first week; step in; step side; but don't dare go back. The kicks came fast and generally quite low. In fact, the front kick and the roundhouse kick were not so different, either one would connect with the lower abdomen very close to the groin with the attacker hardly taking time to line up the attack. I started to spot the stronger more dominant fighter during this intense line up period.

As I had anticipated, Oshima was a handful and being one of the tallest of the club his range was good and his demeanour was more aggressive than most. This was not sparring, but if I didn't move correctly, I was nailed. Too often I would dither as if to get ready or to shift from one of my blisters and a kick found its way home like a heat seeking missile. Attacking with a kick was just as perilous; the counter attacks were always on target to the face. We wore mitts on the hands during this training but I guess that just enabled the punch to go in that little harder without remorse. So, it was then, under the watchful eye of Hideo Tanabe, the attacks went in hard and the counters went in even harder so nobody could complain about being a victim, not that anybody would of course, but swings and roundabouts were in mind here. I was thankful I had spent time in the boxing ring because even though these techniques were snapped back, there was contact, and heavy at times.

Funny enough, I never had a gum shield. During seventeen visits to the boxing ring plus hundreds of rounds sparring with my boxing contemporaries I, of course, wore a gum shield but it never occurred to me to wear one in the Karate dojo. Which I must say does tell of a controlled environment in the world of Karate, which is why

I took in boxing in the first place so that I could experience the fullness of contact fighting. But, I remember, the Japanese students too went without the mouthpiece yet more than one or two smiled with less than a full front row. Stupid really. We had bits of cloth to cover our fists yet nothing to prevent our teeth from being knocked out. Things are different now of course, in the UK and in Japan.

The attack and counter session came to an end and we rounded off training with 'Kihon Gumite' (pre-arranged sparring). I was relieved because I thought we had been warming up for the full sparring bit, which, at the present speed of my footwork would have resembled a duck shoot for any of my opponents

The Wado Ryu style of Karate is a legacy of its founder Hironori Ohtsuka and was formulated to satisfy his thirst for actual combat. He had already achieved a teaching license in Jiu Jitsu so had further enhanced his martial knowledge by studying Shotokan Karate under its chief instructor Gichin Funakoshi. Ohtsuka also trained with other experienced empty hand practitioners of that era and, maybe showing a little contempt for his tutors, decided to blend his Jiu Jitsu technique with his relatively newfound Karate to form his own style. The one thing that Ohtsuka had insisted on during his research of empty hand training was the necessity to fight. Whether in a mock drill exercise or in actual free fighting it was an essential part of training that at that time was considered unnecessary in many circles. Whether it was considered too dangerous or whether the intense practice of basics, makiwara and kata training was considered sufficient is not really documented, but Ohtsuka built his Wado style around many Kumite or fighting drills, therefore adding the practical essence to the training. His Jiu Jitsu technique is well and truly stamped all over these more advanced pair work drills, consisting of arm locks, foot sweeps, body evasion, and economical body movement. His trademark 'nagashi zuki' is the counter punch we had so often practiced in that attack and counter exchange whereby the defender would step in and around an oncoming technique in order to strike first, allowing the attacking move to be avoided.

My knowledge of these pre-arranged drills was a little limited as a twenty-one-year-old first dan but I was able to follow the rest without too much trouble and Tanabe Sensei took time out to demonstrate his broader experience especially as he had trained under, and was still very much in contact with, the Grandmaster. The movement of Kihon Gumite is very economical which was fine for me on this day considering the state of my tender feet. As we went through the movements at a slow pace in order to get things right, I was positively enjoying the experience of the finer points of my style of Karate.

FOUR

It became obvious to me on that second day in the university dojo that training would be much the same on this daily basis. Everything was done as routine for the first couple of hours, in fact you could almost guess the time by which basic technique was being executed or how many kicks had been performed, or which combination we were doing. There was no secret here, no intrinsic or spiritual revelation other than sheer hard work. In fact, if I had made any reference to Ki, an unexplained energy source, or any secret technique that would eventually be taught to only the chosen few then I would surely have been unceremoniously thrown out of the club for being so stupid. Not that I had had any of those concepts in my head before I had left for the Far East, but again at twenty-one you perhaps may have forgiven the notion.

I was proud to have got through this day, even though I had little choice, but I was a little smug anyway. My feet were still like hell on a hot day but I could look forward to a cool shower, more drinks, and a restful night sleep. I jammed some more yen into the machine outside our dormitory building and drank two or three cans of ice-cold orange juice. As I threw back the cold liquid, I thought what a good idea for a business venture back home in the UK. To set up a chain of vending machines like they have over here. In Japan they are more commonplace than phone boxes. And you know how safe the cash in phone boxes are home in England! Nice idea, wrong country.

Hideo Tanabe was jovial at suppertime sharing a joke or two among the brethren. The portable TV in the dining room was serving up some comedy show so I guess he was determined not to be outdone by the twit in the multi coloured suit in some studio with an over compliant audience. After all Tanabe had his own crowd present that would laugh at anything he said. Mind you he could have been the next Bob Hope for all I could understand. I just smiled and laughed along with the rest. And when the dinner was served, I nearly fell about when I saw a hamburger as thick as a slice of bacon sitting on a plate surrounded by cucumber and celery. Now, up to now my ability to use chopsticks had surprised the onlookers. I had a Chinese friend who owned a chip shop so had spent many Sunday evenings digging in to his specialties with a pair of sticks. This was different, how do I do this wafer-thin piece of meat justice with a pair of wooden chopsticks? I mean, I wanted to carve it into several small pieces and enjoy its flavour over a period of time. I didn't want to sling it in my rice bowl as is customary in Japan and eat it in one go. This meat was a crock of gold at the end of a rainbow and I didn't want to waste it. The customary slurping noises all around me hastened my advancement to devour the delicacy. I shovelled the burger into the rice poured on some brown sauce and took it all in one go. I couldn't believe the enjoyment of that taste. A hamburger. Compliments to the chef, it was delicious. Miso soup also assisted the meal followed by some various fruit and I felt well nourished.

At the end of supper after Tanabe had left, Takahashi, a fourth-year senior, made an announcement of some sort. Takahashi was a diminutive figure who seemed too inoffensive to be in a Karate club of this notoriety. He bore the signs however of being on the receiving end with his two front teeth missing. His speech was lengthy and was often interrupted by all juniors shouting "Hai, so!" to press home their full understanding. Then my name was mentioned and it went quiet. He smiled broadly and urged the listeners for an answer. Fujimoto spoke up, so did Oshima. So, it was settled. But I didn't know what. Again, I was embarrassed for I was the subject of conversation I knew nothing about.

On returning to our room, I pressed Enomoto for the answer. At the weekend, he explained, students that lived in the Tokyo area may go home for the night after training. Or those who had relatives or friends may also visit providing they supplied an address and a contact number beforehand. They also must return by early Sunday evening. Sunday was a rest day so students who came from afar would normally go into town and have a day of leisure. Tanabe Sensei wanted somebody to volunteer to take me for a little sightseeing during the approaching Sunday. Hence the reluctance to rush forward and offer to take the gaijin (alien) on a day trip. But it was an order, so two volunteers stepped forward. I felt very popular that evening. Like the last lad being picked for the football team.

The evening was spent around the telly in our room; there was some full contact kickboxing being screened from the States and so we exchanged ideas and techniques for a couple of hours before turning in. All the lads in my room had a 'Walkman' to listen to and as I lay in my futon, I could hear the various high-pitched sounds coming from the small earpieces. I was jealous, for I loved my music and in fact had brought with me several tapes in order to somehow get to listen to them. Yet I had no such modern equipment so was unable to get at my sounds. My feet were still sore and I went to sleep remembering some old wife's tale of men urinating on their feet to toughen them up. Perhaps it was just an excuse after they missed the pan.

Waking the next morning was an experience; not only did my feet sting but my legs ached, my shoulders were tight and I had a fat lip. They say the second day after a hard session is the worse for muscle soreness but I was starting to forget which was the first day let alone the second or third. They all rolled into one. You know it's like when you're on holiday you tend to forget which day it is, well this was no holiday and I had no idea what day it was, only that it was hotter than yesterday. Towards the end of April in Japan you start to sense the coming of summer. I thought it a bit odd then that as the hotter it got the more the captain, Tanemura, wanted to sweat. On this day he was wearing some sort of rubber gear! It turned out to be a fireman's outfit and was the best thing for achieving some weight loss I was told. At the end of our run around the park he would literally wring out the sleeves of the jacket of the sweat within.

At ten thirty the vice-captain 'Fukusyo' told me to be ready to travel with my Karate gi (uniform). We walked from the dormitory through the back streets to find our way to Hachimanyama station. Outside the station was a map of destinations with prices, all in Japanese script. Fukusyo tried to draw my attention to a certain place name, but for me it was like reading tea leaves in the dark. Wherever we were going it cost one hundred and twenty yen, about forty pence. We caught a train to Shinjuku about twenty-five minutes away. This was a different world, a major city within the city of Tokyo. There were shops upon shops just within the station itself and I was grateful to be with Fukusyo for I felt lost among the Japanese signs. We climbed some steps that took us out of the station and into the shopping streets of this notorious attraction. Opposite the station a massive TV screen caught my attention about three storeys above ground spewing out video clips, music, and advertisements. We wandered past camera shops, watch shops, more camera shops, restaurants, coffee shops, department stores and banks. And for every shop at ground level, you could times it by three for all the shops that were on second, third and fourth floors. The atmosphere was like London but everything seemed higher and cleaner. Almost like a Hollywood film set, no litter, no graffiti, and little scruffiness in the thousands of people that hurried past me. Many of the buildings scraped the sky so offered some shade from the bright sunlight and relief from the increasing temperature of the approaching summer.

Fukusyo showed me the main stores as well as the back street shops that contained many of the discount offers which makes Shinjuku one of the most popular shopping attractions. I was amazed at this ultra-modern city. The fact that this was a city within a city was hard for me to understand until we walked up and down the streets, in and out of the avenues contaminated with smells, sights and sounds that were so alien to a west country lad. Yet there was an element of excitement around every corner, and, although we seemed to walk for miles the sounds from the giant screen opposite the station seemed to follow our every direction making it almost impossible to get lost.

After walking for an hour or so we entered Shakey's Pizza Parlour right back near the station. It was one of the many establishments that were situated on the second floor. For five hundred yen you could eat as many pizzas as you liked along with French fries, which was why I guess the place was filled with youngsters. A coke was extra but my wallet jumped at the chance of stretching Mr. Shakey's stock of pizzas. They were not meagre in size these well prepared and tasty pizzas. I went back two or three times to replenish my plate not knowing if I would ever get this chance again. Eventually I had my fill, and then some. Fukusyo smiled and said,

"Aasa, ok?"

"Ok" I replied. Fukusyo was quiet, spoke little English but would often smile broadly which would make the long whiskers on his chin do a little dance. But I was glad of his company even though he said so little, but that suited me as I took in the new sights. Sat in the restaurant I was aware for the first time of being stared at by some youngsters. I realized they were discussing my eyebrows. Now this family trait of mine is unusual on English soil, but eyebrows that meet in the middle just does not happen in Japan so young boys and girls took great delight in pointing and pretending they too were a strange visitor from another planet. They would put their middle finger between their brows and show off to their mates that they were the same as me. Fukusyo scowled at them and they stopped immediately but too late to save my embarrassment.

I could hear the drawl of an American accent and saw two lads in jeans chatting. I wished for their company so I could speak more naturally rather than the slow simple stuff I had been conversing with to my hosts, but we were up and gone before I had chance to think about introducing myself.

Time was moving on and Fukusyo explained we were on our way to Nihon University headquarters for training. This would be the schedule every Thursday so I was to try and recall the route we took that day so I could remember in the future should I travel on my own. At that point a little panic set in for I had never even considered going anywhere in this country on my own, let alone catch a train and pass through the busiest station on Earth, with more platforms than found on a seventy's disco night. Besides, I wish he could have told me before we had left in the morning so I could have perhaps brought a notebook to draw my own map of travel instructions.

We walked down some steps from the main pavement to the underground rail system and another eye-opening experience awaited me, yet more fast, efficient travel with the highest level of cleanliness to match. It was on this part of the journey that I saw the phenomenon of grown men reading comics. Huge paperback cartoon comics that were quite graphic in sex and violence being poured over by men in business suits so engrossed that they never even knew they had shared a carriage with a foreigner whose eyebrows joined in the middle. The time was around four thirty and I was glad to get out when we did for it was getting busy approaching rush hour.

As we left the subway the familiar feeling of anticipation started to course through my body as I wondered how my feet would stand up to another three hours training. Also, there still hadn't been any real fighting and even during the morning sessions with Kobayashi Sensei there was quite some emphasis on no contact. However, the contact during the attack and counter sessions of the previous day had been substantial. All a bit strange and not in any way consistent, I thought to myself. Nevertheless, I knew I was in for another hard session so that was enough to contend with for the time being.

The dojo here was in the basement of Nihon University College of Economics in Suidobashi. It was probably not just a Karate dojo but also shared other sports as well for it wasn't quite the custom-built dojo as the one in Hachimanyama. Being in the basement and surrounded by hot water pipes at head level did not seem appropriate for the type of activity we were to engage in. There were a couple of fans hanging over us on the ceiling but they were probably more effective in keeping the flies at bay.

Five thirty was start time and off we went with our familiar routine of basics and kicks until both Tanabe Senseis joined us to watch the proceedings. On this evening we spent what seemed an eternity practicing one two punches across the dojo. Each of us would take turns to shout one to ten for each double punch performed and we would all do the count; twenty-four times ten with a kiai shout for every SINGLE punch took a lot out of us all. I looked around and I wasn't the only one who found this tough, but my feet were ripping again where the old blisters still hadn't had the time to heal. However, after a fashion the training session seemed to take a different course as this time Tanabe senior took over for a large portion of the training and this time emphasis was on more technical matters. We then practised our Nagashi zuki counter punches for a while. Fumihiro Tanabe was as demanding in his instruction as his younger brother and he was Kantoku coach, overall supervisor for choice of a better word, so Hideo Tanabe remained in the background a little more at times. Being under such hot conditions Fumihiro made sure we stopped and had plenty of fluid. On this day I was introduced to Pocari Sweat, a glucose drink. I had seen Pocari Sweat labelled drink dispensers stacked on a shelf above my sleeping space and wondered all about the meaning of Pocari Sweat. We were now getting it down our necks. It comes in powder form, is mixed with water and is quite refreshing.

As we sat quenching our thirst, Tanabe senior noticed the blood seeping through the tape of my feet and instantly ordered one of the first years to make up some new dressings. This took me by surprise. After I had replaced the tape and gauze, he placed his hand gently on my shoulder and asked “Genki?” Kikuta translated that it meant are you well. “Hai” I replied. He smiled.

I had seen on that night in Nichi Dai headquarters Fumihiro Tanabe bark like the best of them but I had also seen a moment of compassion, and the fact that it was aimed in my direction was a better tonic than the stuff I was drinking. I was up and raring to go just as a result of that gesture.

The evening training was concluded with Seishan kata and I felt under scrutiny from both instructors while they took it in turn to correct my posture and technique. There was very little difference in the way I had learned this kata from the instruction back home, but as I was already accustomed, there is always a slightly different slant from each instructor and I was more than happy to receive as much information as I was offered.

I was aware in these early days that everything was down to me whether my stay in Japan was to be successful. My spirit had to be strong, my technique at its best and my willingness to adapt without question. I sensed the success of the club was as result of its ability to function as a unit. I don't mean to all be the same in the way we fought, although an outsider may argue with that fact, as I probably would have done in the early days I was there, but the logistics of running a club on such a scale depended on everyone falling in line whether they liked it or not.

While I practiced my kata moves in earnest, I was relieved that the physical work for that evening had peaked and I was enjoying the technical training I also yearned. However, I lost count just how many times we repeated Seishan and after probably fifteen times ‘yame’ was called, Fukusyo as vice-captain jumped in the centre of our circle and led us through our twenty or so punches to warm down. It was eight o'clock. The lone Karateka in the corner was still at it and I still hadn't discovered the reason for his predicament.

After training I joined Kikuta, Fujimoto and another, Kenji, for the journey home. At Hachimanyama station we took a small detour down a narrow street and entered a bar that seemed only a little bigger than my parents' living room. The guy behind the glass counter made the customary welcome shout "irrasshaimase!" which I had heard earlier throughout the day with every shop we had entered. Much fuss was made as I sat at the bar and a few locals stared right at me as they were forced to move from their seats to accommodate not only a few new customers but also a 'gaijin'. 'Not many of them in this neck of the woods' was written all over their faces. But the proprietor was pleased to welcome the boys I was with and equally eager to ask about the stranger with them.

"From Engrand" he shouted, "aah so desu ka? From Engrand?" he kept repeating. "Queen's Engrand" he reminded me. "Diana, beautiful" I looked perplexed and I was reminded that Prince Charles and Diana were to be married later that year.

"Hai" I replied "beautiful" and the host gushed with pride for getting that one right. It was more than I could say in their tongue I reminded myself.

"Beer?" asked Kikuta smiling as if he already knew the answer.

"Big beer" I responded. A huge thirst had accompanied me all the way from the dojo and now I was about to extinguish it. Out came a large handled jug full of draught beer and after we clashed glasses and said "kampai" I drunk a good half in one go.

"Aasa big drinka" said little Kenji, "no just big thirsty" I flashed back. They all laughed. I felt great. The happy chap behind the counter brought out some meat and a place at a table was made for us all. A small hot plate was switched on and we were served lashings of raw beef mixed them with sauces and onion and ate and drunk for a good hour. At around nine forty Kikuta sprung to his feet and made a telephone call to our digs. On his return to the table, he indicated that we had to go. "Tanabe Sensei stay tonight" he said so that was an early finish to our evening, but even so an advancement in communication I felt which could only serve to ease the time away from home. On the way back through the twisting side streets only used by pedestrians and bikes I finally got around to the subject of the chap who trains in the corner of the dojo. Kikuta explained that if a student was injured and couldn't train but was well enough to be on his feet then he must attend all classes. He then said that this guy was sick and that was that; I questioned him no more on the matter.

It became apparent to me that despite their initial enthusiasm to join this reputable and somewhat notorious club after maybe a year or two some students wished perhaps; they had chosen something a little less intense. The university system was like the college idea in

America in that the sport they choose will assist in their graduation. However, it was four gruelling years and many of the students who had also spent a couple of years at high school training on a daily basis had gradually lost their initial desire to become National or International champions. So, they did what they could to make things as comfortable as possible in what was a long sentence. Kikuta came from north of Sapporo; you couldn't go much farther north without living in igloos so he spent very little time with his folks. I got the idea he and a few others were a bit cheesed off, but were determined to see it through come what may and I had to admire them for that.

We were back at the dormitory by five to ten so the first years welcomed me when I came in the room. They were a little envious that I had been to the bar, but I was still anxious to sort out my feet before lights out so I didn't seem too keen to entertain this evening. While I sat on my futon Enomoto sat next to me cussing.

"I hate it here" he said. "We are like children to them" he went on. "Like children in pwison" He was referring to the way the first years were regarded by their seniors. He was a big lad was Enomoto, a nice lad, but in the wrong place here I felt. His father owned a garage selling cars so was worth a bob or two and had no hesitation in paying for his son's university fees. But I think Enomoto was between a rock and a hard place. He didn't want to stay here much longer but he couldn't face going home either.

"If you go" I said, "I'll have your Walkman". He leaned across me and switched out the light before a senior did it for us. I don't think he was very happy that night. But then again, I was sure to be having problems of my own and didn't want to be drawn in to someone else's.

For the first time I noticed that the window at the far end was wide-open letting in the sound of the passing traffic. The others too were feeling the rise in temperature and most were now sleeping on top of their futons in the way I had been doing from day one. But middle of the night was a lot cooler and so we would all end up tucked up inside once more. No wonder then that all but me were listening to music or radio stations via their tiny earpieces because six lanes of heavy traffic was a constant din that continued throughout much of the night.

Friday morning was upon me without warning. I was last up, not hearing a single alarm go off. I must have slept deep I thought. I scrambled out just in time to beat the second years who were opening their door to follow us down. The week's training was starting to take its toll and I must have suffered after drinking the beer a bit quick the night before. My feet were still sore as anything and I was still aching from head to foot, but the feet eased a bit when I put on my trainers, which was a positive sign for me. So, after shaking the night's sleep from me I was determined to do the run with a bit more enthusiasm. In fact, I stayed with the one or two lads at the front and tucked in just behind until we were told that was it. I felt better. The stiffness in me eased and I felt like running some more but I kept that to myself. As we did some exercises and stretched down, I noticed the sound of what I first thought were crickets but in fact were cicadas. They are the strange raucous sounding bugs you sometimes hear on Australian soaps nowadays and I remember hearing them before on some tv programmes that typified a warm climate before coming to Japan. I was certainly now aware of these insects as the sound intensified around us, and it seemed they were telling us it was going to get a lot hotter.

After running it was our group's turn in the kitchen. I stood around trying to be helpful with no idea of what was going on so I popped two slices into my toaster and poured the tea for everyone. Tanabe sensei entered and started to muse to everyone about my role in the kitchen. He had a point really. I mean if I couldn't eat their food how was I expected to help cook it? I was asked politely to sit down after serving the tea. With breakfast over and students and teacher absent I stretched out, wrote my diary, a few letters and nodded off for a short while. I guess it was a bit cheeky but the mid-morning sleep did wonders as an anti-dote for the early morning sleepiness that could stay with you for a while. However, I dozed with one ear open for I didn't want to attract negative attention, so every little sound was picked up and deciphered in my sub consciousness.

Later, after a short walk to the post office to mail some more letters home I crossed the busy carriageway at the front of our living quarters and stumbled upon a record store that sold music from all parts of the world. It was another reminder that I was a little lost without my own music to listen to.

Before long I was sat in the dojo ready to go another three hours, reflecting how fast these training sessions came round. I was aware too, once all twenty-four students were sat waiting to begin training that some of these cared not a jot about my presence among them. In fact, they perhaps eyed me with contempt for some reason known only to them. I felt that if I dropped dead in that dojo many would just step over me so as not to ruin their day. Whether it was because I was an outsider or whether they felt that I was simply not in their league I couldn't begin to guess, but I only assumed they were probably a little lacking in social skills and if there were other issues then I'm sure I would get to find out sooner or later.

Amusingly I watched as a little episode unravel in front of me. There were still a few minutes remaining before the start of training and all was quiet except for the sound of the cicadas blowing in through the open door. One of the first years suddenly stood up to ask permission to do something. Now it may have been to go to the toilet, or fetch something he had forgotten, change his pants I don't know but he first ran along to the second years shouting “shitsurei shimasu!” before asking the question. With the consent he sought, he then had to run across to the third years and repeat the same request to which they again agreed. Finally, he ran across to the most senior group, sat opposite us, to get their approval. But this time he was denied the permission he sought so he had to run around to each of the groups in turn and apologize loudly with “shitsurei shimasu” each time for passing them as he went. He then sat back in his place but with his eyes fixed on the captain across the dojo floor. I wondered at this point if there were to be a flash point of some sort between the two for his eyes were firmly on the captain's. A minute or so was held like this until the captain waved his hand and the poor lad jumped up and ran out of that building backwards so that he didn't have to stop to turn to bow on the way out shouting “shitsurei shimasu” from the yard as he disappeared from our view, I only hoped he had made it in time. The discipline was almost comical, but nobody laughed, for this little incident portrayed the absolute respect that had to be observed for any senior grade and was a clear indication of the pecking order that had to be respected in and out of the dojo. In some way I could understand Enomoto's sentiments the previous night.

Once Tanabe Sensei entered at around five thirty, we had just finished a couple of hundred kicks up and down the dojo so we were well warmed up for whatever he had ready to serve up. This time we all picked up some hand weights that resembled little dumbbells and formed some 'teams' at one end of the dojo. From here each line took it in turns to start the relay attacks, which I had already become acquainted with. However today was even more relentless. We did every conceivable combination up and down carrying what once seemed light hand weights but by now were causing our hands to drop further down our bodies. Even though we had a moment or two respite while waiting for our fellow team members to return, there was no real rest as once more we were bawled at to go faster, shout louder and lift our hands higher. Double punches, triple punches, with front kicks, with roundhouse kicks, with sidekicks, every punch had to be with a step so to improve the speed of the forward lunge. I noticed that in order to get more speed and to cover more distance the others lifted their front knee considerably to get extra drive so I began to copy and it worked for a while until my feet again began to tear. Damn my feet I quietly cursed. I pressed on, trying not too hard to stamp my feet to make things worse. At six thirty rest was called and we sat in our little places to wipe our faces. I looked at my small hand towel and it was a reminder of my mum who had made sure I had enough towels to get by with. If only she knew how right she was to insist I packed a few extra.

Tanabe shouted "shokuji" and a few hands went up. I suddenly realized that these were the hands belonging to my little group whose turn it was to prepare evening dinner. Whoever was in the group for dinner could leave training early to get on with it. I looked at these four lads with their hands up and they then looked at me. "You're right" I thought, I'm in your group. My hand shot up quicker than any head block I had previously performed. Great. I was to be on my way, get some fluid down me, rest my feet, take an early bath. But Tanabe's laugh interrupted my thoughts. And as he laughed so did everybody else. Even those who I mentioned earlier who hadn't given me the slightest acknowledgement laughed out loud. The captain who especially seemed to view me with great suspicion was also having a good old guffaw.

So, it wasn't to be. I couldn't convince them in those amusing moments that I had any latent cooking talent so what was the point of letting me leave a valuable training session? I was doomed to remain for the rest of the period. To make matters worse at seven after another intense attack and counter practice period we did an extra twenty minutes circuit training, ran around the field, bench pressed some old weights; skipped and sprinted. What a way to spend a Friday night I thought. I was shattered.

I tried my best to follow the dojo maxims at the end of training "dojo kun; hitotsu reigi o monji; hitotsu jojitsu ni oborezu; hitotsu shinkenmi ni tesseyo!" Elated to be at the end of a blistering session I shouted along with the rest with gusto.

I hadn't noticed at all this evening that we were one person short in our first-year group. I mean I still wasn't really acquainted with every name and character after less than a full week so just as we were departing the dojo, I saw a familiar looking figure approaching, wearing his gi and carrying a small hand towel. He strode past us with a look of intent on his face and disappeared into the training hall we had just left. I asked Enomoto what was happening and he explained that this lad called Hijikata would sometimes be forced to return late due to his studies. Nevertheless, he would then have to begin his Karate training on his return. From whatever time he started he was compelled to fulfil his three hours. Sometimes though he could do a couple of hours during the day and finish the third hour later. However, it wasn't unusual for him to be training right up until ten o'clock if he couldn't get the time slot during the day.

This Friday evening, I was exhausted. I had completed in one week what I probably would have covered in a month at home and the intensity of each hour was like nothing I was accustomed. I was not only tired from the training, but all the new stuff that went with it. All I wanted was complete rest so after dinner I laid out my futon and stretched out hoping for to be left alone. One of my roommates approached, tapped me on my shoulder and held out his hand. In it was a compact cassette player with radio and earphones,

"My name is Asuka (pronounced Oscar) you can borrow if you want, ok?" I jumped up and thanked him and promised to return it as soon as I had my own. I burrowed into my suitcase and brought out the one or two tapes I had with me and laid back oblivious to the room's activities and anything that was happening outside in the corridor or on the street. To be honest it was a bit like lying in a hospital ward. No one seemed to care that there may be one poor soul trying to get a bit of rest. But this time a thrill went through me as I enjoyed some favourite tunes of mine while the bustle around me went unheard and recent memories of my clubbing came flooding back. I drifted off to sleep when the lights were out but was interrupted by some shouting.

"Ichi nen sei!" and then again louder "Ichi nen sei!"

"Hai!" somebody replied loudly from our room. There was some discussion before Asuka jumped up and left the room. Apparently Hijikata had just returned from his late training session so somebody had to make sure there was something for him to eat. A little while later my way to the toilet sometime around ten thirty I saw the solitary figure of Hijikata sat in the brightness of the dining room eating his dinner. He looked up as I shuffled past in the dark corridor and he smiled as he recognized me. I put up my thumb for ok and he did likewise before continuing to eat.

I couldn't sleep for ages once I had been disturbed and I remember hearing Hijikata coming in after eleven and I started to curse when there were more sounds seeping through my earpiece for, I knew that every minute staying awake meant it would be harder to rise in the morning. More slamming doors and I wondered how on earth Tanabe Sensei put up with it all because he was only in the next room.

I woke to the hissing of my stereo as my tape had finished and I realized the loud voices were from Tanabe's room as well as the familiar voice of Kobayashi. I prayed for sleep as I checked my watch and it was now twelve thirty. I cursed as I heard deep sleep from those around me. I was tired, very tired yet I couldn't sleep. I listened to the radio and tried to make sense of any words in the dialogue but with no success. Then one advert for Suntory whiskey amazed me with its clarity. The liquid seemed to be poured from my left ear into my right with the sound so clear it matched the crystal cut glass into which I imagined it was poured. But it made me feel thirsty and I quietly cursed again. I had to get up and make my way to the large trough like sink for some cold water from the tap. I looked out of the window that was propped half open and watched the traffic sail by in both directions and wondered where each car was heading so late on a Friday. I wondered too about home and all its comforts and looked around me at the starkness of the building in which I was living. At around one in the morning at that moment I was as lonely as I had ever felt and realized the honeymoon period was perhaps coming to an end.

I slept a little but was awake again before anybody else. It was now five thirty. I dreaded getting up in half an hour. I had hardly slept despite things being a lot quieter around me. Just one of those nights when you just know sleep has passed you by. I lay still until the first alarm clock erupted and then was first up and out. It was undoubtedly hotter this morning and of the familiar sights I was becoming accustomed none so welcome as when Kobayashi emerged last from the building. My Japanese good morning was as loud as anyone's and he nodded curtly at me before we set off for the park. Needless to say, there was a full quota of six laps to be done this morning and I was a little more up for it for some strange reason. I ran with the front lads once more and this time tested my feet with a cheeky little sprint at the end to finish first. That was a bit daft because although I had a little longer to rest than the others it took more out of me than I had anticipated.

In his wisdom, Kobayashi decided to get everyone doing a few sprints plus more light sparring so I had more than my fair share of exercise that morning. But that was nothing in comparison to what he had planned later that morning. After breakfast at around nine o'clock just as I was getting comfortable stretched out in my room listening to my newly acquired sound system Kobayashi interrupted me and asked what I was doing. I was obviously doing nothing and he didn't like it. He instructed me to grab some hand weights and follow him up on to the roof. Here was an area of some considerable size part of which was occupied by a few washing machines and some horizontal poles for drying. The rest was a flat surface area big enough to hold a small five a side football game. However, football was not on the agenda today. Unfortunately, two fourth year students the captain, Tanemura, and Hakoishi were stretched out in the sun so they too were drafted in for some extracurricular training. We spent an hour and a half practicing the five pinan katas plus more partner work, every move burdened using the hand weights. There was no shade, only heat that intensified as the time approached midday when thankfully our mentor put a stop to the impromptu training. As soon as we were done, we dashed downstairs and had a cool shower. Not much was said as the seniors took their shower in a grumpy mood; no doubt they tacked the blame on to me for their interrupted sunbathing.

I had of course now accidently discovered where to get my washing done so before lunch managed to jam as much clothing into a machine and sat for a while taking in the view from this new vantage point. To one side of the dormitory block there were other buildings like the one on which I was stood, featuring hundreds of balconies of residential homes. Across the dual carriageway at the front, I could barely see behind the line of trees that ran the full length of the road opposite but then looking closely I could distinguish the location of our morning training venue following the footpath to what was a clearing that contained the park. I could also see huge netting somewhere further in the distance that obviously was a venue of some ball game or even one of the many golf-driving ranges that are scattered up and down the country.

I was summoned to the dining room by one of the third-year boys and joined both Kobayashi and Tanabe sensei for lunch. I had earlier told Kobayashi that my favourite food up until this point was the curry rice so the remaining students had prepared this dish for my benefit. However, Tanabe was not amused for it was Saturday and curry rice was always served up for supper. To be honest I would have welcomed it for breakfast too if I had my way but I was grateful for it twice this day. So, on this seventh day I had succeeded in annoying not only my senior senpais but also the club coach. If there were to be any fighting later today it wouldn't be too difficult to find a partner, I thought.

FIVE

I was still a bit mystified as to why I had spent my first week here and not yet fought under any circumstances. Not just for me of course, but there was an absence of free fighting that I thought would have been in abundance. It wasn't my place of course to ask the nature of the training schedule here, nor was I going to ask anyone "hey, how about a fight then?" It would have been a wasted journey if the emphasis was no longer on the facet of Karate training for which this place was so famous.

Well, fate has a way of bringing together thoughts and deeds in a most coincidental way. Kobayashi was in full attendance for our afternoon class and after our two-hour routine of basic training he ordered for some mitts to be distributed. Well, they were poured out of a bag onto the floor and we helped ourselves, in order of seniority. I picked up a pair of scruffy off-white frayed mitts that had dried bloodstains etched over the knuckle part and pulled them over my hands. Kobayashi called my name and then Tanemura, the captain. I wondered at that moment whether indeed my opponent standing opposite had put in a special request to have my head. We bowed to each other and my opponent surged forward quickly and aggressively with a front hand punch toward my face. I managed to avoid his attack and moved around. He was a bit apprehensive as he stood off and so I gave him my trademark roundhouse kick to the head that slapped him around the face. Kobayashi berated him and so he came in fast looking for a leveller of some sort, but again I moved comfortably out of the way and traded a few punches with him, but nothing was decisive. Tanemura wasn't heavy enough in his attacks to unsettle me in any way and in fact he was more nervous of my impending kicks as I was obviously looking to set him up again. The first pangs of nervous energy had coursed through my body, but I now became a little more relaxed and was able to settle down and comfortably control this first encounter on foreign soil. This was a typical feeling whenever I fought, the nerves at first affecting my initial movement before getting into my stride. Of course, the harder the opposition the longer to get to that relaxed state.

I sat back in line sweating profusely from this brief encounter and managed to get my breath back while I watched intently how the others performed. I noticed the nature of all present was to get stuck in as quickly as possible. There was virtually none of the movement I had been used to back in England, where often competitors would bounce around for long periods of time before mounting a challenge. This was not at all what I saw here. From the word 'Hajime' (to begin) there was no time wasted and once an encounter was ended it was back in again for more of the same. The spirit I witnessed was impressive from all those who took to the floor, all of them showing little respect for each other as they attacked relentlessly. The pattern of technique was much the same too. Lots of punches to the face and low kicks to the body, usually front kicks, or on the other hand a roundhouse kick that travelled very narrow and fast that was difficult to distinguish from the front kick. The white belts were showing just as much spirit against their seniors even though they were often outclassed. It made no difference, full steam ahead.

I was up again and this time faced the vice-captain Fukusyo, who had treated me to a pizza earlier in the week. He was a bigger version of the captain so had the reach advantage, but I felt under little threat as I moved in when he attacked and was able to greet him with a punch to the face as he also caught me. As he stepped away, I once more connected with a roundhouse to the face which caused another stern admonishment from our watching instructor and Fukusyo replied with a loud "HAI!" and a furious attack which caught me off guard and open to the face. The punch was hard and my eyes smarted from the blow but I managed to return with a strong reverse punch to the body. I was put under more pressure and we continued to smack each other in the face a few times out of sheer stubbornness until 'Yame' was called.

I was told to remain on the floor as another opponent stood quickly in front of me and as 'Hajime' was announced I was set upon even quicker than the two previous combatants. This guy was on a mission. He looked young, perhaps a second or third year, but he had strong kicks and he was determined to close me down, probably to avoid my face kicks. I felt his powerful kicks to the body just above the groin, which caused me to drop my hands, and then I caught a hard punch to the mouth. For the first time I was unnerved and fought back with face punches to put him off. His shouts too were piercing and along with his relentless attacks I was struggling to remain with his tempo. As I tried to make space to raise my knee to kick, he would instinctively step in close to thwart my attack so again we would stand toe to toe and trade. I managed to sweep his front leg and he lost his balance enough for me to slot a punch right in the ear. He reacted furiously. Back he came and I did wonder if there was anybody else fighting at the time because I felt a little tunnel visioned as I took on the seriousness of this match. Our fight seemed to go on for ages and I was no longer comfortable as fatigue took over as well as the demeanour of my opponent was unsettling. I was mad at wanting this exchange to end, because I was momentarily defeated in my head and too tired to do much more than just stand and trade. Kobayashi called a halt and we stood and glared at each other before our bows and "Arigato gozaimashita" (thanks for a good fight we'll do it again sometime)

His name was Kishiyama, a second year, Enomoto later told me.

"Aasa, nice jodan mawashi" Enomoto congratulated me on my face kicks, though I was less than happy with my fight with the second year. I told myself to be quicker off the mark in future to match their speed of attacks, and to be more aggressive. This was not randori but serious fighting without any worry over a little contact.

I was relieved to be in the deep bath that night. I had a few knocks from the fighting so felt relaxed after the shower and felt a little sleepy once I was immersed in the deep tub that was so hot, I felt like a bit part actor from Shogun the movie. That unfortunate soul was boiled alive.

I discovered that for the previous two weeks all students were undergoing exams in their various studies so there was a 'no fighting policy' for that period. Now the exams were at an end and the fact that there were some serious contests approaching there was to be plenty of fighting to go round. Enomoto also told me that Nihon University was consistently among the top three universities all styles team in the country and Tanabe was adamant this position was held.

After supper there was very little disturbance for the rest of the evening as I sat with the first years and watched television. A few of the others commented on my nice kicks and one also challenged me to a race on the Monday morning but I for one was looking forward to my first whole day off that week.

It was a luxury to sleep until around eight o'clock the following morning. No one seemed to be in a hurry to do anything. We all took breakfast around eight thirty. I was starting to exhaust my stock of bread for my toast so I reminded myself to pick some up on my travels.

Fujimoto, Oshima, and myself left for the station at about nine and I found myself on a familiar route I had taken earlier in the week and so we ended up in Shinjuku. There was no urgency on this day so I was able to do a little more shopping; some postcards and a Japanese to English dictionary. I was keen to transfer the words I was hearing to my own language determined to learn what I could while I was here. I was once more taken to Shakey's pizza parlour, but being a Sunday there was no special price at all, but I enjoyed the food and a large beer that was ordered on my behalf.

From Shinjuku we travelled to Harajuku where young Japanese people go to express their identity. Now I considered myself still a young person but I failed to identify with any person I saw on this day. On this day this area is closed to traffic and is a showcase to many different types of fashion. There were young punks; there were rockers; there were punk rockers. Teddy boys with teddy girls, different coloured hair, pins in noses eyes and ears. This was a freak show to music and the more we stared and mocked the more they seemed to enjoy their status. Yet there was still an innocence about the whole charade. In fact, it was a charade because they were simply clones of an identity they had probably seen on the telly. I'm sure before they returned home, they would remove any sign of their double identity and slot straight back in to their disciplined society. I looked closely to see if I recognized anybody suddenly thinking how I'd crack up if I saw captain Tanemura dancing round his rock box with red hair or Kikuta greasing up his quiff in his leathers.

Harajuku is situated in the impressive Yoyogi Park that also houses the Meiji Jingu Shrine situated in its centre. This is a place of worship for the Shinto followers in the Tokyo area. It is dedicated to the Emperor Meiji who was responsible for the demise of the Shoguns and the advancement to a more modern Japan. This shrine has a huge wooden gate at its entranceway under which we walked to make our way along the gravel path to the sanctuary of this holy place. People were washing their hands and faces at a small fountain before entering the shrine; a large wooden constructed building with all the characteristics of the ancient architecture of Japan. How strange, I thought, that within these grounds away from the traffic and high rise modernness you could imagine being in a society over one hundred years old, yet only a few hundred yards away a group of youngsters were trying to disassociate themselves from anything traditional. They couldn't have picked a more symbolic place.

My guides for the day did a good job considering their limited English. We exchanged small talk about English stuff in comparison to Japanese. They were similar in character; quiet, modest, not in any way brash. I knew already that Oshima was in the serious bracket of Karate exponents at the university, I knew on the other hand that Fujimoto was not. They were both third years so the same age as myself and I felt this was relevant as our communication that day was well balanced. We had fun but we didn't overdo it.

We passed the street punks again in order to grab some food from the hordes of take away stalls that were set up along the cordoned off thoroughfare. We ate hot dogs and a little barbecued chicken, which was delicious and washed it down with a cola. The three of us then headed back with Hachimanyama, and all that it meant in our thoughts, as our next destination.

We returned to the dormitory and me to my room around five o'clock. I chatted with the first-year students and I noticed one of them write on a calendar hanging on the cupboard. I looked closer and he explained that he would cross off the days as they went. This lad was Iidabashi, a handsome, slightly built lad who was always telling me about some American soul artists called Sam and Dave. I'd never heard of them. "Aasa" said Iidabashi, "you like running?" I told him I did so he said that he wanted to race me the next morning. So, it was settled, the others were excited and we looked forward to the competition.

Once more rain had fallen through the night. This along with the overcast sky cooled the air a little. The rain had stopped so we headed for the park and so to my little race with Iidabashi. We all set off together but Iidabashi went off like a jackrabbit so I went after him. I sat right on his shoulder and kept with him every step of the way. It was a strong pace and I was wondering if I was doing the right thing by accepting the challenge.

That was it I suppose; I wasn't happy unless I was up for some sort of challenge. I had lost a few fights at school because I was always 'up for it' against older or bigger boys, but I didn't have the ability to see it through. I guess there was always some intrinsic reason for me to start some form of martial arts rather than the aesthetic reason that was an attraction to so many. As always when you begin something that may be a tough undertaking you wonder if you have done the right thing. I can vividly remember travelling to Bristol as a sixteen-year-old to join in the South West squad training sessions that were held every so often under the guidance of Fred Kear. The fighting was intense and there were always the incidents you wouldn't want repeated. My mate Bob Flowers kneed me in the groin in the morning session that dropped me like a stone. Fred said, "Sorry Bob but no can do, nice technique though". In the afternoon session someone smacked me in the face and gave me a beautiful shiner (no mitts back then). From then on, the little jaunt up to Bristol in the back of my mate's Ford Cortina was always a nervous one. But for those sessions, which instilled 'the get back in there' mentality, I doubt I would have taken on this trip in the first place. I remind Bob every now and again that I still owe him one.

I decided, sat on Iidabashi's shoulder, to force his bluff. I was a little tired from the pace of the run but I still had some left in me. I passed him and took up the pace hoping to give him the impression I had loads left in me. My little ruse worked, for just as I was wishing I was simply jogging with the rest, after half a lap or so he gave up the chase and I pressed on to take gold. We shook hands at the end and we both enjoyed the light-hearted episode.

My feet, thankfully, were a lot better and I was looking forward to training later this afternoon. My scrap with Kishiyama was on my mind, which often happens after a tough one. A confrontation of this sort causes the mind to turn over the fight time and time again; the good bits, the bad bits until there is some sort of favourable result at the end of the analysis. I have known people lose a street fight convincingly, but after a short while are arguing how well they did, even to the point of claiming a victory, sounds nutty I know but very true. After a week or two however, they're taking another hiding. I knew that I didn't fare too well against Kishiyama and I was convinced I was caught unprepared so I was determined to correct it. Thus, he was to be my 'bogey man'. And in every club, I have trained there has always been one of them. Somebody who is either very good or just likes dishing out a bit of rough. Often, they are the reason for people to quit. The best thing is to decide that he is the person to beat however long it takes. Learn from him watch him and plan the takeover.

Tanabe was in his room most of the day and only emerged to instruct one or two remaining students to sort out some lunch for us. The four of us sat at one table and enjoyed a stew of some sort. I was hungry so it went down well and I began to realize that Japanese food was as varied as any other. It was just that initial shock of eating 'natto' that had put me off and I knew I would be foolish in hoping to buy my own along the way. On this day I decided to decommission the toaster after all and turn Japanese.

After lunch Tanabe sensei invited me along for a cycle ride and just as we were about to set off Kobayashi drew up alongside in his trusty Toyota and so the three of us travelled to another complex belonging to Nihon University only two minutes' drive away. This was where Hideo Tanabe worked. He was professor of physical education and here I saw a sports complex that catered for so many different activities. While I stood in the huge sports arena there was a fencing class, trampolining, gymnastics, and basketball all taking place at once such was the magnitude of the open area. There were young kids running flat out around the balcony that circled above our heads and I thought there was some kind of running battle taking place until it was pointed out there was a running track marked out beneath their feet.

I followed both instructors into an office and while they were in discussion, I browsed through the manuals that filled the bookshelves around me. There were mainly Karate books but some were old manuscripts with pictures of Ohtsuka and Shotokan karate's founder Funakoshi plus many more old photos of people I didn't recognize but all from an early generation. I now understood that

Tanabe worked here most of the day before cycling through the back streets to return to his passion of the Karate club. The realization of Hideo Tanabe's world began to dawn on me that day. Having spent his youth training and then graduating from his beloved university he was to spend probably the rest of his working years and more committed to its cause. He had a fierce reputation as a fighter and so was the best man for the job.

Once I had returned from the afternoon visit a second year came running to tell me that I had missed a phone call. Now that sounded strange because I was halfway around the world, had only been here a week and the only people I had met all lived with me. Apparently one of my old instructors, Wakamei, who had made a few teaching visits to my hometown of Bridgwater had learned of my arrival. Wakamei Sensei too had graduated from Nihon University before traveling to England. He spent several years teaching under Tatsuo Suzuki so he was keen to contact me and ask how things were going. The messenger told me he would call back again. Katsumi Wakamei, I remember, was a young instructor who brought vitality to his instruction based on his experience as a fighter winning many tournaments in Japan as a top competitor. His instruction too was of the highest quality and he was able to switch from innovative fighting techniques to the refined kata movements so important to the students of the UK back in the seventies. He was also a handsome young man and made the most of his freedom from the restrictive Japanese lifestyle in favour of the more adventurous one of the London scenes. I was certainly keen to hook up with a familiar face especially one who could speak English so well.

A few hours later I was sat in the dojo pondering what was next in store. It was six o'clock and we just had spent two hours doing more of the same as last week only this time we had just finished a countless number of punches on a pad held by a partner. The emphasis was initially on the speed of attack, but after we had performed a quick one two combination on the small round target Tanabe sensei was having a fit on anyone dropping their hands as we moved back to prepare for the next attack. As we were theoretically backing off from an opponent (God forbid) we were reminded of our need to guard our face. This sounds more than obvious I know and for anyone reading this who trains I can understand them thinking 'well I do that as a matter of course' but bearing in mind we were about two hundred combinations in when our hands got more than a little heavy and so the need to drop the hands for a little respite was probably understandable. Yet Tanabe stood behind us all and waited for the inevitable so there would be a smart kick up the rear and a slap around the head for the culprit who let the side down. And while one took his punishment, we would all stand to attention and shout "Hai, so!" as if we were all guilty.

"Mitto" Tanabe shouted and out came the bag of mitts, which were scattered across the floor. My stomach turned over and the adrenalin started its journey around my body. I had one eye on Kishiyama who funnily enough shot a glance in my direction. I watched the first wave of combatants and started to make a mental note of how people were faring. The third year Oshima was up and putting up with no nonsense with his opponent. Time and time again he connected with his front hand and I wondered if his poor adversary had realized it was the front hand that was hitting him in the face or whether he was looking somewhere else. There was another impressive fighter too, Kawano, a stocky bear like character who was extremely agile for his stocky build. He was giving my roommate Enomoto a hard time. Enomoto certainly had the reach advantage over anyone in the dojo but at this moment he was not putting it to good use. Kawano was hanging back out of range momentarily before sending a vicious front kick to the belly and then following up with the trademark face punch that connected every time. I sometimes looked at Tanabe sensei to see his reaction when a punch landed a bit strong but his face remained impassive. He wandered from fight to fight stopping them from time to time to give his instructions before waving his hand for them to resume. Then I saw one of the first years backing off from his opponent. It was Tanaka, the doctor look alike. Whether he had just been hit or just felt the pressure was getting a bit much for a moment I hadn't noticed but Tanabe was up behind him so quick and bellowing so loud that he instantly charged forward, only as far as a vicious punch in the face. I guess that was safer than the full wrath of our instructor. The intensity this day was far greater than the last session because of Tanabe's presence. Kobayashi could berate and scold; Tanabe could breathe fire in comparison. Every student was working at full throttle just to keep from any unwanted attention from the roving resident instructor.

"Aasa"

"Hai!" I shouted and jumped up.

"Takahashi!"

"Hai!" and he was up. The manager. The little fourth year who had arranged my sightseeing trip on Tanabe's request. We bowed and stepped forward and I noticed he had a strange way of holding his front hand. It was held high to give maximum protection to the face but he also waved it annoyingly around in front of my face almost at full stretch. I opened with a feint or two by raising my front leg as if to kick but he moved straight in ready to jam the kick and counter. But my feint had created this reaction and I leaned back and hit him with reverse roundhouse to the side of the head resulting in a satisfactory sounding slap. By the time my foot was on the floor however the undeterred Takahashi closed me down and hit me twice; front hand and reverse punch, I guessed because I didn't see them coming. I just felt the two belts around the mouth that sent my head reeling. Takahashi senpai darted away from me as quick as he came in and kept his front hand once higher and more outstretched waving a small imaginary circle, perhaps he was trying to hypnotize me I wondered as I tested the ground between us with a lead front hand. Again, he stepped in ready to counter punch Takahashi wasn't heavy so I didn't feel threatened by the power so much, but I could see I was facing an experienced opponent, gutsy too, for he was more than willing to move in without hesitation. With good timing the lighter fighter can still do damage and his tactics were to be in and out, finding the space to connect with the Wado Ryu trademark 'nagashi zuki' punch. I did my best to keep the fight at length so to negate his objective but it was inevitable that his speed and tenacity would tell over my rather pedestrian movement. We exchanged a few more face punches before time was up and another opponent was mentally recorded for future reference.

I sat and waited after my first fight and watched little battles developing in front of me. I wondered if Tanabe knew I had had a tough fight at the last session. I wondered too if there was any communication between him and Kobayashi about my training so far. If they were to see what I was made of then surely, I was to be put under pressure early so they could form an impression. I wondered a lot of things while I sat with my mitts waiting for my name to be called, perhaps to fight somebody who despises the fact that I'm even here and who, if given the chance would simply steam in and take me apart to send me back to where I had come. Early mind games with myself and I wasn't coping too well. At that moment I thought how things would have felt any different if I had travelled with a mate. Somebody I could team up with or simply chat to when things got a bit tough. A bit of friendly banter on the battlefield, so to speak. There was a pal at home who I had trained with from the first months of joining the Karate club. He was a few years older than me was Ian and already a green belt when I came along as a beginner. We became inseparable training partners. He was the only person skinnier than me at the time, like a pencil, but if he kicked you in the face, you were over. He would have won the summer course tournament in Southport '76 if a youthful Bob Flowers hadn't popped up and punched him in the head in the final. In my opinion Ian would have undoubtedly made an international fighter but he decided to wreck all that and join the army. I was devastated. A guy who trained as much as I did, was fast and gutsy, deserted me. I knew too that if it had not been for the army, he would have been here lapping up the training doing his best to knock someone over. I mentally smiled at the thought of there being two of us here.

"Kikuta!" Tanabe shouted

"Hai!" he was up.

"Aasa" and with a quick response I was on my feet. We fought for several minutes but with little passion. I sensed Kikuta wasn't that bothered so he went through the motions of attacking now and again so I caught him with a couple of counter gyaku zuki, reverse punches, to his midsection. I threw a couple of face kicks that caught him off guard, but I purposely had no desire to prove anything to this uninterested adversary. I felt his ambition to become world champion had deserted him long ago so there was nothing to prove here except a little show to keep Tanabe happy.

I did a few rounds the rest of that session with my first-year colleagues and although we were kept at it until seven o'clock, which was a lengthy free fighting period, there was not the level of competition I knew would be waiting for me from several other hungry fighters. I did conclude by now though that most of these students were more than a little unprepared for my face kicks which perhaps reflected in their training. Their own repertoire was mainly a mixture of lightning-fast head punches with direct low kicks accompanied with a spirit of extraordinary bravery, but so early on I had exposed a weakness simply because they did not seem to practice the kicks which had become fashionable on the European circuit. I thought back then what a formidable combination could be developed from this observation. I also knew that the faster the opponents came in, to a degree, there was a predictability to their method and if I stood my ground and applied the logic, the easier they were to hit. Putting such ideas into practice was to be the hard part. There was to be plenty of opportunity, I reminded myself, but this day was over. I felt good after a tough three hours. My body was a little more accustomed to the duration and repetition of technique and in particular my feet were well on the mend, just chunks of dried skin waiting to peel off. That should give me something to do later should the evening be uneventful.

Returning and having dinner was becoming a pleasurable experience. I had the feeling that I had achieved something when evening came around. There would be a light-hearted mood too among the first years in my room, as they would discuss the day's events, often bringing me into the conversation. They had been at university no more than two months prior to my arrival so they too were still finding their feet and learning the ropes. I watched the first-year boys as they compared notes on their training session. They would often get so animated and worked up while demonstrating certain techniques they had either performed or been successful with that one of the other lads had to pretend to be Tanabe sensei to bring things to order. This was when we discovered the hidden talents of young Hijikata, the student who would often be training until ten at night. In fact, he explained to everybody that although he was a bit hacked off about training at unusual hours there was a small dose of satisfaction along the way because there had to be a senior grade to monitor his training. After all, one might take advantage of being in the dojo by oneself and just sit around and shout a few kiais every now and again to add a touch of realism. Of course, the seniors weren't stupid, they weren't going to deprive a needy student of their training commitments. Until they had to baby sit for a few hours trying to create an atmosphere for one when usually there were two dozen. This was where Hijikata had the sense to reverse the psychology and gloat at the fact that the guy who was sharing his space for an hour or three probably hated every minute of it. Hijikata would then start to impersonate the senior who had been watching over him the previous training session. His facial expressions plus his physical antics were hilarious and the more we laughed the more he continued with impersonations of other seniors, then instructors, both Kobayashi and Tanabe. I fell about, not just at the impressions but also at the thought of Tanabe present in the next room hearing us laugh and not at all aware who was the subject of the hilarity. Hijikata then went on to mimic famous sportsmen of Japan such as baseball players and I still laughed even though I had no idea who these people were. The trouble with having a bit of talent however, was that it would soon become common knowledge and we would not be the only ones to encourage Hijikata to supply the funnies.

I lay in my bed that night listening intently to my tapes that brought me closer to home. There are certain songs that can remind you of certain people and places. The problem was, every song I listened to became a symbol of a place in my hometown. George Benson, Michael Jackson, Barry White, and all the soul stuff brought back memories of my nightlife in a flash of pre-Japan. I began to realize that Kikuta's reluctance to elaborate on the answer to my question about nightclubs was obvious. I guess he was too embarrassed to tell me straight, so let me down lightly. Quite simply for us there was no nightlife, just Hijikata's performances before ten o'clock lights out. Now and again, I would switch to a radio station on my borrowed music centre and pick up some jazz music for which I also had a penchant for, if it had a beat to it, and then I would make a mental note of the artist and make sure, given the opportunity, I would look out for the record played.

Each day I started to develop mental mood swings. I was into the second week and daily life had taken on a grim reality in stark contrast to the first. In the mornings a feeling of "oh no, not again" would swarm over me as I rose early to do the run. The thought of another three hours later in the day plus facing another line up of over enthusiastic head hunters would also add to the dread. Yet after training there would be an almost euphoric feeling of accomplishment and relief. In the short evenings after training everybody seemed in a happy mood, relaxed, friendly. I suppose then I wasn't on my own experiencing this roller coaster of emotion.

SIX

After breakfast one day during only my second week I decided to put my spare time to a bit more use. The weather was now warming to a considerable degree as May approached and I felt an Englishman abroad would be considered rude not to make the most of the amenities on offer. So, wearing only a pair of shorts and carrying a measly bit of washing in case my position was compromised, I ascended to the roof and stretched out in the sun for a while in order to darken the pasty white skin a little. I was interrupted after half an hour by Fukusyo, the vice-captain. He invited me to go along with him to Hachimanyama station where he said there was a place that sold English speaking newspapers. So away we went for the ten-minute walk through the maze of back streets that was finally becoming familiar. Sure enough, there was a small newsstand that sold The Japan Times, and with that in hand I followed Fukusyo into a noodle shop that sold an astonishing variety of noodle dishes served up in a big bowl of a hot broth like soup. This was not only delicious but surprisingly filling. All for a cost of around seven hundred yen, which worked out at about four pounds. I sat regally in that noodle shop that day, with the vice-captain of Nichi Dai, and read my paper. I felt anything but a foreigner who had only been in the country less than a fortnight. As I sat reading my paper, I became witness to the phenomenon of slurping, which is considered good etiquette in Japan. Everybody slurps when consuming soup or noodles. This being a noodle shop there were a variety of shapes and sizes sat around me dining and the variation in noise was phenomenal. I think there was a pattern here, like an impromptu chorus of their national anthem.

Sat in the noodle shop drinking tea, I asked Fukusyo for a few pointers on the Japanese language. First, I needed some clarification on the after-dinner speech that was customary whenever a meal was finished. Remember, up until this point I would just open my mouth pretending to know the words so as not to look out of place or offend anyone. A bit like being at a wedding when the hymns are sung or the Lord's Prayer recited, you know the feeling. 'Go sauce the chestnuts' was a close facsimile of what was said and I felt I could get away with it among twenty-four other voices, but I would be a bit stuffed if I were on my own in different company. I repeated 'go chi so sama desh'ta' several times much to the amusement of those in the shop. Also 'oishii' was another word relevant that day, meaning delicious. I left the noodle shop fluent in two phrases that day and leaving the proprietor looking a little smug.

Returning to my room that afternoon I stared at the belongings around the room hung up at various places that denoted our sleeping places. I looked too at my suitcase in the cupboard, which contained everything I had in the world and felt more than a little lonely. Passing the time away here was one of the hardest parts especially when much of the day was spent alone. I looked through the paper I had bought and searched the jobs page hoping to get a little inspiration there. Most of the vacancies advertised were either for candidates with university degrees or those with a student visa. I had neither. When I had taken the trouble to travel to the Japanese Embassy in London prior to taking my trip, they laughed when I asked for a student visa to study Karate so I could stay a full twelve months. They said I could study something a little more cultural like the language or cookery, but that I needed some certificates already of proof of study. I had certificates of Karate, but I guess that simply wasn't Japanese enough. I therefore came to Japan on a six-month tourist visa with plans of my own to extend that period.

As the weather warmed so the training took on a new challenge. It's funny how a small window just above floor level can attract so much attention. While sitting, during our breaks, I, like a few of the other first years, tried to get as much air as possible from this poor excuse of a window. Considering there was very little breeze blowing anyway there was nothing to gain even if I could have stuck my head through.

From where I sat, I could see through the window on the opposite side of the dojo above where the fourth years sat. I could make out the top of a large house which was right next door to the dojo. I wondered who lived in that house, and whether they had air conditioning. Funnily enough after training I never thought about that house. In fact, I never saw it at any other time other than when I was training. I remember just seeing a couple of first floor windows and the top of a large tree that probably grew in their garden. It was a bit like The Secret Garden, a place only I visited. I imagined a place of grandeur with a western style decor, even a piano, and everywhere in the house was cool and spacious. Everything this dojo was not. I was sat flushed in the face and with the cotton karate gi clinging heavily to my sweaty, tired frame.

On this Wednesday of my second week, we had just finished the weighted kicking section and were lining up at the back of the dojo ready to begin our relay of another several hundred kicks or so when a couple of strangers strolled in wearing crisp white Karate gis. These two were quickly followed by another, plus Tanabe. As we continued to train, these three, who I guessed were in their late twenties, nonchalantly limbered up and admired themselves constantly in the mirror. One was a heavy chap while the other two seemed in better shape, but all had a demeanour that was foreboding. Tanabe Sensei too emerged from his mirrored changing room and adopted a similar presence, warming up as if he were going to fight somebody. As we continued to train and sweat and shout these four circulated among us and gave instructions of technical detail to every individual. The three newcomers ignored me, not due to my superior technique I might add, but rather I felt, they didn't want to risk looking a fool in trying to communicate with me.

Tanabe on the other hand was having a field day with me. Telling me to keep my front hand up, to snap back my kicks, move faster and so on. I had the feeling that he was indicating to the other three that his language skills were a lot more advanced so he would take care of the foreigner. Typical Tanabe. This continued right through the next hour-long punching session before we finally sat for our break until the last hour commenced. At this point there developed a familiar feeling of trepidation. There was always the likelihood that there would be some serious fighting next and I remember often thinking, 'not today, let's do it tomorrow instead'. At times Tanabe would shout "kata!" or "kihon gummite!" and a feeling of relief would sweep over me. "Mitto!" shouted Tanabe and they were poured unceremoniously onto the floor for us to salvage. The three amigos also donned a pair of mitts and started to demonstrate their handiwork by shadow boxing around the dojo.

I was first up today opposite a young lad from the second-year group called 'Akii'. He looked fifteen. We bowed and he closed the gap in super quick time, kicked low which I just had time to cover with my front hand but which left me open to the face. For the first time blood was drawn, and it was at the opposite end from my feet. The punch that followed the kick hit me straight in the mouth splitting my lip. This kid in front of me took the direct route and it worked. I was furious, with him, with me. My front hand shot up to hold a high guard, rather after the horse had bolted so to speak, but I was determined to make amends for my dithering. After Akii had pulled away to register his opening gambit in acknowledgment to himself, I stood off him a little and dithered some more, he came in again and I stepped in with a strong reverse punch. Now I am left-handed, a southpaw fighter in boxing terms, so many of my better punches come off the left side. The left punch connected to his body and so did the right that followed to the head, which knocked the little fellow back somewhat. Which proved my theory if you step in quick enough you should get there first. But like Kishiyama this boy was strong and determined so he came right back at me, which was no more than I expected by now, so my left hand once more drove home to his body and knocked a little wind out of him. This time I had the room to kick and so brought the roundhouse up to the face which he too was aware of and so moved skilfully out of the way. For a young lightweight Akii was a match for anyone and I cussed as I chewed my fat lip when the proceedings were called to a halt and I sat to wait for the next rally.

I then watched as Oshima faced one of the visitors. Oshima was as tall as this young man in front of him so I imagined a close contest, but Oshima was taken apart by the technique and ferocity of his opponent. This certain individual had an array of technique that I hadn't seen among the present crop of students. His legs were quick and versatile and his hands were controlling Oshima in every way. The contact too was solid and despite the valiant effort of our third year, the man in front of him punched him at will, knocking the head back on more than one occasion. Typically, though the beaten man did not know when to quit until Tanabe's shout broke the campaign. They bowed to each other and Oshima's uttering of 'arigato gozaimashita' was loud and purposeful. He really meant the fact he had enjoyed the beating!

There were several more fights for us all that day and I fought with Tanemura again, the captain, plus one or two third years but these guys didn't have the fire in their bellies like one or two of the second years. My opponents, however, were quickly adapting to my wanton high kicks and so endeavoured to close me down at every opportunity. I would have to consider from here on how to cope with this change in their tactics.

While I was doing my usual raid of the vending machine immediately after training to quench my raging thirst, Kikuta and Fujimoto joined me for a chat and I asked about the newcomers that day. The three strangers were ‘old boys’, students who had graduated from the ranks a few years earlier and were still active on the contest scene. So as much as possible they came back to use the facilities and the personnel to aid in their training. By all accounts there was a contest approaching and they were looking for some sparring partners. The biggest of the three was Tachizawa, elder brother of one of our second years. The guy who had fought Oshima was Murase an international fighter of some repute and one of the finest of recent years to have graduated from this club. He had a reputation that even his training partners found him hard to handle even when just going through one or two drills, such was his level of commitment. I wondered if it would be sooner or later when I too would stand in front of Murase.

The next day took on much the same pattern as the previous and I guessed the routine would be much the same from here on. The day was uneventful, a little more time on the roof in the sun, a little walk to a cake shop where a little old lady sold custard and curry filled doughnuts. I started to gain more confidence with my limited Japanese and put it to use in these simple situations when there wasn't too much pressure. Asking for and buying items was no longer a mountain to climb. I spent the time studying during the day and asked for help from students in the evening and so started to gather a fair amount of vocabulary. I would also hear short stock phrases said so often around me that the meanings became clear naturally, rather than having to decipher them. Learning a language is best done with native speakers and so I took on as much as I could. The problem was that a few students spoke good English so this didn't encourage me enough. We would sometimes try to have a Japanese only spoken evening in our room, but my vocabulary would dry up too quickly. Picking up the colloquialism of those around me certainly helped and I was determined to learn more.

Training on this day intensified and I got the impression that something was afoot. The old boys were back and once more strutting their stuff. We spent an eternity on the various striking shields and focus pads. A punch bag was erected at head height for the use of high kicks. We struck the makiwara punching post until our knuckles bled so then had to continue by using the elbow until the full quota was performed. Even then there had to be permission from a senior student to change from punch to elbow. He would first check the damage on the hand before allowing the change. The mitts came out, but this time my temperament was ahead of the game for I was expecting to fight and therefore actually looked forward to whatever came my way. First, I faced Enomoto. His kiai shout would always be up before him, in other words he was charging himself up ready for battle. He was the tallest of the club and when I bowed to him, he towered over me. I took a leaf out of Takahashi's manual of little people and stretched out my front hand a little to secure a guarded face and give Enomoto some distance to worry about. He too however had picked up a few tips in recent days and was firing his front hand out like a pro boxer. I charged in quick knocking his front hand away with my right and punched his body with the left, stayed in close with my front hand open once more in his face to back him up a bit before using my left to punch his head. This was a common tactic in this dojo whereas often, back in the UK, once a technique is considered a score the two adversaries would simply back off and start again. Even in the absence of a referee it was considered fair play, but unrealistic. The fighting in this dojo was constant, nobody stopped until time was up. If you were backed up against the wall then you remained there or fought your way out. Enomoto struggled at close range so I kept tight as much as possible until he too shoved me off then opened with a front kick that caught me perfectly in the solar plexus, I was winded and badly so. I knew to stop would be disastrous; I moved around to buy some time groaning quietly as I went. Tanabe was shouting at me to attack for I must have delayed any forward motion for at least five seconds, which was unheard of. I shouted with a firm 'Hai!' and that helped to rally my spirit before stepping forward onto a face punch that snapped my head back. I saw red for the first time grabbed Enomoto's front hand and let him have one of the same with my favoured left hand. I had underestimated my fellow roommate and paid for it. A lump on the side of my cheek was growing quickly and I was thankful we wore mitts because I could have had my face split open. I enjoyed the fight however. There was a feeling of euphoria in such a scrap, my fitness was improving and I felt I was adapting to the intensity of the fights, but I was still making errors that were of an elementary nature. I told myself to be a little more ruthless and dominate from the outset.

The session was far from over. I fought no fewer than six others that day each fight probably lasting five minutes. All the while Tanabe would be prowling the perimeter coaching and yelling, sometimes stopping the proceedings altogether and all present would stand to attention and listen intently and shout loud responses for every point made. Tanabe demanded our undivided attention and we were obliged to give it. He had a habit of standing behind one fighter and coaching the opponent opposite. This made me smile for my old boxing coach would do the same. It was a little distracting at first for I could see my opponent's eyes flickering from mine to something over my shoulder. I thought at first it was the start of a conspiracy to finally be rid of the Englishman, but this was one of his many coaching methods. It would be a long time before he did the same for my benefit I felt.

The old boys present concentrated on the other lads and in a strange way I felt jealous that perhaps they didn't consider my ability worthy of their attention.

Training concluded that evening with the advanced partner work of the Wado style and I paired with Fukusyo who insisted on putting me right in a few places. I didn't feel out of my depth at all during some of the technical training, just happy to learn from anyone. Tanabe would again float about and correct me saying that in Japan we do it this way even though Suzuki Sensei, who was my chief instructor back in England at the time, does it differently.

I was as hot as I'd ever been that day. My gi stuck to my body

from the gallons of perspiration
I had secreted and my throat was desperate for some liquid. We drank nothing during training even when sat in the rest periods so it was a long wait for refreshment. I was always first to the machine outside and it became an in-house joke to stand out of my way while stepping into shoes outside the dojo. Even at the dinner table there was often an irritating wait because our food and drink sat looking at us but nobody could touch a thing until all were present. And Tanabe would take his time just to wind us up. The food I could wait for, just, but the fluid was essential to my overheated system. Enomoto and I quietly discussed our fight that evening over dinner and then in a whisper told me that today's training was the first time he had ever witnessed a heavy bag hung at head height for kicking.

"Because of you I think; Tanabe is not happy about students being kicked in the face."

I was stunned. To think I had in any way made an impact was a revelation. I walked a little taller that evening even though Tanabe had never complimented me in anything I did. That didn't bother me at all for I was used to that back home. It just wasn't in the instructors' nature to throw niceties around when you were expected to get things right anyway. But this was to me a symbol of Tanabe walking up to me and slapping me on the back and saying 'thanks for kicking some of my lads in the head.'

'That's all-right governor I'll stay on a little longer for that' would be my reply. 'And while I'm staying how about a little more refreshment in the dojo?'

As if the surrealism of my thought patterns influenced those around me! After my shower I was summoned to Tanabe's room where he was sat with the three visiting old boys. I was introduced and offered drinks, which I thought would be rude to decline. Kikuta was summoned and he poured our drinks while he translated. He too drank a little of the wine on offer and then some sake which was served from a huge bottle which came up to my chest, well, I was sat down at the time. It was here I noticed that the old boys too would jump up to pour the drinks for their former instructor and light his cigarette as soon as it hung from his lips. Espying his glass almost empty, I too sat up on my knees and picked up the bottle of sake and offered it forward. Tanabe looked satisfied as if he had just trained a monkey from another country to fall in line. In a way, he had. In Japan it is considered etiquette to pour your senior or friend's drink. It is in my opinion a great gesture. Although I could only imagine what would happen if you should try to encourage this in England. If you should pick up your mate's pint to top it up before it was finished there would be a row before there was a chance to explain.

SEVEN

Tanabe sensei held court in his small domain. The conversation was all his. The three old boys simply interjected from time to time and laughed along at the appropriate moments. Because of my presence he would tell me about England and the English customs as if to impress his listeners. In fact, Tanabe sensei was one of the first Japanese instructors to visit England and he would dig out some old souvenirs and show the five of us proof of his tales. He said he had a girlfriend somewhere in London. Then again, he said he had a girlfriend in Italy, Spain, and the United States. He asked me which part of England I was from and I told him near Bristol and he recognized the city in an instant telling me of Philip Kear, brother of Fred, now residing in Australia who had many years earlier also stayed at this university. I of course knew this, for it was talking to Philip during one of his brief visits to the UK that inspired me to come here in the first place. Tanabe sensei then said he had a girlfriend somewhere in Bristol. Tanabe was as enthusiastic in his entertaining as he was in his teaching in the dojo.

The three old boys left for home or some other destination. Kikuta went back to his room but then Tanabe beckoned for me to follow. We jumped on a bike outside the front door and cycled quarter of a mile or so to a small apartment. Here Tanabe fished out more souvenirs of worldwide travels and photos of him at various training courses. He also presented war memorabilia and photos of young kamikaze pilots taking their sake on the airstrip before departing to another place. Tanabe then drew the blinds in case of unwanted attention before revealing a magnificent samurai sword of historical value.

Tanabe waved me away as he dried up with things to show me and so I cycled back alone to the dormitory block. I felt I'd had a drink or two by now and was looking forward to some sleep. However, I didn't manage to make it to my room for there were a few third and fourth years milling about making the most of Tanabe's absence. They were a little taken aback on seeing me and for a moment they looked past me to see who might be in my wake, fearful at the thought of being compromised out of position. The time was around eleven thirty and they figured Tanabe was not coming back so they could extend their evening a little in his absence. Fukusyo approached asking about the situation before relaxing after I had explained I had tucked Tanabe in for the night. I could sense also that the vice-captain was half drunk. He urged me to accompany him downstairs out on to the road where a hundred yards or so along the way was what appeared to be a workman's hut. There was a plastic curtain surrounding the hut under which we stooped to enter. Inside there was an old fellow behind a counter cooking and chatting to another old fellow sat on a bench. Fukusyo ordered two beers and some food and joined in the conversation while I sat quietly amused at the scene, a mobile fast-food hut. The drinks were poured from bottles into our small glasses and Fukusyo, along with the old man and the punter, chinked glasses with me and uttered "kampai!" Fukusyo welcomed me to Japan. At this rate if everyone takes it in turn to welcome me to Japan I could eat and drink free for a month, I mused. Another bowl of noodles and lots more slurping was had before we turned in for the night.

Next morning with a slightly thick head I rose early as normal. What wasn't so normal was the game of soccer that followed. We were led around the back of our building onto the sports field and separated into two teams. For the next forty minutes or so we chased a ball around the field representing some sort of organized game. The young first years of my room were filled with excitement as they raced up and down tackling the senior grades and then briefly stopping to apologize before continuing to press for goal. The final result was lost in the glut of goals that were scored, but to see the likes of Takahashi, Fukusyo, Tanemura, Oshima, Kikuta and all the rest mix it up with their junior kohais was a warm sight in what is usually a tense and torrid atmosphere. The weather seemed hotter than the day before so Hijikata was sent to get some drinks and we each shared our fluid with the next man.

Laid outstretched on my futon after breakfast I reflected on the last twenty-four hours, the visit to Tanabe's room, then to his flat, the late spell with Fukusyo and even the soccer game in Tanabe's absence. If I was perhaps a little homesick in these last couple of days then maybe one or two people had picked up on my mood and designed a way to help settle me in a little. I felt embarrassed, but a little honoured at the same time.

Today was Thursday and at around two thirty I joined Kikuta and Oshima to travel via Shinjuku, where we ate lunch, to Suidobashi for training. More intense fighting for a half an hour or so and Fumihiro Tanabe joined his brother in monitoring every clash with great interest. I still sensed there was something afoot with the intensity of the sparring and the visit of the old boys who graced us with their presence again this evening.

While getting prepared to leave with the rest of the lads after training I was invited along with both Tanabe brothers plus the three old boys to a nearby restaurant. We walked a few minutes in the balmy evening before entering a small eating-house where both Tanabe instructors were obviously regular visitors. The lady in charge fussed over them, brought forth bottles of beer to a table and introduced me to a few of the locals before I settled down to listen to excited conversation for half an hour or so without any idea of its contents. Fumihiro Tanabe finally spoke to me and asked if I liked fish to which I replied in the affirmative so he ordered something on my behalf. Fifteen minutes later I was served with something on a bowl of rice.

"Unagi" said Hideo. "Eel" he added. I was grateful, but I'd rather he hadn't told me. The eel was spread over the rice in a rich looking sauce. I prodded it to make sure there was no life. It didn't have a head or anything to resemble its former life form, but just the same I prodded away. I picked up the meat took a mouthful and surprisingly enjoyed it. The sauce too was delicious so I tucked in and cleaned up all in my bowl plus the tempura that had also been served. Tempura is a dish of fish or vegetables cooked in batter, not unlike our own fish and chips but nowhere near as greasy. My glass of beer was constantly replenished and so I reciprocated whenever possible. Fumihiro then raised his glass and welcomed me to Japan and the others followed suit. They then spoke of Shiomitsu Sensei and the old days and asked whether I liked Japanese girls. I think personally they lived such a sheltered life that possibly they hadn't seen a girl for such a long time and was wondering what one was like.

The meal was followed with a little presentation of a Nihon University sweat towel, which I knew I could put to good use. Perhaps it was a hint of some sort. I was also given a lapel badge with an NUKC inscription across the front. I knew then in my own mind I was here for the whole nine yards. Ok, the kind gesture could have simply been a good public relation exercise in order to maintain the good name of their establishment throughout the Karate world, an offering they make to any overseas visitor. But for me it was to become a symbol of my determination to become a more accepted Karate student, more than a visitor, perhaps even a bonafide Nichi Dai boy.

That evening I travelled back by taxi alone. Fumihiro Tanabe paid the fare and instructed the driver of my destination. I was chauffeured through the bustling streets of Tokyo where there were as many taxis as there were cars on the road. Throngs of people filled the narrow streets, many still in their business suits looking perhaps a little less like the sober office workers they were at the start of the day. Amusingly some were leaning on one another staggering on and off the pavement. Despite the obvious signs of inebriation and alcohol-fuelled revelry there was not a punch up in sight as we narrowly avoided striking them down. My cab twisted and turned in and out of narrow streets that seemed hardly big enough for a cyclist before we joined a larger road that eventually became familiar when we drew up outside the dormitory. It was midnight and I looked forward to a good night sleep. I crept quietly up the stairs along the corridor not wishing to attract the attention of anybody who may want to have a chat. Fortunately, my stealthy entrance was successful and I was tucked up in my futon ready for sleep. I had been here a little less than two weeks and I had seen so much. I was overwhelmed with my hosts and I had trained like never before, but two weeks out of fifty-two was but a fraction and I knew there was much to do.

The following day after an easy run and breakfast, I took a trip to Shinjuku with Kikuta so I could change a traveller cheque. I was expected to pay my first month's fee for my accommodation any day now so I needed a bit of cash. The train journey was becoming a little more familiar, so were the dozen or so stations along the way. On board there were scores of people who would use their journey as wisely as possible studying, working, or catching up on the sleep they had missed the previous night. I wondered how many of those dozing around me were out on the town the previous evening consuming vast amounts of their favourite tipple with their colleagues. The sleepers in the carriage would often be leaning to one side inadvertently resting their heads on a fellow passenger's shoulder. A gentle push would then find them leaning to the other side and so to another unwelcome headrest. A gentle game of push the head would ensue until the train pulled in at the right destination when the sleeper would suddenly be up and out without hesitation, seemingly oblivious of the mild annoyance caused to others. There were few foreigners along this route so I would often be the subject of scrutiny not just from the kids but from others secretly looking me up and down wondering about the fair-haired young man in jeans and his purpose among them. I was always comfortable in the company of my fellow students. This wasn't because I felt threatened in any way, on the contrary, there was an easy-going safe atmosphere everywhere I went, but I felt I belonged and had a sense of purpose about my being there unlike that of a tourist frantically searching for clues on destination and train times. Although it was inevitable that sooner or later, I would be travelling on my own so maybe then I would look every bit the nervous tourist.

At the bank I was finally issued with my yen in return for my traveller's cheque which was not a formality, but followed quite a palaver of passport inspection, address in Japan, a ten-minute wait before I was called to the desk;

"Meek sama!" A stern looking manager type stood with my details in hand. I wondered if I had been successful, or whether I was about to be reported to Interpol for some inexplicable reason. Then a big smile and "dozo" whereby I would collect my cash before he and all staff of the first floor would politely shout after me "arigato gozaimashita" as I left.

After another Shakey's lunch we were 'home' by two thirty to relax before the dojo training. However, Kobayashi was present and he ordered me to be ready for another trip to one of his dojos. I was relieved to say the least. We left just as the rest of the lads were making their way next door. I had a feeling of guilt and relief all rolled into one, and to be honest if I had been given the choice, I would have stayed for I was getting to grips with the intensity and didn't want to lose the momentum. But in his wisdom Kobayashi had decided I go with him so I was going to enjoy the break. We drove in silence to the neighbourhood dojo I had been before and this time there were only two students; that is to say one child in the first class and one adult in the second. I was ignorant at the time for I now realize they were probably private students rather than a dismal turn out, but I happily trained alongside both students.

The atmosphere was unbelievably sedate even though I was training hard. Compared to the last week or so I was having a rest. Technically however I was under the scrutiny of a perfectionist. I was under no illusion that my technique of Wado Ryu Karate was in any way near proficient. I had come here to learn and I wanted only the best for my tuition. Who better than a man who has devoted his life to training and teaching? The lesson was always formal and rigorous with little rest. We would however spend much time on the syllabus of which I was already accustomed back home in England. Kobayashi was a devoted student of Tatsuo Suzuki and continued to teach his methods in his own dojos. We practiced the many combinations of various kyu grades before running through the 'semi free fighting' partner drills which had been devised by Suzuki. We performed these so diligently that it was as close to the real thing as was possible. Punches, kicks, sweeps, and throws. The Wado style owes much of its advanced pre-arranged sparring to the throws of Jiu Jitsu so these too were executed with vigour and we would drive each other hard into the wooden floor. I was thinking at the time that it would have been a good idea to spread out the Aikido mat before training rather than after. We finished that evening with the customary free sparring. I first fought with the brown belt student who for the last half an hour had been watching from the side-lines when Kobayashi gave me the benefit of his skill and experience. Kobayashi was never heavy handed, but the contact to my face was frequent as if to remind me I had slipped up.

The journey back to the dormitory was becoming chattier as

Kobayashi would ask about certain friends he had left back in England. Some people he mentioned I knew, some I didn't. His laugh was deep and infectious and often he would laugh at something trivial which would set me off because I laughed at his laugh. He would often turn up the radio in his car when a well-known tune would play and announce “this is a good song” to which I would reply "hai, good song". The Beatles, Carpenters, Jacksons, they were all “good songs!” and most of the way home would be spent listening to The Far East Network, an American station devoted to their countrymen serving in the armed forces in Japan.

The return to my room would often cause a little fuss because my roommates were keen to know where I had been, and then without fail Kikuta would wander in and ask the same. They would listen eagerly and enviously as I told them about my little trip and I would ask about training so they would fill me in on as much detail as possible.

On this evening one of the second years ‘Hara’ came in waving an envelope saying “Aasa, for you”. It was my first letter from home and was from my girlfriend. I looked at the lads and they retreated so I could read in privacy. The letter told me everything was ok at home that my Mum and Dad were missing me like mad as did she. She told me that the nightlife was a bit dismal without me around. I thought of the lack of nightlife I had here and, in a small way, felt better. The boys of my room gathered around and we spent the rest of the evening talking about our girlfriends, although I got the feeling that in their youthful bashful world, they exaggerated more than a little. The letter had an inspiring effect as my girlfriend wrote about how proud people were of what I was doing. She also asked how training was going. I felt close to home that day because of the letter and hoped for more news soon.

The next morning was Saturday exactly two weeks after I had arrived. We were up and out sharp as ever and I felt rejuvenated after my little break and some inspiring words from England. For the first time since my arrival both Tanabe and Kobayashi were present for our morning run. We did our full quota around the park and then some shuttle runs before the light sparring. Tanabe was on my back telling me to move faster, and then sorting out my posture and telling me my hair was a little long, so just when I was on the brink of maybe settling in there was a reminder not to be complacent. I think also Tanabe was making a point in front of Kobayashi that it was fine to slip away occasionally, but while Aasa is here, he's mine.

Nonetheless, I took no criticism to heart and was suitably content that morning while washing out the showers and toilets. I even insisted on helping the juniors with one or two seniors’ gis to take upstairs for washing. It was Saturday so presuming there would be another day of rest the next day I sensed the mood around the camp was a little more cheerful.

Many of the students still went off and studied on Saturdays, but the lads that remained that day were treated to some chicken and rice for lunch with spaghetti. Both instructors were in humorous mood and took it in turns to mock the students present. Tanabe insisted his spaghetti eating technique was superior because his Italian girlfriend had taught him how it was done. Kobayashi asked Tanabe her name and he pouted in defiance of the insubordinate question. And we saw the funny side as Tanabe realized he too was being set up.

As I trained that day during the first hour I began to try and remember the names of those around me. Every now and then Tanemura would shout a name followed by an instruction, for example

"Asuka, takai" (stance is too high) or

"Fujimoto, osoi" (too slow), and from these verbal coaching tips I started to learn names of students I hadn't even spoken to. It was just a mental exercise to keep things going. When the repetition of technique started with the kicks it was often taken in turns to count one to ten. My little knowledge of Japanese had included the one to ten counts so I was glad to join in, but their colloquial count was a lot lazier than the textbook form. It sounded quite different, almost like we would say 'un , oo, ee, our, ive, etc. so within these two weeks I felt a little stupid because I was probably sounding like a toffee-nosed posh kid from a Japanese version of Oxbridge with my clear-cut Japanese. I dropped the consonants and got with the slang.

The pad and bag work today were even more relentless and it was real relief to hold the pads to get a rest. While I did so I could study the form of most of the fighters as they belted the pads and try to work out little counters to their technique. When, for example, I watched Oshima I knew he would use his superior reach to dish out the one-two punch to the face. I imagined dropping underneath and catching him with my left-hand reverse punch before following up with my right to the face. This was an old boxing combination of mine, except I used to often right hook my opponent instead of punching straight. Same body moves different technique. Hook punches here were not part of the repertoire but a ridge hand was common, that is, a similar strike to the hook but with the inside edge of the open hand without the follow through of the boxing equivalent. Casting my eyes over the rest, I knew also that the bear-like Kawano's strength was in his forward rushing tactics so I would have to be quick in moving off his attacking line and strike to his face from an angle and then be away even quicker. He also tended to grab and pick up his opponents before dumping them and punching what was left.

So many different types of fighters filled that dojo and up to now I had barely fought a third of them, but I was mentally preparing for the inevitability of each one. Both Tanabe and Kobayashi joined us this afternoon and so out came the mitts.

Today I faced Hakoishi, the one senior fourth year student I had never spoken to, nor him to me. A little taller than me he always seemed disinterested in most things happening around him. He normally did his chores of the morning with the least amount of effort. He was always last on the run if in fact he ever broke into a running stride. His demeanour, as Kobayashi looked on and started the free fighting with "Hajime" (begin), was one of an old pro boxer who had had one fight too many. He shuffled instead of sprang on his toes and his hands were low. Above all he had an annoying smirk, which seemed more intentional this day because of the fact I was in front of him. He didn't seem too keen to get on with things so I tested him out with one or two feints with my hands and he stood impassively covering the shots as if he'd seen it all before. He then shot out a low front kick that was in fact very low and deliberate. I too covered it by slightly moving back so it fell short. Kobayashi barked at me for I was probably doing just what my opponent had hoped, slowing down to his pace, and playing too cautious. We started ten seconds ago and I hadn't done a thing. I stepped forward with the most obvious of front kicks to his body, which he attempted to block with his front hand, and then I leaned in to my next shot. I switched the front kick to a roundhouse just near the point of his block and let him have it full in the face. Now there was no intent to the amount of contact and to be fair he did well to stay on his feet, but the smack echoed around the dojo and for once his smirk was well and truly wiped off his face. Instinct and temper drove him forward and we were away exchanging punches for fun. After a brief spell at close range, he broke away and was struggling for breath a little so I closed him down again and drilled my left hand to the body followed by the right to the head. He saw neither and he was now out of his depth physically so couldn't sustain his intention of filling me in. We continued lightly for I knew the fight was out of him and I was not in any way going to make things more difficult for myself by getting cocky. I felt I did enough and left it at that.

Kobayashi called an end and summoned for me to join him in some kumite and what followed was another demonstration in free fighting from someone who was still in good shape a dozen or so years older than me. I pressed as much as possible with various attacks, but my learned opponent read the moves and avoided the techniques. Now and again a lucky punch would filter through and Kobayashi would always acknowledge the move and say, “ooh nice one” before turning on the style a bit.

I sensed that with both instructors present things were going to warm up a bit in the latter part of this session. I also had a feeling the instructors enjoyed matches for a chance to see a flare up. Kishiyama was called up and I looked intently at the floor in front. I was dreading my name to be called for I knew that a tough time was in store should we face one another. Yet I had thought about this situation time and time again and was hoping it would arrive sooner in order to clear the mental stammer I had over this young upstart.

"Aasa!" I jumped out of my place as well my skin and stood opposite Kishiyama. We were both breathing hard from previous fights and I felt he too was trying to control his nerves in order to get a good start for he took a couple of deep breaths. Tanabe shouted for us to begin and we both bolted forward. I knew he was expecting for me to kick so he was trying to close me down to avoid my legs, but all I wanted to do was punch him in the face. My front hand got there first as I stepped around him with an avoiding 'nagashi zuki' and the connection was firm. He reeled back from the impact and a loss of balance and so struggled to contain my follow up. I chased him as he backed off to avoid falling and my roundhouse kick caught him low in the abdomen. He shouted loud to rally some spirit and grabbed me for some respite. I tried to break free and momentarily exposed my face, which Kishiyama gladly punched. It too was a firm punch and we both broke away to gather our composure. Straight away I was up with my leg to try and score the golden shot. I thought with a little space between us was my best chance but his front kick was there first followed by his head punch. In the section of pad work we practiced every day this was a routine combination; low front kick followed by head punch. Akii caught me before with the same two moves and once more I fell foul of this route one assault. Tanabe bellowed at me for dropping my hands before I was about to kick. At least I think that was what he meant by his loud shouting and his impersonation in caricature of me trying to kick with my hands around my knees. He was mocking me and I almost laughed myself at his funny mimicry as I stood to attention but I was smarting too much from the punch, which had caught me on the nose. When we continued to fight, I was now not bothered by the technicality of the fight I was in, I only wanted to hit my opponent once more in the head. It sounds crude but a little extra aggression was what was called for here and I was fed up with moving to the side, or trying to set him up, I just wanted to give him a smack. We were more level now than before but I wanted to come out on top. I attempted to close him down on several occasions but he was reluctant to stay in one spot and finally 'yame' was called. We bowed, thanked each other, and returned to our seated position at the side of the dojo. The fight I felt was a good one and I had now adjusted my own level of contact to suit the situation.

I studied closely the fights that followed and once more mentally fought one or two of the performers in my head. Kishiyama was called up again and this time Tanabe stood opposite him. It was the first time I had seen our club coach face an opponent so I watched intently. Tanabe stood quite high up on his toes and advanced with an outstretched front hand gradually moving in on Kishiyama, who was clearly not going to make a fight of this. Tanabe backed his prey into a corner without so much as a single technique being thrown and his opponent stood waiting with his hands up offering some sort of token resistance. I saw Tanabe's right hand raised by his right side cocked and ready for firing. Everyone in the dojo was silent. Tanabe then used his right leg to sweep away Kishiyama's front leg causing him to drop a little and then wait for the follow up. Instead of a punch an open hand smacked the side of the face of the already defeated young man. Tanabe strolled proudly away and shot me a look as if to tell me 'That's how it's done'. It was not impressive. I didn't doubt Tanabe's ability but there was something of inevitability about the conclusion and I thought there was nothing to be learned from that little display.

Back in our room we disrobed our gis and compared red welts and bruises on parts of our anatomy. I checked my nose to see if it was in any way disfigured any more than before and the lads were excited about my fight with Kishiyama. They all said that he was too strong for them despite being only a year older but they felt that he didn't like fighting with the foreigner. I said, I didn't think he went much on fighting with Tanabe either. We all laughed at the unintentional joke and at the fact that Enomoto was also giving one or two seniors a hard time too. An exclamation from Iidabashi interrupted our mirth and he was stood by his hanging calendar, pen in hand, with a deep puzzled look. Somebody had already crossed off his day before he had got to it. Everyone looked around at one another as if something of value had been stolen, until I confessed to have been at it earlier in the day. Once more laughter broke out and we turned to Hijikata to give us a few more impersonations.

Being a Saturday night there had been talk with Kikuta during the week about perhaps going out to a club or somewhere. As luck would have it, Tanabe had laid down a curfew for everyone so we were all confined to 'barracks. At about nine thirty there were the familiar shouts of "chop, chop" or more accurately "chawa, chawa" as important seniors had entered the building and there was the sound of running feet in the corridor and slamming doors as juniors were ordered to fetch this or do that. Finally, Tanabe's door opened and slammed shut and things quietened down a bit.

Half an hour later just as I was stretching out on my futon ready to listen to my favourite sounds, Hara, the regular postman, entered with "Aasa for you" There were two letters, one from my Mum and Dad and one from my old training partner Ian Roland. Mum and Dad's letter was in fact Mum's sentiments all over. There was an anxious tone to the message even though they were pleased they had heard from me, that I had settled in ok, that I was eating the food, listening to my music, and generally enjoying myself. I had left out the blister problem, the number of front kicks we performed with leg weights, the fight with Kishiyama and even the foreign language for fear of causing worry, but there was anxiety written all over this letter in my hand. Still, they filled me in with the latest gossip by telling me Chris, my brother, had got a new job and that they may send me some money. I read that bit again. Yes, they were going to put some cash in the post. I was close to home that evening, closer than I had been in two weeks. Ian had written to me congratulating me on finally getting here and I thought again about the time we could have had here teamed up together.

Of all people Kishiyama entered our room and everybody stood to attention as normal, but kind of looked in my direction. I simply looked and waited for his purpose of standing in my doorway about two feet from me. It went through my head that perhaps he wanted to continue our head-to-head after hours.

"Aasa" he whispered almost apologetically

"Tanabe Sensei wants to see you"

I jumped up, donned some jogging bottoms, a tee shirt and went next door. Tanabe was sat crossed legged on the floor at his usual place at the small square table. Around the table also sat three other gentlemen of smart attire. I was introduced to all three but only one name registered in my brain, that of Fujii Sensei. He shook my hand instantly and beckoned for me to sit down. I was impressed with Fujii's English for it didn't have the accented tone I had been accustomed. I had heard of Fujii but only from Shiomitsu Sensei. He was charming, polite, and showed interested in my ambition. Here was a gentleman who had polished his communication skills in my home country. After graduating from Nihon University and winning the All-Japan Championships he was a prime candidate to be one of the first instructors to visit Europe in the sixties before eventually settling in England where he spent four years.

For the first time here, I was completely at ease with a senior respected old boy because he was talking at my level, an ability that very few senior people could achieve. Fujii Sensei spoke about Shiomitsu with great excitement almost as if he were a kid thinking back to a few cheeky misdemeanours. I knew there was mutual respect between the two and I was honoured to be in this man's company. I drank some wine until my presence in the room slowly faded into insignificance as the others took to their own conversation. An hour or so passed and I fidgeted uncomfortably in a cross-legged position until eventually Tanabe waved me away and I thanked them all for their generosity and bid goodnight, relieved to be on my way to some sleep.

The next day we took full advantage of the day off by sleeping in until after seven. Breakfast was a more relaxed affair and students were dressed differently in casual clothing ready for a day out or simply looking forward to a lazy day in their rooms. I sauntered back to my room and thought about tidying up around my suitcase which should take all of two minutes when a third year came in and told me in very bad English that I was to go with him for the day. He looked as if he had just picked the short straw, which then of course gave me all the enthusiasm of a hare going to the dog track. He introduced himself as Minamidae and he looked a little on the rough side. Handsome he was not and the two front teeth missing made his smile frightening. From the bike ride to the station there wasn't a word spoken and I feared it would be a tough day. He had also been one of the guys around the club who had never spoken to me, not so much as a nod, so what he felt about organizing my day trip was anybody's guess.

We took the train and once more ended up in Shinjuku. I wondered if he had thought of that all by himself. His speech was monosyllabic, monotone, and morose. What was this guy doing opting for head of light entertainment on this priceless day off?

However, there was a slight breakthrough when after an hour or so of silently looking around the shops my chaperone suggested, or rather grunted, a coffee. Well, it was mid-morning and I thought it not a bad idea; a nice chat over a cuppa should help pass the day. But I was in for a cultural surprise, for coffee shops in Japan are more a leisure idea than simply a few tables of cups and saucers. Everywhere were video games. The coffee tables themselves had glass surfaces covering 'space invaders', 'pacman' or 'asteroids'. Games that are of course more or less extinct today but which were very much the modern screen pastime of the era. Sitting at the table you couldn't resist putting a few yen into the slot and starting a game that would then develop into an ongoing vendetta with your partner. Well, without having to say a word between us Minamidae and I started to battle. For over an hour, and even under the efficiency of the air conditioning we perspired as we fought it out. He was good at 'pacman' gobbling up his prey at a phenomenal rate, ordering more coffees as he leaned to one side and then the other getting the best angle of vision and attack. But my forte was the 'space invaders' having spent a few of my own hours in the pubs at home perfecting my technique knowing someday it could come to this; a battle for supremacy against a being from a foreign land who couldn't understand our words or thoughts. We moved from one table to another to play the two games desperate to be the victor. I was mortified when eventually he won the one game, which I had considered my own. I was even a little uneasy when my foe smiled in all his toothless glory at his victory. He wasn't just happy he was glorifying in my defeat. But I offered my hand and he readily shook and said, “Aasa ok”. Now that could have been a question, it could have been a statement, it could also have been a compliment on my ability to play space invaders, but his dull intonation gave no indication of his meaning so I just thanked him for the game and said I would get him back some time.

“Back?” he asked

“Forget it" I smiled; you will know when it happens, I thought to myself.

Our day continued when we took a tube to Roppongi, a place of sanctity for foreigners, especially English-speaking visitors, for everywhere were nightclubs, hostess bars and drinking holes all advertised in the language I could understand. For example, outside one place was written "happy drinks for all to love", then another caught my eye “party to the one who cares”. The messages seemed like cryptic clues but were a reminder to me of the shopping bags that are carried on the arms of many a young woman that show a couple of smiley faces and the words “love is on a plate in your heart” or some kittens frolicking and a message “kind love show some spirit” just nice words thrown together. I was trying to think of some nice words for Minamidae but I struggled so I thought of perhaps having a nice time in one of these places. But this was an early Sunday afternoon and the most we saw after climbing to the second floor of one promising club was a private party with no admittance. I was encouraged at the prospect of eventually hitting Roppongi with a few of the lads. Minamidae and I had a game of pool in an empty bar but we were both bad pool players so there wasn't the same emotion in our game as earlier. I won, but it didn't seem to matter to either one of us. I must say after a day in which I'm sure both of us had spent against our wishes we had both come up with a result of some sort. I had learned a bit more of my surroundings and my guide had discovered there is something to smile about occasionally. I did ask him about the loss of his front teeth and he mentioned some old boy who had visited, but he didn’t go into any further details. I bet Murase would have been a good guess.

We had a lunch of spaghetti that I had chosen from the window display at the front of the restaurant. Luckily enough if you don't understand the menu in most places, you simply escort the waitress outside on to the street and show her the dish, which is displayed as a plastic replica in the window, easy! I must say the spaghetti bolognaise was delicious and by the way Minamidae slurped I guess he enjoyed it too.

By three o'clock we were on our way home. It had been a day of interest despite our initial sentiments. I think even Minamidae had taken huge steps in learning to communicate, perhaps even with his own species.

Suppertime that evening was a light-hearted event. Tanabe sensei was absent so the chat in the dining room was flippant. There was a lot of joking among the third and fourth years but the first and second years remained quiet and enjoyed the banter between their seniors. Suddenly Hijikata's name was mentioned and he was summoned to the front of the kitchen. The TV was switched off and our first-year comrade was stood at the front of us all looking far from comfortable. The word had got out that Hijikata could make people laugh and now he had to prove it.

Hijikata then produced a performance to impress the most humourless among us that evening. He cleverly impersonated the recorded message you can hear at railway stations. Now, I had only been witness to these messages one or two times but as soon as he started, I knew where I could be; stood on a platform being warned of not stepping too close to the edge, what time the next train was expected and where I could buy a sandwich or a cup of coffee. Hijikata was hilarious and the way he covered his mouth with his hand to copy the speaker system just added to his polished performance. He was applauded, cheered, and jeered. We all laughed, we all joined in the mocking, the hooting, and the clapping, unaware that he was now a marked man, doomed to be an entertainer for a long time to come.

After supper the young men of my room would begin to prepare their clothes and books for the start of the week studying. Nihon was known as the university of economics. I did some home economics at senior school and that was another name for cooking, but I didn't see any aprons or cookery books here on display anywhere so I guess it was to do with the business side of things. There were also students studying physical education but their days were generally taken up with the usual school stuff of maths, science, and English language. On top of all the preparation of their college stuff there were also the seniors' Karate gis to sort out. Some had to be sewn up a bit as well as washed and ironed and folded with the precision of an origami master. The mood of the room would be a stark contrast to that of the night before for it was on our minds that next day it all started again. The early run, the three hours in the dojo and the intensity of the fighting. Each one of us would go into our own little world and so the conversation would begin to dry up a little.

This evening though Fujimoto, Oshima and Minamidae dropped in and asked if I wanted to join them for a beer. There was no need to wait for an answer for I was soon up and out and cycling along the pathway leading to the bar near the station. I often wondered to whom the bikes outside our dormitory belonged, but I never asked, so whether they were the property of the university or individuals I couldn't tell. Inside the small bar a small crowd had gathered around a small TV. There was a baseball game in progress. The owner welcomed us with the customary shout and said hello to me in English. I replied "konbanwa" the Japanese for good evening and he mockingly praised my Japanese. Encouraged I continued with "beer o kudasai!"

"Hai!" he shouted.

It worked I thought. When learning a language, you're never sure at first whether certain words are said correctly so when a response is positive the confidence grows. I had just ordered a beer and I was on a roll thinking quickly about another thing to say. There were lots of things I had recently learned but they didn't fit into this situation. I mean asking the time would have been a bit lame, 'that girl has a pretty face' useless in an all-male bar so I asked him where the toilet was. Now that would have been fine but he pointed to the far end of the bar and looked at me as if to say it hasn't moved since the last time you were in here. I had to go anyway just to make it look good.

A bar in Japan is not just a drinking venue. The drinks are always consumed along with food. Sometimes just snacky nuts and sugar-coated crisps are served though often the barman will prepare and cook food to order. Many places will have their own little specialties, like the eel I had in Suidobashi with the Tanabe brothers. Here in this bar, I was introduced to yakitori, barbecued chicken and it was delicious. It would be cooked with onion on a wooden skewer and handed over to the customer on these little wooden sticks so there was no need for chopsticks, just dip in some sauce and pull off the food with the teeth.

Fujimoto's English was basic but he kept the conversation going, Oshima couldn't speak much English but would interject now and then with what little he knew, and quite loudly at that, especially once he had downed a beer. Minamidae was just staring and grinning. I think he was happy, but it was difficult to tell. I must have made an impression though that day for he did obviously want to come this evening so maybe I had done something for his insular personality. Fujimoto then reminded me that there had been another call to the Karate club, this time from Yamanashi Sensei enquiring about my progress. Yamanashi was another young instructor who had lived in England for a while teaching and he too had visited Bridgwater more recently and had graded me to brown belt. So unlike Kobayashi he did remember me from his teaching visits. He had left a number, which Fujimoto held in his hand and urged me to phone from the bar. I rang his home and was delighted to speak to one of my previous instructors and was taken aback when he wished me well and invited me to visit him some day.

I was flushed with a little pride that senior instructors took the time out to ask after me and once more I reminded myself about sticking things out and not letting anybody down. I told Fujimoto about the invitation from Yamanashi but I didn't realize how far away his home was so it looked unlikely I would make the trip. I would however log the prospect in my head.

After another beer and more conversation, the phone on the bar rang and the owner called to Oshima. It was Kikuta ringing to say Tanabe had turned up at the dormitory so we ought to be getting back before the ten o'clock deadline. So, this then was their little system. They watched out for each other and were able to enjoy the privileges of their third-year status if they were sensible. I, on the other hand, was lucky that I was of their age and was considered an interesting party to mix with so I could also enjoy a little freedom in their company. The first years had each other to fall back on and in a way so did I, but things were a little less desolate for me being able to have a beer and some conversation with likeminded companions, Minamidae apart that is. Anyway, I think Tanabe had instructed I feel at home as much as possible so this was in a way in accordance with his wishes.

With the excitement of the weekend over it was time to focus on the week ahead. But that was beginning to become a daunting prospect. Once the morning run was over and the breakfast tables cleared a silence spread over the building in which I lived. It was the beginning of May and the heat of the approaching summer beckoned me outside. I strolled the now familiar route to the station area where there were shops of all kinds. Two days earlier I had dropped in a camera film to be developed so I picked up the photos and eagerly looked through the images of my last few weeks before departure. There were photos of my last days of work, a night out over the New Year with my girlfriend and another couple and some sparring pics with Malcolm, one of my training partners. All a reminder of the familiarity of home and all its comforts and I felt a tug in the heart department. I needed, I felt, more to occupy myself with during the day but what the solution was I didn't have a clue. A part time job or even a chance to study Japanese at a school would have kept me busy, but money was the key issue. Without some form of work, I couldn't pay for any extracurricular activities. On my return from the shops a few students were in the dining room preparing lunch so I took advantage of the free meal and light conversation trying once more to pick up more of the language.

Before training I was told there were a couple of contests approaching which explained the visits of the old boys. They too needed some extra training and sparring partners so they were free to drop in and exploit what was available. That also explained the increase and the intensity of the fighting during training. Apparently one or two students along with Tanabe were soon off to Taiwan for a competition, and shortly after that there was to be some area university championships. That meant all students would be up for some form of selection. Training on this day consisted of the usual basics, the countless repetition of kicks and the continuous racing across the dojo performing lightning-fast punches. Then the familiar line up of students at the front of the class while others would attack. On this occasion the attack would be a quick one two punch combination to the face. The defender, holding the same stance as the oncoming foe, had to time a counter punch with the front hand between the oncoming first and second punch. This started a game of one upmanship. The attacker was ordered by Tanabe to ensure both punches were as fast as possible. The man at the front was told on no account to fail with the side step and punch. It was not a game for the weak willed. Tanabe roamed around behind the defenders ready to kick the legs of anybody he felt was not stepping in the right direction. The attacker could adopt any stance left or right and so the defender had to quickly adjust to exploit the open side of the guard. There was the usual skill level of control needed in this exercise but of course punching at the face every time at this sort of speed brought the inevitable collision. I got caught on several occasions and wanted to stop and check for damage but the next attacker was already lining me up so I held my ground and lashed out indiscriminately to protect myself. It was often the younger juniors who suffered the most and there was no alternative for them but to tolerate the situation. As always, before every encounter, there was the customary bow and “onegai shimasu!” then afterwards “arigato gozaimashita!” as if to say, “the punch in the mouth was a bit heavy but thanks anyway”. I often marvelled at the irony of this situation as a first year would be belted and thank the offender for his trouble. Things were a little different however when the conflict was between higher grades. For example, the difference in ability dividing the third and fourth years was often slight and so more competitive. Especially when there was a team place up for grabs.

On this day there was a flare up between Kawano and

Oshima. The former being only a second year and nineteen years old but built like an African rhino while the latter was lean and mean with a year's advantage and the seniority to go with it. Kawano, from what I could make out, had done his usual intimidation stuff at close range, which we were all encouraged to do in order to keep aware and psyche out the opponent, you know eyeball to eyeball. However, Kawano probably left his stare in there a fraction too long and so Oshima took exception and delivered an added punch to the face to remind the youngster who was who. Kawano must have forgotten the script for he did his usual bear like grab and picked up the startled third year and attempted to up end him. Oshima's head came forward and butted the shorter man with the speed of a woodpecker not once but twice forcing the grip to loosen. Tanabe shouted while Kawano grabbed the lapels of Oshima to continue the scrap but one or two students stepped in and parted the pair. Oshima cocked his head from side to side as much to say I was just warming up and Kawano smirked with an impudence that probably only he could have got away with. A trickle of blood came from the nose of Kawano but he ignored it like he did his senior for the rest of the session.

I had been completely unaware up to this point that there were in fact some keen Kata competitors among us. I had only really expected this club to produce fighters and considered the Kata practice as merely a necessity of the Wado Ryu grading requirements. I had expected us all to be fighting after the attack and counter drills but I was pleasantly surprised when Tanabe sensei shouted;

“Kata!” I think a general relief swarmed over us all. It was hot, humid, and temperamental after the little spat between the two big fellas. Our instructor in his wisdom probably also sensed the need for a bit of order and calm so switched the training, but unfortunately not the intensity. There are five Pinan katas which are considered the fundamentals in progressing through the first grades of our style. The application of each kata however was not explained when training here. They were merely a supplement to our physical training and to keep our minds sharp. After a two-hour stint it's surprising how easily the concentration can be diluted.

"Ichi, ni " Tanabe counted continuously as we moved in unison starting with the most elementary Pinan Nidan and moving through the other four kata. Occasionally a student would make a mistake so would shout;

"Shitsurei shimashita!” drop to the floor, do ten press-ups, then up to repeat the move again, but correctly - with a kiai shout. This would be the usual pattern for kata training. On this day however we would perform each kata twice and then a third time but in reverse, in other words starting right side instead of left and so on. This was a deliberate ploy not only to improve our ambidexterity but also our fitness. Up and down, up, and down, we all fell foul to the unusual directions of a normally familiar kata. Put it this way; try to eat a roast dinner with a knife and fork in the opposite hands without dropping any food. Press ups for each pea spilt!

After an hour had passed, we were mentally preparing to finish for the day when Tanabe shouted: "Kushanku!" my heart sank. This is the longest kata of our Karate style and consists of over sixty moves. We were all physically drained. Mentally we were vulnerable to make even the simplest move a challenge. I started to think everything I did might be wrong. There was doubt in even telling the time wondering whether the hands should be the other way round. Was it really ten past seven or one thirty-five? Most of the others were faring no better. To make matters worse, if somebody erred, all students joined in the press-ups. Some were obviously kata enthusiasts. Takahashi for example was hardly putting a foot out of place and performing the techniques not only correctly but also with an element of pride in his performance. Kikuta on the other hand was butchering his way through the moves and drawing attention to himself in the process. We got to one point halfway through Kushanku and Tanabe was trying to get Kikuta to perform a technique correctly, or should I say, more correctly. No matter how he moved it wasn't right. We were all hitting the floor with Kikuta's words ringing in our ears "shitsurei shimashita!" time after time. The looks on the faces around him showed their discontent. Kikuta knew this and, physically, he was desperately hanging on. Psychologically, he was worse. I felt sorry for him at that point, but I don't think it was this technique that had annoyed our instructor, it was the demeanour of the early part of the kata. We all felt the desperation when we started doing the overtime but Kikuta displayed the adverse emotion and was now paying for that weakness. I had seen so many crude breeches of the so-called controlled techniques during the fighting here. Yet no one, Kikuta included, moaned, or showed the hurt from a resulting slap. That was a weakness that was considered a cancer and could not be tolerated. But in kata why should it be any different? Obviously, this message was for all to see.

The time was five minutes to eight when 'yame' was called. My legs were aching from the deep drops and jumping kicks that are characteristic of Kushanku. Furthermore, the arms were numb from the press-ups and I had lost count at around one hundred and ten. Lactic acid had pooled everywhere in my body and I was desperate for a shower and the hot bath that followed. But we then had to sit and watch one or two guys perform kata for their approaching competition. I was relieved to be sat cross- legged, mopping my sweat-soaked face and neck. I watched Takahashi perform Chinto kata with a freshness that I couldn't believe. His performance was impressive considering he too had trained like the rest of us. Yet this diminutive figure expressed none other than a spirit of a wanton warrior and my respect for this man leapt dramatically at this point because of kata and the way it was handled that afternoon. Okano, a quiet almost anonymous second year showed us Seishan. This too was a polished exhibition.

"Aasa!" shouted Tanabe. For a moment a shot of adrenalin raced around my body as I thought I heard my name called. Surely there was an alternative explanation for what I had just heard. There was probably another student whose name I was unaware of but which resembled mine almost exactly. I looked at Tanabe and he was looking at me. I was mortified. I had just trained hard for four hours, watched Kikuta get taken apart, witnessed two exquisite katas being performed by two karatekas on their home soil and now I had to follow all that with a demonstration. My reaction though defied my body, for Tanabe was still waiting.

"Hai!" I replied and jumped up. I walked to the centre of the dojo and stood ready.

"Bassai!" I shouted. Away I went, performing a kata that I probably hadn't done for about three weeks, but which was one of my favourites so I thought it should be my best chance to avoid a disaster. Well, it went ok in as much as I didn't go wrong anywhere, but I don't think I was a threat to the National team members. My kata concluded the day's training and we all filed back silently to our barracks without a word spoken. There wasn't the usual jokey atmosphere that usually followed a hard session. I was even too tired to get some change to visit the drinks machine. We were all knackered and demoralized. Kikuta was a lone figure carrying the burden of a couple of dozen annoyed comrades, but just before he disappeared into his room, I playfully prodded him in the back. He reeled around quickly in surprise and I winked at him. He smiled weakly and went in. I thought about how he had been around to talk to me in the past couple of weeks, take me for a burger, a beer, maybe even let on that I was a little homesick, so I wanted him to know that the press ups didn't matter to me.

As I sipped some ice-cold appleade that Hijikata had fetched for us all I could hear there was excitement in the rooms opposite our side of the corridor. Tanabe was in and out of each room talking loudly, organizing, and laughing even. There was further commotion as arriving visitors brought about the usual fracas from students greeting them. Kobayashi had turned up, along with Fumihiro Tanabe and they were helping with preparations for the trip to Taiwan the next day. The contest was planned for the weekend, but they would spend most of the week pre-training, even sightseeing a little. Tanabe senior came into our room to say goodbye, a gesture that fell a little flat among the occupants, despite the standing to attention and shrill responses. The chief coach then approached me and with a hand on my shoulder said;

"Aasa, genki?"

"Hai, arigato gozaimasu" I replied.

"Ooh, Nihongo jozu desu ne" he commented that my Japanese was good. Well, it wasn't but it was an improvement I thought to myself. I found Fumihiro Tanabe considerate and affable although I was sure he could be the opposite, but it was thanks to this man that my stay here was possible and for that I was grateful.

With all that was happening around us that evening we were more than ready for sleep after the extra hour's training. I concurred with my roommates that I would rather have done more fighting today than the marathon kata session. Funny enough nobody said anything about my kata performance so perhaps it was ropey and they didn't want to tell me. Likewise, I didn't want to hear of anything adverse so I didn't ask either.

EIGHT

Kobayashi led the run the next day and then told me to be ready early after breakfast for we were to travel. I sat with a few things packed in a bag and waited for three hours. Finally, Kobayashi returned from chauffeuring somebody somewhere and told me to be ready soon. I then waited another two hours before it was time to go. Sensei explained that because there were a few people travelling abroad that week along with both Tanabes it was a chance for me to visit his part of the country while things would be quiet at the dojo.

The busy road that ran past our dormitory block headed one way straight into Shinjuku. However, travelling west in the other direction, we picked up the Chuo expressway that took us from the busy Tokyo outskirts to a rapid change in scenery that became a lesson in geography. The transformation in a few miles was astounding as we drove from the closely packed houses of the city dwellings past fewer and fewer houses until there were only farm buildings dotted in and around the mountains that seemed to fill the windscreen of our car. Each mountain was covered entirely from base to peak with thick green lush forest. The road meandered in and out of mountain after mountain and there were at times no sign of civilization except for the electricity pylons and cables and the occasional pipeline running down the side of the mountain looking like a dry ski slope. In comparison to the monotonous city traffic this was a beautiful scenic route, breath-taking in its contrast to what I had been accustomed.

We drove for two hours, the journey all the more fascinating as I picked out the various rural houses, or fields of different crops and the picturesque scenes were complete with the old folk working in the fields wearing their wide brimmed hats to protect against the glare of the sun.

Kobayashi explained we were heading towards Yamanashi Ken. Japan is divided into forty odd 'ken' in the same way England has counties. Our destination was not far from Mt. Fuji where he promised to take me for a visit the next day. We drove past further beautiful landmarks, in particular a huge lake that nestled beneath our road and the mountains opposite.

We made our way to a high school in a small town where there were twenty or so teenagers, wearing Karate gis, waiting in a gymnasium for our arrival. Most wore white and green belts and lined up quickly as we entered. One youngster rushed forward and placed a small damp towel on the floor beside each of us on which we wiped our feet. Kobayashi urged me forward to introduce myself, in English thankfully. I then stood on the end of their line and trained alongside the boys for an hour or so enjoying the relaxed but technical lesson. We bowed out to conclude the training and we were quickly in the car again for another hour until we reached Kobayashi's hometown of Uenohara. Immediately we went straight to a dojo where about twenty-five children were waiting outside. This time I was asked to help a little and I could see why, not only because of the numbers but also due to the different grades and the odd unruly kid. It seemed every student looked up at me in horror, aghast that a person from a different land was within touching distance. I doubt there was much contact with foreign nationals of any description in such a remote town.

The lesson was a basic affair and the mixture of ability was broad to say the least. I was by now accustomed to seeing a club of experienced young fit fighters at Nichi Dai and it kind of gave me the impression that every Japanese Karate club would be of a similar ilk. Of course, I couldn't have been more wrong as this club was like any other in any public domain. There were slim kids, overweight kids, keen and sharp students as well as the ones that just wanted to play around. Kobayashi sensei pretended to be stern with one or two, putting on a serious voice but it didn't always seem to work too well. I wandered over and stood silently behind one or two and that seemed to do the trick. I knew the eyebrows would be useful sooner or later. I could see however that at brown belt level there was a standard that was nothing short of impressive. Their Kata practice was appealing to the eye and one or two showed abilities far beyond their years.

During the short break Kobayashi sensei stood at the head of the dojo while each child lined up and stepped forward to receive two pieces of fish each. Now I'm not talking a battered cod or anything I mean a whole fish of sprat size, which was quickly devoured by all. I had wondered about the gesture and later discovered that sensei was concerned with everyone's health and made sure they all had enough calcium in their diet. I was quietly relieved when there wasn't enough fish for everyone.

I continued to help that evening when the second class of about ten senior students got under way, comprising of white and green belts. Sensei then asked for me to spar with one or two and asked me to demonstrate a few fancy moves I might have developed while training with the UKKW squad. Happy to oblige, I threw one or two high kicks plus a spinning one now and again and that seemed to do the trick. In all the time I trained at Nichi Dai I never tried that once.

By nine o'clock we were finished and by ten past I was walking through the door of Sensei's home to be greeted by his charming wife. Mrs Kobayashi spoke good English with a little accent, a reflection of her six-year stay in London with her husband. Two little boys came running up to meet their father but stopped abruptly when they saw me stood in the kitchen. Sensei laughed and scolded them, then urged them forward to say "hello, how do you do". 'No way' was written across their cute faces but finally the older one said "herro" so that was good enough.

Kobayashi's home sat on the edge of a narrow lane and was a typical wooden country dwelling. However, it was bigger inside than I had thought from my first impression. As I walked through from the compact kitchen, I stepped up into the tatami floored living room. This too was a small room with a bookshelf along one side and a TV in one corner. I sat and watched TV for a while before the two children plucked up enough courage to join me followed by their father. The three began a game of rough and tumble wrestling and I laughed to see the two children charge into their father time and time again soon becoming oblivious of my presence. A couple of black and white pictures of elderly people hung at head height and I asked who they were. They were sensei's parents both of whom shared the house upstairs. It is customary in Japan for married couples to share the home with parents usually for generations where the same house can provide valuable accommodation in the expensive housing market.

I was urged to have a bath before supper. Until now the reason for my bath or shower had been the same as at home, obviously after training and then a soak a couple of times a week. I thought the big bath at Nichi Dai was for a bit of the male bonding you see after the rugby games back home. Bath time in Japan is a ritual. Every evening, before supper, the bath, which is often taller than it is wide depending on the bathroom space, is filled with piping hot water, and then covered with a plastic cover to keep the heat constant. Washing must be done outside the bath on the tiled floor where you soap and scrub yourself down and then pour copious amounts of hot water over the body to rinse away the soap. Only then when you are already clean can you enter the bath. The temperature of the water is always very hot. I mean so hot that it's a very slow process to finally immerse fully. The bath water is not emptied until all occupants of the house have had their turn in the tub.

I came out of the bath not only sweating, but also with an instant suntan. There was a loose-fitting patterned cotton dressing gown, or 'yukata', for me to wear so that I could cool off a little easier. All I needed now was a pair of shades and I would have looked like I had just stepped off a Hawaiian beach. There was no air conditioning in the house but a large fan stood in the corner of the living room. I sat right next to it and deprived everybody else of the breeze it generated.

I then enjoyed a supper of potatoes, cooked fish, salad, and chips. It was a great combination for a young man hungry for a full square meal and I reckon the chips made it just that. Sensei had a bowl of rice with his fish plus other more traditional dishes but I was too engrossed in what was in front of me to care about his palate. Out came the beers, ice cold from the fridge and we made further small talk of England and its contest scene before fatigue set in and I was shown to my room. The small rooms were all divided by the traditional sliding doors and windows and when I pulled my door shut not a sound could be heard, unlike the last two weeks listening to half of Tokyo's traffic sail by. However, I had to open the door a little to let things cool a bit for I was already sweating again. I managed to find one of my small hand towels in my bag, sneak to the bathroom soak it in cold water and cover my face with it before finally drifting off to sleep.

I woke the next morning when Kobayashi gave me a shout at around eight o'clock. There was an eerie silence to the morning to which I was unaccustomed. The previous night I had entered the front of the house and because it was night, I hadn't noticed the surroundings at all. In fact, when I was sat inside the living room there had been curtains drawn at the back of the house. When I made my way to the living room this morning the curtains were open revealing a view of outstanding beauty. The house overlooked a meandering river about one hundred metres away and I suddenly remembered we were in the middle of the countryside on the edge of a town far from Tokyo. Despite the high temperature I hadn't slept so well since I had landed at Narita airport. The complete silence and my relaxed state of mind the night before was instrumental in sending me into a good night's sleep.

Mrs. Kobayashi was busy in the kitchen and after our good morning greetings asked if I wanted tea or coffee. Personally, I'm a coffee drinker first thing so this was in fact my first early morning cup in this green- tea drinking society. To follow was a plate of toast plus salad and then chips. I got the feeling my hosts weren't too sure what I liked to eat so they gave me a choice, only I ate it all. In fact, my revered instructor had the same breakfast put in front of him but passed it over to me and ate his preferred rice and natto. I wasted no time in finishing the bonus meal before his kids were up.

Once the breakfast was over, I took a stroll outside in the warm sunshine and for the first time noticed the presence of mosquitoes. Obviously, the proximity to water, plus the country air, was a haven to the little tykes. I doubt if the Tokyo smog had quite the same attraction.

I strolled along the narrow lane which appeared no wider than a farm track yet there were several houses either side continuing down towards the river. Just across from the Kobayashi home was a house with several large paintings propped up against the fence outside. The young artist appeared from the house and I watched intently as he put brush to canvas and added to the already beautiful scene with a couple of strokes. He was painting a meadow that was obviously from memory yet the picture he painted with its colours and contents was as good as a photo. He chatted briefly in English explaining he would sell enough to make a small income. It occurred to me that Kobayashi and this artist had much in common. Although miles apart in their choice of recreation they both seemed happy to live a humble almost basic lifestyle with no room in their lives for big ideas or dreams of earning big bucks. They made good neighbours.

At eleven that morning we left for the hour's drive to Mt. Fuji or 'Fuji San' as it is called. The journey was not without more splendid scenery of mountainous forests and lakes either side of our twisting climbing highway. It was almost as if I was enjoying a starter before the main course. The road started to climb more steeply before I was told we were on the climb of the mountain itself. There are five 'steps' denoted by roadside signs indicating various heights on the ascent. The fifth step is the final stop for all vehicles. A large car park sat shelf-like off to one side of the mountain and I was surprised to see a tourist area with its own shops, restaurant, and shrine, not to mention the metered telescopes scattered about to entice all to view the scenery. It is possible to climb to the summit from here allowing for about six hours for the journey, or a bit quicker if you were to opt for the donkey. But we settled where we were for the weather was perfect giving us a crystal-clear view from this fifth stage of the snow-capped summit above us as well as the towns, villages and lakes which spread out around below. The view was breath-taking and despite the sun shining there was a cold wind that reminded me I was several thousand feet up.

After a photo session we left the magnificence of Japan's sacred mountain and descended to visit one of the five lakes, Kawaguchiko, near the town of Fuji Yoshida. Here, several kilometres away are the signs of Fuji San's last eruption around 1700. Not only the lake itself but the caves and the hardened molten ground beneath our feet. We had lunch, another new but tasty discovery for me; 'yaki soba', buckwheat noodles. I knew this was safe because I had by now learned anything with 'yaki' attached to it means it is cooked. 'Yaki' means 'to burn," so anything I was to eat in a country where raw food is a delight was welcomed in the burnt context.

Following lunch, we travelled to a high school in the nearby town of Fuji Yoshida where a Karate club was waiting for our arrival. Young students eagerly came forward to take our bags, provide us with wet towels to wash our faces and damp cloths to wipe our feet before entering the dojo. I was prompted to introduce myself to this class of mainly beginners all around fifteen years of age. I then joined the ranks and trained for about two hours and enjoyed the basic training plus the little sparring that followed. I was urged to fight most of the boys present and considering there were about a dozen in waiting this kept me busy. With training finished at five thirty we were on the road for another hour to yet another school for more training. About thirty children of all grades plus three instructors greeted us in a large gymnasium. The training was more varied reflecting the differences in grades among the students. I trained alongside the three instructors under Kobayashi's instruction and enjoyed the free fighting techniques he added for our benefit. Kata training followed and the four of us were put through our paces while the children sat and watched. I got the impression watching the three instructors of this club that they were from a different background to that of our instructor. In other words, there was not the relaxed confident technique I had seen even from the youngsters at Nihon University. They were practicing Wado moves but not as I had been used to even back home in England. I didn't know anything of their background, nor did I ask, but something told me that they too were privileged to receive their instruction from the pedigree of Kobayashi Sensei.

After training there was a photo session plus small talk as so many children wanted to speak a little English as it was part of their curriculum at school. I was only too pleased to do for it was a pleasure to see the smiling faces of these kids instead of the scowls I had seen in public beforehand. Kobayashi was presented with a case of wine before we left to get changed.

We left the school at around nine thirty and drove for another hour before finally returning to Uenohara. Just as I was mentally preparing for my bedtime, we pulled into a coffee shop cum restaurant owned by a good friend of Kobayashi and before long we were supping a beer while our host rustled up something for us to eat. We ate a burger sank one or two more beers before returning to sensei's home. I was hoping there wouldn't be a Mrs. Kobayashi waiting for us with more supper and a beer for the guest but at nearly twelve o'clock I think sense had prevailed and I was able to hit the sack, once I had taken a bath.

I was dead to the world when Kobayashi sensei woke me at nine o'clock. I don't think I had slept in so late since I had been here which made me embarrassed. I dressed quickly and joined my host in the lounge. The scenery through the rear window took my attention and I sat near the window for a while until I was brought some coffee. Mrs. Kobayashi had gone to work teaching English in a kindergarten so her husband provided the nutritious breakfast. There was a bowl of rice, some seaweed, a raw egg plus plenty of soy sauce. A bit of tomato and cucumber and one or two pickles were also on offer so I did my best and tucked in.

During the rest of the morning, I wrote letters to both Shiomitsu and Suzuki Sensei to assure them both I had settled in well and was enjoying the hospitality of the university as well as my current host at his home. I later had a light lunch, which resembled breakfast and then rested in my room for an hour or so before we were ready to return to the local dojo.

I helped my instructor sweep and clean out his dojo before his first class at around five thirty.
In came the kids and one or two were smiling in recognition from the previous training. Each one would approach the instructor on arrival and say "Sensei konbanwa!" a greeting of good evening. It didn't seem to be a lazy greeting in any way for there was genuine compassion in the words spoken. Their respect was genuine and I guessed this too was an indication of the society in which they lived where, despite the small minority trying to emulate a western way of life, like the teenagers I had seen at Harajuku, seniority held an automatic position of esteem. Now one may say this reflects a way of life enforced upon them in their imperialistic almost clandestine history but it has its rewards. For instance, not at any one time did I see Kobayashi sensei bother to lock his car door especially in the grounds of the several high schools we visited. I think it would have been considered fair game if the same situation were in England even if it were just a target for some unwelcome jocularity.

While I helped keep the kids in order during training, I couldn't help notice as I passed the windows, a man of around thirty years of age, fifty yards or so from the dojo, weight training in his small front garden. He was stripped to the waist and displayed a powerful physique. For the duration of the hour this fella pumped iron in the early evening sunlight. An impressive sight even though weight training to me has only ever been a small supplement to my Karate. I could see many hours of training had produced a fine result and I admired the dedication in that.

The junior class came to an end and the seniors started to arrive. I greeted them with 'konbanwa' and they replied with 'hello'. I smiled at the irony. Then a familiar face appeared and I realized it was the weight-training enthusiast I had spotted earlier showing off his muscles to his neighbours. I greeted him and he joined the rest of his colleagues in warming up.

Kobayashi conducted the class with the preliminary basic training followed by kata, which I followed in line with the others. I was then asked to teach a few contest techniques and demonstrate various moves I had developed from training with the Wado Ryu England squad. So, I did what I could to make the little instruction interesting. The senior students in the class were no more than brown belt grade so I didn't feel I was trying to preach to the converted. I was then asked to spar with some of the class and first up was the body builder. He wore a green belt around his waist so I took it at face value and began to spar at a light and well controlled pace. I delivered a few light kicks but my opponent suddenly rushed me grabbing hold of my gi and threw me to the floor. I was up immediately, a little startled but continued in the same manner keeping things once more on an elementary level trying also not to show the obvious annoyance of being thrown. Before I knew it my cheeky opponent had bolted forward again with the tenacity of a terrier on heat and once more, I found myself lying flat on my back. I was rattled and this time took up the challenge I had earlier neglected. I first stepped up the speed of my attacks plus the power but above all the level of aggression. My opponent backpedalled quickly ending up in one corner where I kept him pinned. He tried from here to mount a last-ditch assault by stepping forward to punch followed by another attempt to grab me. I took a small step back to allow for his punches and grabbing hands and then opened with a combination of punches to the face plus sweeps to his legs and kicks to the body which simply became too much for him to deal with. Although I made very little contact except for one or two sly body shots my opponent remained in the corner dropping to one knee until Kobayashi sensei called a halt. It wasn't until later I was told this student was a dan grade in Judo so felt naturally compelled to resort to his style of fighting. It was a lesson for me. Maybe had I known from the beginning my opponents background I would have been more wary and fought differently. But when are you ever given advanced warning of the opposition? Even so after I had reflected on the result of my opponent backed into the corner, I also thought about the two occasions I was on the floor at his mercy. If the scenario had been a little different, I perhaps wouldn't have been so lucky.

From this training session we jumped in the car and left behind the relative tranquillity of Yamanashi prefecture and headed back to the traffic tangled Tokyo district of Setagaya- ku where the familiar darkened complex of the Nihon University building sat forlornly on the roadside. I had been travelling for three days and trained each day with the best of instruction, but I felt I had in some way played truant from class. When I returned my roommates were asleep and I couldn't help thinking about their time here when I had been away.

NINE

I was back to reality with the sound of what seemed a hundred alarm clocks. The last couple of mornings I had been spoilt with a bit of a lie in so this morning was a stark reminder of what life here was about. The boys of my room greeted me as they hurried in their slumberous preparation for the morning run. I was last to be ready for I was still in the mode of the countryside and wishing I had just one more morning left in Uenohara's sleepy town. The run was a struggle and ironically, I cursed the last few days away for I had been settling in to the university way of life before I was whisked away for a bit of a break. However, after talking to Enomoto, I was assured that training had been much more relaxed, as there hadn't been the seniors to oversee the strict regime so it then became apparent to me why Kobayashi had taken me with him; to ensure I kept up my training.

Shortly after breakfast two teams assembled with Kobayashi and Hideo Tanabe, who I thought was in Taiwan, and left for the weekend to attend a contest. Considering there were still one or two in Taiwan that left only a handful of bodies remaining back at base.

At eleven o'clock Kikuta, Fujimoto, Kenji, and I went to Denny's restaurant where we were soon met by a friend of Fujimoto who had come by car. Before long we were on our way out of town on the freeway listening to some loud music and pretending, we were leaving for good. In the frantic conversation I took no notice of our direction or surroundings until we pulled up at a lake about an hour later. There were some pedaloes bobbing on the water at the end of the pier so we took advantage of the boats for hire and pedalled frantically around the lake creating a minor skirmish in the normally still waters. Looking around at the mountainous beauty surrounding our location I asked where we were. “Sagamiko!” shouted Kikuta. A shiver went down my spine. This was only one stop from Kobayashi's home town Uenohara. Sensei had shown me this lake just before we reached his home on the first evening. I knew that all our instructors were out of town and that technically we weren't really doing anything wrong, but I warily checked out the personnel in the ice cream shop sensing any minute that our position would be compromised by an undercover Nichi Dai agent. By two o'clock however we were on the return journey in order to be back at the dojo for four.

There were only eight of us for training that day. All the fourth years were away so that left Fujimoto and Kikuta in charge of afternoon practice. Now normally the warm up and stretch with a partner consists of a little light massage to loosen up the back and shoulders as well as pushing the partner to help the stretch a little. On this day the massage lasted a full half hour so we were well and truly relaxed for the training to follow. Our basic training consisted of a couple of punches one-way two more the other way and 'yame' was called. We sat and rested. Our rest lasted about twenty minutes before Hijikata was called up followed by Yatabe, another first year, and then Hara, a second year. It was decided they were to do a little test of physical strength by hanging from the window- sills by their fingers. We watched and laughed as they each brought their feet off the floor and hung from the windows like monkeys, determined to be the last to give up. The pain started to register in their faces as they each reached one minute and they looked at one other in turn to see how the opposition were faring. It was then that the kohai senpai system became a little interesting. Hara in his wisdom started to nod his head to Hijikata as if to say "drop down!" Hijikata would shout a stifled "hai!" but then Kikuta would intervene with a curt order to remain as you are. Hara continued this desperate urging of others to give up before finally Yatabe, who to be fair was a little on the heavier side, dropped with a thump to the floor. The two remaining young men hung in limbo, Hijikata and Hara both had the look of fierce determination on their faces as they hung for dear life as if they surely faced a drop to their death should they fall. This was about pride and here was a chance for a first year to get one over a senior grade without recrimination. Hara's feet were getting desperately close to the floor and Kikuta barked to urge him to lift them up and stay in the game. Seeing this Hijikata gained the extra confidence to see out the remaining seconds before his adversary finally gave up and slumped embarrassed to the floor. Kikuta mocked both but the moment belonged to young Hijikata and the first years that silently cheered him.

We spent the last forty-five minutes of class that day practicing Naihanchi kata and with good spirit too. I think the third years in charge thought that we had better do something a little more worthwhile for the remainder of the time, after all it was a rare occasion that so many senior grades were absent and we had already exploited the situation. However, there was no reason to be completely irresponsible. It was while we were half way through our Kata training when an 'old boy' suddenly appeared in the doorway to look in on us. He lived nearby and was walking his dog so decided to stop by. We all stood briefly to attention while he had a quick conversation with

Kikuta. Satisfied all was in order he continued his way. We continued with our kata shouting even louder in the appropriate places to send our visitor on his way with the knowledge that we were at it full tilt. No doubt he could have been briefed by Tanabe sensei that we were instructorless that day so it may be a good idea to drop in. If it had been fifteen minutes earlier then the sight of three young men hanging by their fingernails could have been a little awkward to explain.

After supper things altered somewhat from the usual routine. Beers were brought in, plus the snacks that go with them, and I was invited into the third-year room for the first time since I had been here. I was quick to take advantage of the beer on offer plus some wine, which appeared from nowhere. Kikuta, Fujimoto, Kenji, and the second year Hara, exchanged conversation with me the best they could. As the drink in us started to take us to a different level of entertainment so did the bravado. I asked about using the telephone in the kitchen that now and again rang for certain students. Kikuta said it was possible I could ring home, but it was only a local phone so therefore I would probably have to use an international operator and reverse the charges. That was it, before long we were all crowded around the green payphone as I stuffed some yen into the box and rang. Yes, I could phone England if they would accept the call charge so without hesitation, I gave my home number and waited.......

"Hello" It was my Dad. I started to speak at ninety miles per hour with every intention of telling him everything that had gone on since day one but he interrupted me and asked whether I had been drinking. Now there are certain times that considering the context of things said you quickly sober up and calm down to talk more rationally. But I was halfway around the world, not knowing if I would ever get this chance to phone home again and absolutely delighted that there were friends in my company to help a little.

"Yeah, Dad I've had a few and I intend to have one or two more" I said. 'And I've missed you all like mad and sometimes wished I hadn't come over here' was what I wanted to add but thought better of it because my Mum would only worry even more.

"Ok son but you're not driving, are you?" Considering my two-hundred-year-old Ford Cortina was sat on his drive and it was highly unlikely I had access to a motor since I had been here it was just another cliched question from the family album. I wondered for a moment if my Dad had remembered where I was or whether he thought I was in town having a late night out. But it was three o'clock in the afternoon in England so I guessed he knew the score. My Mum unfortunately was at work but my brother Chris was at home and so he came to the phone with a modicum of common sense and quickly filled me in on the local gossip. He asked me about the Japanese girls and I quickly set him straight. Dad came back and talked with a sense of true realization and encouragement and before we said goodbye I was on the right lines with my old man, which meant a great deal at that moment.

My four friends looked at me compassionately for although they understood very little of what was said they knew precisely the mood of conversation so dragged me back to their room for another drink. The cans were empty so at eleven thirty Hijikata was awoken from his slumber to cycle to the nearest store and replenish our stock. Ten minutes later my first-year roommate entered with a carrier bag of beers and was invited to stay. He smiled very wearily for I knew at that moment he wanted to go back to bed but once he sipped his first beer he was as much an accomplice as the rest of us. Then some whisky appeared, and that was consumed, although, in small doses with lots of water. Kikuta then suggested we go to a nightclub. Well, there was no stopping us from that point. While we rushed to change into something half respectable Kikuta phoned for a taxi. At half past midnight the five of us piled into a taxi and headed for the glow of neon lights.

I knew nothing of our destination until we stopped outside a crowded entranceway with a couple of black bouncers. We paid our way into the club and went straight to the dance floor and behaved like we were at a school disco dancing together in a circle oblivious to anyone around. This was unbelievable, I was at home with the atmosphere and lights and the sounds that filled my head. The music played was the music I had been listening to prior to leaving for Japan; stuff like Quincy Jones, Earth Wind and Fire, and the Crusaders. We did our bit on the dancefloor for a couple of hours before it was decided to return to our abode.

We only had one drink each since we had been in the club except for Hijikata who had a bit of catching up to do. While we were messing around on the dance floor, he had been sampling the best of the bar stock so when it was time to go, he was acting like Norman Wisdom; smiley, incoherent and very unstable. We got him to the taxi but halfway home he was leaning out of the window spewing the various contents of his stomach across the streets of Tokyo. The taxi driver was trying to stay polite to his customers but was having trouble containing his true feelings. However, the address of Nihon University Karate Club in Hachimanyama seemed to temper his emotions for it has been said that former members of Nichi Dai have found their way into the Yakuza, the organized crime 'family' of Japan. Considering the Yakuza control much of the night life that is on offer in and around Tokyo the taxi driver thought twice about causing a fuss. We were back about two thirty. I was knackered but euphoric at the same time for I had a chance to let my short hair down which was no less than I needed after the stiff military like environment of which I had eagerly become a member. With this one night of freedom out of the way I felt I had got something out of my system.

The alarm clocks rang the next morning and everybody jumped as normal but we all stopped when at the top of the stairs and waited. Tanaka and Yatabe were holding up Hijikata for he was still half drunk. I couldn't imagine him running anywhere except to the toilet. There was no movement from the third-year room or the second years for that matter but still we waited. Even though I had been a guest of the third years' evening I was in no way taking things for granted and was prepared to get back to the first-year activities as was expected. Gradually though we realized the run was off and so we sauntered back to our beds and quietly lay still for fear of reprisals. One by one we all drifted back to sleep.

We rose at around seven thirty so one or two took their turn in the kitchen while the rest set to sobering up young Hijikata. He was still in a drunken stupor and needed straightening out otherwise he would draw unwanted attention which could in turn reflect on the others. While most of us ate our breakfast the two first years who had been keeping him from falling over earlier now took him to the nearby park to walk off the hangover. I thought about explaining the ‘hair of the dog’ theory but balked at the idea of attempting to make any sense of it in Japanese when I don't really understand the English philosophy behind the phrase. I also didn’t want to see anything but tea get past Hijikata's lips that morning for I too would have been running to the toilet.

At ten o'clock that morning a call came in for me from Mr. Wakamei. He decided, as there was no serious training going on this weekend and with the prior permission, he had gained from Tanabe he would stop by and pick me up for a short stay at his house. I was to be ready for two thirty.

I spent the rest of the morning washing some clothes and then grabbed a light snack from the little shop near the post office. The little old lady seemed pleased to see me, as I had not been around all week. I explained with my improved vocabulary that I had been to Yamanashi Ken and to Fuji San plus a nightclub. She laughed and it wasn't until I had left that I realized it had sounded as if the nightclub was on the mountain. Well, I knew to speak the language could be a little hazardous.

Wakamei was at the door at two o'clock so in no time I was in his car and away. The other lads too were planning to get away after another light training session so we were all destined for a full break before the following week started. Wakamei spoke enthusiastically about my stay in Japan. His English was smooth and fluent and being only thirty years of age was a little more up to date on his conversation. He spoke of his love for the English way of life and the happy times he had spent in London but he was destined to return to Japan when a family illness had forced him to return.

The Japanese people love to show their visitors as much as possible of their country and Wakamei was no exception. He took me to Akasaka, where we briefly viewed the Akasaka Palace. Wakamei explained that it was originally built for the Crown Prince and was constructed with Buckingham Palace in mind. We passed by the Houses of Parliament and finally the British Embassy. It was here in Akasaka that Wakamei worked. As we drove around, I asked about his training. He said he was unable to practice much because of his job. This had become a familiar tale with many of the original Karate pioneers who had travelled the world. Unfortunately, their commitment to business provides little time for serious training. It is not unusual for company employees to be in the office until late into the night. I had witnessed this recently when travelling by car at night the number of high-rise office blocks fully lit when at home in the UK there would ordinarily be darkness.

We moved on from Akasaka to Ginza. On the way Wakamei did say however that he was hoping to fight for selection for Kanagawa prefecture soon. I wondered about his chances considering he no longer trained seriously. I knew that Wakamei had a very fine background in fighting; winning area titles and reaching the All-Japan Championship final but that was in his prime. Time had moved quickly on and circumstances had altered dramatically for him. Still, I hoped to get chance to see him make his comeback.

The well-known Ginza district of Tokyo has a reputation of expensive shops and up market restaurants and clubs. The beauty of Ginza is its night scene for along its main street are huge advertising panels attached to the many buildings either side of the street and the neon lights that light up these panels reflect onto the road below. It seemed we were driving between colourful waterfalls, and it felt we were on a river of people that flowed either side of us. I had never seen so many people in one place and they all appeared to be walking in the same direction, and because it was bumper to bumper on the road we were going no faster. Eventually we had parked the car and entered one of the many restaurants. Not wishing to be a spoilsport I opted out of the sushi and went for the Teriyaki beef which was delicious. A couple of beers and a couple of small glasses of sake and I was well fed and watered. A hearty “gochisosamadeshita” from me outside the restaurant brought a smile to my host’s lips and he commented he could see the little differences in my attitude after I had spent the recent weeks at Nichi Dai Karate club, or the 'brainwashing' he added jokingly.

We made our way that evening to Wakamei's home where I met his wife and two-year-old daughter. The house was small, particularly in comparison to the spacious home of Kobayashi's but I imagined the cost of such a home in Tokyo would be frightening. I chatted briefly with his charming wife and daughter before I was urged to take a bath before bedtime. I took their daughter's room while she slept in with her parents and I was grateful to have my own room in total peace and quiet. However, the tininess of the room and the fact there was very little ventilation made it a little claustrophobic, but eventually the little alcohol I had consumed pulled me under.

Next day was Sunday and so nobody had to rush anywhere. Mrs. Wakamei cooked a full English breakfast at nine o'clock. We laughed at the irony of being in Tokyo and eating egg and bacon considering there probably wasn't a chicken or a pig within a hundred miles of our breakfast table. But it was another example of the fantastic hospitality I had received from two instructors who themselves had lived in a foreign land and understood about home comforts.

There was another day out for me to spend sightseeing, so straight after breakfast I said farewell to Mrs. Wakamei and their little girl and we were on our way to Kamakura which was probably only twenty miles away but took us about two hours because of the Sunday traffic. Kamakura is noted for its seven-hundred-year-old giant bronze statue of Buddha that sits regally in the 'lotus' position hands clasped serenely in its lap. The forty-foot statue was surrounded by tourists and so I took my place among them and was photographed on the steps in front of the huge representation of peace and tranquillity while listening to hundreds of people shout instructions of how to look their best. If I had a pound for how many times I heard "cheezu" from the photographers urging their subjects to smile I could probably have paid for a private counsel with the great Buddha himself.

All around the vicinity of the great Buddha, who represents all that is tranquil with the need only for enlightenment from within, were as many gift shops as I had seen at any seaside holiday resort home in England, which kind of made me smile a bit. There was a buck to be made here irrespective of what the great man himself would have thought. We looked around the various shops and to be honest prices were reasonable and the wares were novel to say the least; Buddha shaped rings, pendants, candles; tee shirts with the bronze image as well as hats, carrier bags and playing cards. My former instructor and companion bought me an ornamental teapot as a present and I ended up splashing out a few thousand yen, about fifteen quid, on a short sword that took my fancy. I had my first souvenirs of Japan but afterwards I felt a little reckless in spending so much money in only my first month here. We had a light lunch here in Kamakura before making our way back to my final, familiar destination that day.

It was Sunday afternoon so most of the students from Nichi Dai who had been away would also be returning to Hachimanyama for their return to reality. And in a way that was what my trips away this week had been, journeys of not only discovery but of a surreal break from a lonely environment.

Wakamei stopped the car at one point so we could watch a couple of local games of baseball taking place in a park, much the same as in England where you would see a football match or two but without the swearing, the attitude and maybe even the passion from these smartly dressed athletes.

I was back among familiar surroundings at five o'clock. Wakamei promised me he would take me out again in the future before he left me to get back to normality of six days a week training. The rest of the evening I helped tidy up our first-year room before supper and a quiet reflective period was spent before shower and bed.

TEN

I was well prepared for the return to training for I had been away for almost a week, for one reason or another, from the intensity of the usual Nichi Dai stuff. The early night meant I was up easily for our morning run. We were virtually back to full strength in numbers and it was Kobayashi sensei who escorted us around the park.

After breakfast there was extra training for anyone who didn't have classes to go to. Five of us went up to the roof with dumbbells in hand and Kobayashi led us through all five Pinan katas plus Chinto and Seishan as well as some partner work. We wore only shorts and tee shirts but already the weather was becoming increasingly sticky with the humidity that increases as summer approaches. Up to this point we were still technically enjoying spring but now the sun was even higher in the sky in the early part of the day. We sparred lightly to finish off and we all had a cool shower to prevent heat exhaustion.

Later that day the final few students returned from Taiwan and the manager Takahashi popped into our room bearing little gifts and souvenirs of his visit. These were shared among the first-year students. He also proudly displayed two trophies he had won for kata and kumite making a clean sweep in winning both categories.

Things were back to normal that day. Training was fierce, although without any fighting, but we trained on until seven thirty doing extra fitness work with Hideo Tanabe at his barking best. It was almost as if he knew there had been a little 'r and r' around the place so it was time to instil the rigorous practice for which we had missed. In fact, the two days that followed the weekend were the same; lots of running with Kobayashi in the morning, extra training for 'elevenses', then three and a half hours from four o'clock.

That Wednesday I travelled early with one of the second years to Shinjuku in order to get to the bank only this time he continued to college leaving me to mooch around the shops before returning on my own. The purchasing of a ticket in Shinjuku to get back to my destination was no mean feat and I had been lucky until now while others did this for me. Shinjuku station has several entrances but I had to make sure I was at the correct side to get to the Keio line. I stumbled upon the right area and then had to purchase a ticket from the many machines on the wall. Looking up at the chart on the wall of destination and prices gave me no idea at all so I braved some Japanese to ask a passer-by. One or two were simply too busy to stop but eventually somebody gave me the information I sought and so I continued with ticket in hand to the platform. The Japanese rail system is both efficient and reliable but one thing I hadn't been aware of was the different kinds of train to catch. In other words, there is a slow train which stops at every station, there is a medium fast train which stops at most stations, and there is the super express which hardly stops anywhere but gets you there very quickly.

When travelling previously with my Japanese friends I hadn't taken any notice which train we had caught and sometimes we had changed trains for no apparent reason than for a quieter carriage. But those had been changes to a carriage that would be sure to stop at our destination. So, on this day I stepped onto a train that was waiting to go in my direction. That was easy to work out because Shinjuku is a terminal for the Keio Line so it could only go one way out. But I hadn't a clue which train I had boarded. I did however think it was a little empty as I sat and read my copy of The Japan Times and opened a sandwich I had bought at the newsstand. The train left Shinjuku and I looked at the little light which denoted our travel on the electronic map overhead and there were name places in English that I could understand. I picked out Hachimanyama so was safe in the knowledge I was going in the right direction, but then a slight worry crept over me as stations flashed by me in a blur. I knew after a couple of minutes that we would normally have stopped at one or two stations by now but this train was stopping nowhere. Panic started to set in as I looked around the carriage to see if anybody else was at all looking a little anxious. I thought for a moment we were indeed on a runaway train. The mood on board was one of nonchalance, a stark contrast to what was inside my head. I looked again at the little light on the diagram on the carriage wall and watched as it fast approached Hachimanyama station. There was no way it was going to stop there when it had already passed every other. I looked at my watch. It told me I had two hours to go before training. I didn't know where I was heading at high speed but I was hoping I could get back from there in time to be in the dojo.

The stations I was familiar with immediately before Hachimanyama sailed by in a blur and I knew then that I could be heading further away from Tokyo than I had ever been before. Finally, what I had dreaded happened. The train sailed past my destination, Hachimanyama, which up until now had been a station of dread and nerves as it meant I was only a short time away from three hours of training. Now it seemed a beloved old friend who had not been there when I needed him. In the coolness of the most efficient air conditioning in all Japan I was sweating profusely. One station, two stations then three and I feared the worse. I had no way of contacting anybody and I wondered how I was going to explain my absence from training. I espied the emergency chain and compared the consequences of being arrested with that of missing training but common sense prevailed. Suddenly the train began to slow and to my relief came to a stop in Tsutsujigaoka, which according to the map was just four stops further along the track. I leapt out of my carriage and dashed to speak to a station worker and screamed only one word "Hachimanyama". He pointed to the other side of the track to which I sprinted. After a wait of fifteen minutes or so I boarded a train that stopped at every station and was relieved to be off at Hachimanyama. I hurriedly made my way through the narrow streets and along the main road to the dormitory safely back by three.

Another hard lengthy training session followed that day with the relentless fighting combinations that saw us racing up and down the dojo. However, there was a rest from the free fighting and emphasis later in the class was on the advanced pair work, Kihon Gumite. More circuit training and makiwara followed this before the session ended. I was in my fourth week and I never knew at this point if there was any pattern to the fight training, why we fought so much during one week and then not the next. Looking back, I figure there was a lull in the fighting immediately after a contest so physical training became the priority until another contest approached. I wasn't sure what the recent contest was all about because nobody explained, but I did discover there was a bigger tournament on the horizon and so I was hopeful I might get a chance to fight.

Following training and supper on this Wednesday I was eager to get to bed. Whether the stress of the train journey that day had took its toll or the fact the humidity was closing I wasn't sure but I had a headache and needed the rest. I spoke to no one and laid out on my futon and slept soundly.

The following morning, I awoke before the alarm clocks with a pounding head and the shivers. I was cold and then hot so I knew I had a problem. This was compounded with not knowing what I should do about getting up. My mind raced at the thought of not training and how the seniors would receive it. Today was Thursday so it was to be headquarters training at Suidobashi. When the lads around me got up I stayed where I was and told Enomoto how I felt and he said he would pass on the message. I drifted back to sleep until my roommates returned from the run along with one or two third years and little Takahashi. I was given an ice pack to place on my forehead, which I must say brought some relief and was finally left alone to sleep off the remainder of the day.

The third year Kenji came in around lunchtime and served me up a little dish of melon and banana plus some orange juice, which was refreshing, replaced my ice pack and departed for training. I was happy to be left alone to sleep again, relieved that I would not be training later for I felt lousy.

I awoke later with Enomoto shaking my shoulder. He said there was a little supper for me in the dining room. I couldn't believe I had slept so long. I joined everybody for a bit of rice and some battered pork plus a little salad. I was relieved my head was not as painful as earlier but was keen once more to return to my bed. On this night Tanabe sensei was absent so the third and fourth years were enjoying a bit of a late night. However, with the enjoyment of some soon came the harassment to others. I had witnessed before the constant disturbances of seniors when they were in and out fetching things from our room or wanting an errand run by one of the first years. In fact, I abetted the third years quite recently when we 'hijacked' Hijikata for some more beers and then finally took him with us to town after he had earlier been fast asleep. I was not well this evening and all I wanted was good night's sleep so I could get back to training the next day. Kikuta, who by now was a little drunk, kept interrupting our sleep having a private joke with one of the boys until finally I asked if he would leave us in peace for, I didn't feel well. He in fact apologized and left so we all returned to our sleep.

Much later I was awoken by the light being switched on, then off again. I looked up and stood over me was the fourth year Hakoishi leaning against the doorframe flicking the light switch to his heart's content. I asked him politely in English to stop but he looked at me with complete disdain and smirked then switched the light back on. I sat up and once more politely asked him to stop. He ignored my request. This time I stood up and said firmly in a raised voice;

"That's enough!" He eyed me again with no sign of complying. He was drunk and couldn't care less about me, my condition or for that matter about me raising my voice. He was a senior and that was that. He switched the light on and off again and my temper got the better of me. I grabbed his arm and shoved him out into the corridor. Only then did I realize what I had done and the consequences of me having a scrap with a fourth year.

The commotion brought the attention of one or two spectators stood in the doorways of the rooms opposite but there was nothing said as we stood a couple of feet apart. I had made my move and remember thinking I would accept the consequences if I had to give this lout a smack. Hakoishi seemed to shift uneasily in front of me, either from indecision or the beer he had consumed, and for a moment

I anticipated a sudden attack from him. I wasn't going to let him have it though unless it was absolutely necessary. There was no chance of that for he shrugged his shoulders let go a little sigh and drifted back to his room. The incident created a buzz of excitement in my room as I laid out in the darkness for, I could hear my name mentioned once or twice as those who had been sleeping were awoken and filled in on the details from the eye witnesses. One nil to the first years I thought as I curled up to get back to sleep.

I awoke the next morning feeling tired because of the interrupted sleep but better than the previous day so I was keen to get up and train. I was a little worried about the confrontation with the fourth year and hoped it hadn't spoiled my position in the club. Hijikata and company were beaming at me as they quietly mimicked my "that's enough!" and added their own drama to the incident by jumping into an exaggerated fighting pose. As we left our room, they were taking it in turns pretending to knock down all the seniors with jumping kicks and wild punches. It was almost as if I had started the idea of a revolt and the first years were warming to their task until we stepped into the corridor and there was complete silence as they reverted to their previous life as cowering lowlife for fear of disturbing the all-seeing, all listening seniors on the other side of their doorways.

There was more rain this morning to greet us as we stepped into the awaiting daylight and after the limber up Takahashi ran alongside me and told me not to worry about the previous night as Hakoishi is a 'little crazy' and nobody cares about him anyway. That put my mind at rest and we avoided each other for the better.

It was now approaching June, which is often considered the rainy season in Japan but on this morning, it was decided, even in the absence of instructors, to do our bit because the rain was quite light and fairly refreshing as we jogged lazily around the park. The odd tramp could be spotted huddled closer to the trees to get cover from the rain, their cardboard houses folded away for fear of spoiling in the wet. It was ironic that in a country of so much wealth and technology that there should be poverty and destitution so flagrant to my eyes. Then again, the plight of these pour souls was well hidden from the millions that passed by the shrouded park. It was almost as if the homeless too knew their predicament should be better out of sight in order to save face on behalf of their country.

It was another day when I was left with just myself for company. This was beginning to take its toll when the days could be long and without interest and so I would spend further hours tripping into Shinjuku and wandering the streets hoping to gain a friend. This proved impossible for everyone seemed to be walking with a purpose and had no time to meet my gaze, even if I smiled at the odd passer-by. There was also the look of suspicion from one or two, as I must have appeared on the brink of mugging somebody as I wandered aimlessly among the crowd. I knew that coffee shops were places of meeting people but I'm afraid my modest English background prevented me to hang around drinking copious amounts of coffee in order to chat about the weather. I guess the evenings would have been a better option, especially in the Roppongi district where Minamidae had taken me, but that time of day was out for me and so was the money needed to frequent those places.

ELEVEN

After another day spent in town I returned for training where Kobayashi turned up unexpectedly so our time in the dojo that evening resorted to more fighting. I stepped up on this day to face Oshima, the confident and very capable third year. By now I was starting to pick up the fiery starts to my fights which had rubbed off on me from the training and before I realized I was steaming into Oshima with the traditional one two punch to the face. This had some success as my second punch made the lightest of contact; he stood his ground though and countered with a wicked back fist that caught me flush on my left ear. Personally, I've never been a great fan of throwing a back fist for I never really considered it a knockout punch but some people can execute it with ferocious power. One such person was Bristol's Fred Kear who caught me out when, as a green belt, I tried to kick him in the head and my knees wobbled as he sidestepped and the punch hit my temple. The punch that Oshima caught me with just hurt like hell as my ear momentarily rung like the bell in the school yard that used to be swung by the headmaster of my old grammar school. I kept up the pressure though and kicked low and hard with my left roundhouse from my southpaw stance to catch his lower abdomen unguarded. Again, he immediately responded with a counter reverse punch to my face with a little contact but this time I grabbed his front hand and smacked him back. It was punch for punch and I felt I was putting pressure on one of the top boys until an unexpected low roundhouse kick caught my front thigh and I staggered back like a bird with a shot wing. The kick had connected perfectly on my outer thigh giving me the deadest of dead legs so I had to change stance to reduce the weight on the affected leg and to remain in the fight. I kept my weight over my lead left leg and could only really punch to keep Oshima from giving me a right tanking. Not realizing my problem, he seemed a little unsure at my change of stance and I managed to use my left hand to his face, as he came in, to jam his attacks. I grabbed with both hands to tie him up a bit just like a boxer would to spoil the opponent's combinations. It worked for long enough until time was called when I looked forward to stepping to the outer edge of the dojo to massage my leg. However, Kobayashi seemed to spot my predicament and kept me in the middle to fight again. Kobayashi sometimes displayed a slight weird enjoyment in seeing people struggle. The word sadist would be far too strong a description for there seemed to be a reason to this; like my encounter with the Judoka there was an element of seeing how one can cope in what could be a demoralizing situation. I now faced Hara who I wouldn't ordinarily have anticipated as a serious problem but my handicap proved a real bonus for my opponent who waded in bull-like to close me down and intimidate me in the process. I again had to revert to close quarter boxing tactics to minimize my leg movement and punch it out toe to toe. Hara wasn't blessed with the finesse of a gazelle but he had the stoutness and attitude of a wild boar and so was in his element at this distance. A couple of times I let go with a hook punch which brought a derisory shout from my watching instructor but I was in it up to my neck unable to move with my leg in spasm so I was going to fight any way I could to keep this situation under control. I made good contact and felt Hara back off a little. He tried to kick, which was a little comical even from my situation because his short stout stubby legs seemed to groan in their attempt to come too high off the floor. It made my opponent easy prey and I stepped in and punched his exposed head not once but a couple of times to keep him away. This slowed him up enough for me to hold my ground comfortably on my good leg.

I fought no more that day and was relieved to get to the showers and a hot bath. My thigh was badly swollen and I attracted Oshima's attention to the fact that his kick was a little low. He laughed as if to say he knew it was and laughed even louder when he saw the lump on my leg. "But Aasa strong" he said complimenting me that I was still able to give him as much as I did, despite the setback. Oshima and Kikuta then jibed me about the incident with Hakoishi the night before and they too told me his head wasn't all there by putting their forefingers to the side of their head and twirling them in a circle.

After supper Kobayashi told me we were to go to immigration the next day in order to finalise my period of stay in Japan hoping maybe to convince them to allow me to remain for one year. That almost seemed like a sentence being passed down to me. I had nearly completed one month here and my time could now be extended to twelve for good behaviour. I just hoped I could cope with the thought of being here alone for much of the time.

After a full training session in the park the next morning and a full breakfast consisting of scrambled egg, a rarity I can assure you, I was once more a passenger in the mustard-coloured Toyota. It was Saturday so traffic was slow and the warm weather made the journey unpleasant. I knew then why public transport was so popular. It was preferable to this. We drove to Ikebukuro a district to the North of Shinjuku where one of the tallest buildings in Japan had recently been built. Aptly called Sunshine City this skyscraper measured two hundred and forty metres high with over sixty floors containing offices, shops, restaurants even an aquarium. There was an observation deck at the top that gave us a stunning view over Tokyo. We were however here for the government offices and so to immigration we went. After a wait of an hour or so I was politely told that approaching three months into my stay I could apply for another three months and then would have to go home. Because I had entered with a tourist visa it could not be changed or extended. A British citizen was permitted a six month stay. So that was that. But I had heard that it was possible to leave the country for a few days and then return with another three-month visa so if I were still keen then that would have to be an option. For the time being though I was perfectly happy with the thought of staying six months, as it didn't seem too much of a life sentence. I was in two minds and would see how things panned out.

From the impressive Sunshine City, we made our way to the Nichi Dai headquarters in Suidobashi where we picked up Fumihiro Tanabe and Takahashi and drove to Chiba, a prefecture to the East of Tokyo. There was a high school all style Karate contest taking place at a leisure complex and so I watched as many teenagers fought out their matches with as much spirit as I had seen from the seniors at Nichi Dai. The contest though became a little tedious, as one bout resembled the next; there were lots of fast punches very few kicks and very little flair. The ladies kumite was much the same and there was also some full contact on display, but they were so heavily padded and protected that their movement was restricted to no more than a slow slugging match.

At four thirty we left after we had witnessed the final of the male category. The winner had been an impressively strong character who seemed far older than his years. Often, he would perform some form of pick up and finish off the opponent while they remained in a crumpled heap. That was flair, and there was an abundance of it in his stocky frame, and, along with his ability to kick and punch he was an all-round complete fighter at such a tender age of sixteen. Fumihiro Tanabe indicated that he was to try and persuade this young dynamo to come to Nihon University. Not only for the young man's further development but also, I suspected, for the purpose of nurturing a future talent for the prestige of his university. It was almost like the football league back home in England. To ensure the position and reputation of the club there was an element of scouting to be done to 'sign up' the best talent. Even though the university club I had took it on myself to train with was of the Wado Ryu style I learned that quite a few of the students had joined from other styles so had to adapt in some of their fighting methods as well as their traditional Karate training. This was quite a surprise to me but only because of my viewpoint concerning styles back home. A fighter is a fighter no matter what his style. After all, I had boxed for a while with the same aspect of refining the rules of another system to add to my existing experience in order to compete within the ring. Styles had to be interchangeable as well as understood: to defeat an exponent of a different style it is always best to figure out their principles and their methods.

We returned to Tokyo, took our senior instructor home then continued our journey on to the Nippon Budokan. There was to be a Shotokan contest the following day and Kobayashi was to attend a meeting this evening so Takahashi and I were left to dine in a nearby restaurant. The Nippon Budokan is situated in the Northern parts of the grounds to the Imperial Palace. It is a prestigious venue and is the home of many Martial Arts tournaments throughout the annual calendar. It was in fact originally built for the Tokyo Summer Olympics of 1964 to host the Judo, hence its name to mean Martial Art Place. However, its impressive octagonal building has been a well-known venue for many famous rock concerts since the Beatles graced its presence.

I found Takahashi to be a serious martial artist with a likeable disposition. His English was fair and he was keen to help with my Japanese so once he had ordered from the menu, we drank a small beer and practiced a few phrases and some new vocabulary. He would laugh easily at my mistakes but there wasn't a condescending attitude toward me, in fact he openly said that he admired me for what I was doing so far from home. He said he missed his parents and they lived not that far from Tokyo so that made me feel a little reassured. He was in his final year at the university and was intending to work in the civil service near to his home so that he could also continue with his Karate and help teach at the club where he had begun his training.

Our food arrived and there was a plate of sushi as well as tempura. I was hungry and keen to get stuck in to whatever was on the table. Sushi is a traditional meal where small handfuls of rice are packed tight with a piece of raw fish placed on the top. It is customary to eat sushi with a little green mustard called wasabi plus a final dip into some soy sauce. There were various sushi toppings on the rice from mackerel to tuna and shrimp and they all tasted good. The accompanying tempura and rice made a complete meal, which I enjoyed immensely. Miso soup was also served and this was a bowl I now looked forward to at meal times. The restaurant was spacious with western style tables and chairs but I noticed there were low tables at the rear of the restaurant on a raised floor with tatami mats where the customer could choose to sit without shoes cross-legged in the more traditional manner. I suppose it was essential to cater for all tastes as we were in the centre of Tokyo yet as I looked out of the window it seemed quiet for a Saturday evening, although we were a little further away from the busier streets of the district within a stone's throw of the Budokan.

We walked to the Budokan after dinner and entered its monumental structure. There was a little diagram inside the entrance that gave relevant information to the visitor. There were in fact three main halls with a total of fourteen thousand capacity for spectators. While we waited for Kobayashi sensei to appear, I watched a Kendo class practicing in one of the main halls. There couldn't have been a more fitting demonstration for me to watch in this National stadium as the twenty or so Kendoka trained diligently in the art of their ancestors displaying the same martial spirit I had become so familiar with in the past weeks.

Kobayashi joined us and we left to return to our own martial art abode in another part of this huge city. Back by eight thirty I was told to be ready with my gi for nine and I thought for a moment I would be making up for a lost day in the dojo by training alone until eleven, but I was to travel once more in the Toyota to Uenohara.

Mrs. Kobayashi warmly welcomed me when, at ten thirty we were walking through the door of her home. Sensei's mother and father were also up and I bid them good evening in Japanese and she smiled shyly then nodded her head slowly to reply "konbanwa". My sensei was in a good mood and cracked open a bottle of wine that he had received from the club we had visited ten days earlier. The family went off to bed and so we continued to talk and drink plus snack on the usual bits and pieces which are always close at hand on any family table. As the wine flowed so did the chat and before long, we were talking of the funny characters of the present club. Kobayashi once again displayed his infectious laughter and would say, "Yes! Yes! That's it" when I prompted him about a member who was a bit comical. Then I mentioned Fukusyo and his slight bow-legged run and up jumped Kobayashi to run around his small living room impersonating the bandiest legged creature I had ever seen. I laughed not only at the joke but also at the hysteria of my revered instructor who in my presence was letting his guard down a little by acting the goat. It was also a unique moment for during this period I was still in need of some light relief to keep me from thinking of home too often and this was certainly a fitting tribute to the idea of home entertainment. Our evening finished around midnight, for I was duly informed we were to be off to a children's contest the next day.

I was roused the next morning at six o'clock and with a slight hangover I ate another of Mrs. Kobayashi's excellent breakfasts. Kobayashi had borrowed or hired a minibus and so at seven we were outside his dojo packing as many kids into the bus as possible. The kids were excited not only at travelling to the contest but also at the prospect of shouting out English phrases to the foreigner. Their instructor, while driving, encouraged them all to speak to me as much as possible. There was first, “hello” then “good morning” coming from the back of the bus. As the time passed their confidence grew and before long, they were shouting “hey you!” or “come on!” in thick American accents no doubt remembering scenes of a film. As soon as I responded with “come on then!” and then “I'm gonna get you! “a shriek of laughter would erupt around the bus and so we volleyed these one liners back and forth much to the delight of everyone on board.

We arrived at or destination two hours later further out into the countryside towards the West of Yamanashi prefecture. A large sports stadium was the setting for the children's contest and by ten o'clock there were probably one hundred and fifty children of all ages lined up in their Karate gis as the opening ceremony got underway. In Japan nothing gets going until there has been a speech or two. Just before the various dignitaries addressed the children the chairman at the head table noticed me stood to one side and quickly made a space for me at the table so that I could enjoy the contest in comfort. After one or two lengthy introductions I too was then asked to contribute by way of addressing the competitors. Bearing in mind I knew nothing of the contest, or the teams present, apart from Uenohara, and no idea who the important people alongside me were so it was a little difficult to know what to say. However never too shy to say a few words plus the fact I had basically introduced myself to every Karate club in Yamanashi prefecture I felt confident enough to do my bit. So, with Kobayashi sensei interpreting I thanked everyone for inviting me to this special day and wished all the competitors the best of luck. I think I scored with the most applause simply because I spoke the least. I was then told that they would be delighted to see a demonstration from me later in the day. A round of applause again for that one as I bowed deeply and quietly cursed.

The competition went like clockwork. Kata began the day and I was impressed not only with the intensity of the contestants but also of the other children sat quietly waiting their turn. I was looking around for unruly kids playing chase in and out of the buildings or parents having a fag in the doorways of the emergency exits or even the odd father having a pop at the officials. But these things didn't happen. Everyone sat cross-legged around the outside of the three areas and quietly applauded each kata performed. I thought it would probably all kick off when the fighting starts but inevitably the kids were left to do their stuff without interruption or delay.

After the lunch interval Kobayashi sensei told me to get

changed and so I went out a little later and gave an impromptu sparring demonstration with one of his teenage students. I showed off a bit with the usual high kicks and spinning back fist and kept it short and sweet. I was dreading he would ask for a kata performance so I quickly left the centre after I had bowed to my young opponent. I had seen enough fine kata that day and I didn't want to spoil things with my performance.

The Uenohara contingent won five kata trophies and the young lad I had demonstrated with came fourth in the fighting so there was a little disappointment with the rest of the fighters. We headed home weary and with less excitement than the outward journey.

The following morning, I joined Kobayashi sensei for an early run at six. His daily jaunt would take him through the town to Meisei High School where he would run around the grounds of the school once or twice before returning home. Most of the children of Uenohara would attend this school and Kobayashi had one or two afternoons instructing Karate here. In fact, Hijikata too had come from this school before joining Nihon University. After our run while having breakfast Kobayashi told me that the principal of the school was planning to go to Korea later in the summer and maybe I could get a chance to join him as an option to extend the visa. An excursion to Korea sounded exciting, the extension of my visa I wasn't sure about. I was however happy to go along with the suggestion because it would have been rude to seem indecisive.

After breakfast of melon, ham, lots of salad, which my host insisted was ‘good for health’, we walked the half mile or so to his dojo where we cleaned up and mopped the floor. While Sensei did a little paperwork, I looked through some old karate magazines that were piled up inside the door. There was no recognizing any of the text for it was all in Japanese script but as I studied the photos from competition reports a familiar sight caught my eye. On many of the competitors' gis I spotted the two characters of Nichi Dai emblazoned on the left breast, an unmistakable symbol, and a further reminder I was to be heading back that day to join the ranks.

TWELVE

I was back in my room by two o'clock after Kobayashi had dropped me off. He was off elsewhere to teach. I hung up my gi by the window to air it out a little which was futile for it must have been twenty odd degrees outside but in this heat, things tend to get a little mouldy so what breeze there was could circulate around the crumpled uniform. I sat by the window and watched the traffic flow by and reflected on the weekend I had spent with my instructor, his family and club students. I was grateful for the break from this place. It wasn't so much the training but the whole grey environment in which we lived that brought a colourless outlook to every day's proceedings as if the real test of character was surviving the confines of the dormitory. Waiting to go training didn't help either. In fact, while there was nobody around in the room, I would begin to stretch to relieve some boredom and to get mentally prepared for the forthcoming session.

This day was unusual as Tanabe was back early from work and so he was with us right from the start of training. This was a first for me to endure and we were sweating buckets just in the first hour of basic training when normally we would coast a bit to take things easy before the more demanding stuff later. As we trained in our neat lines up and down the dojo Tanabe walked among us bleating and barking at our sloppy stances, our poor technique and weak spirit. I knew this was going to be no ordinary training day for our club coach had an attitude as big as the Budokan and we were going to be the beneficiaries of his foul mood. My name was in the frame as much as anybody else's as he demonstrated in front of me a poor punch delivered in the manner of the pathetic punches category. My kicks too were just as bad and I wondered if I had done anything to attract so much attention but as I wondered he went off to pick on someone else. Our extra effort for speed and power in this first hour raised the temperature in the dojo and I wished there were some decent air circulating but I doubt things would have been any better if the roof could have come off. I did wonder if I might suggest they invest in some air conditioning like the excellent systems on their underground railway but it was merely a notion of fantasy, but the thought of cool air filling the dojo, for a moment, seemed a delight.

I sat in my space with my towel to my head wiping away what

sweat I could before another load dripped down my face. I studied the house outside the window wondering if the occupants were sipping a cold drink while listening to some sweet music. The usual ten-minute break was cut to five and we were up with our leg weights and counting out the tens with more effort than we were accustomed. This seemed a bit like starting a twelve-round fight like a raw novice, hard, fast, and suicidal. I had the feeling there had been a little complacency somewhere along the way and Tanabe was out for retribution. Because of the heat however we were allowed the extra momentary stop to wipe our faces with our towels that by now were as wet as we were. We were lashed by the instructor's tongue should we wipe our faces with our sleeves. Yet we did when his back was turned. We lined up after our ankle weights were discarded and started our relays up and down the length of the dojo. This time the second row was immediately sent after the front row in an effort to catch them up and this started a panic to avoid a kick in the back. The front-runners were motoring like they were escaping from a rabid dog and the guys behind were enjoying the chase, especially the junior kohais after their senpais.

This continued for a half an hour or so and was a cat and mouse chase the whole time. Several times Tanabe shouted when somebody was caught and kicked so there was double trouble for those culprits being too slow. Once or twice, I could sense somebody closing me down. I could feel their presence with a sixth sense of panic and increased the speed of my kicks almost to the point of running with my back arched waiting for the belt in the back. This infuriated Tanabe for it was really defeating the object of the exercise to see so many students developing a parody of some ridiculous 'funny walk' character. So, in all his wisdom to get the best out of us backfired a little.

I was as tired as I had ever been during this training session. Usually there was a chance to catch a little breath when waiting for other students to catch up but because of the chase idea there was so little time to rest. I did catch on however with the idea of kicking a little more efficiently. I noticed the other guys after snapping back their kicks would stepped further forward for the next kick in order to gain more ground. This probably saved three or four kicks every time they travelled one length of the dojo so after half an hour or so that's a lot of effort saved. I routinely copied this movement and felt happier that I was covering more distance a bit easier. The kicks we performed were of every type and in numerous combinations. High front kicks, low sidekicks, double kicks, treble kicks, any which way there was, we did. I had gone past really caring how fast or how strong each technique was I delivered. I just did what I could and hoped it was good enough. I wasn't on my own for I knew this was making everyone suffer for I could see it in the faces around me that they too were all spent.

'Yame' was finally called and 'kyukei' followed, which meant we were back in our little places for a rest. Tanabe shouted something and first the fourth years jumped up and shuffled out into the yard where from where I was sat, I could see them drinking from a tap in the yard. I had been here a month and never knew there was a water tap. I guess it hadn't been considered warm enough to justify any need for its use. We waited our turn after the other groups finished and we were ushered out to get our fill. I knew the danger of taking on too much water during training but I was as thirsty as a rabid beast and I gulped as much as I could. It felt so refreshing I wanted to shower under the crystal-clear cool cascade. But as I drank with my head under the faucet, I could feel Enomoto pushing to get his turn of the water so I ran my head quickly under the flow of water and quickly regretted what I had done for I knew it would be obvious to everyone from my wet hair that I had doused myself. As I returned inside, I quickly grabbed my towel and wiped my face and hair to hide the evidence. I felt I had stolen something from everybody and was looking on the floor to avoid detection.

We resumed with the next routine of punches using hand weights. We again relayed up and down the dojo with the small dumbbells in our hands as we performed more combinations; front and rear hand, then the other way around, then three punches in quick succession followed by four. Each punch had to be delivered with a step so the tops of the legs burned from the constant driving forward to cover more distance. My shoulders slowly began to ache from the extra weight in my hands and I had the familiar feeling I was just hanging on. I remember thinking at these times if I had to fight anyone, I would be easy meat for there was nothing in the tank. Yet we continued, for to stop was unthinkable. Even though it was probably in the foremost of our minds to want to stop everybody continued. From my point of view, I wasn't going to be the first idiot to call it a day. We still shouted and gave it all we could but the once proud 'kiais' were pathetic. Each time we turned at one end of the dojo I prayed it was the last but then 'hajime' was repeated and off we would go again. I looked at Tanabe in his smart uniform with his neat and tidy hair and quietly cursed him. We were all looking as shoddy as shipwrecked sailors in a sandstorm but the top man was immaculate even checking his features from time to time in the mirror. I despised his presence that day for he was out to demoralize us with his continued ranting and demands for more effort. The hour finally came to an end just as I feared I might collapse. I took my place to rest and I thought I probably couldn't get up again. No sooner than we had sat down when Tanabe shouted "mitto". I thought I was hearing things for he couldn't possibly expect us to fight after the last two draining hours. Tanaka jumped up and fetched the bag of mitts and I looked out into the yard and thought about getting up and walking straight out the door without saying goodbye. I could see myself walking to the tap then next door to pack my gear and finally to the train station to board a fast train to Tokyo then on to the airport. It all happened so vividly in my head yet I remained rooted to the spot and was prompted by Enomoto to get some mitts on.

I felt I had surrendered all I had to give in the previous two hours. The thought of 'mixing' it with a few lads to appease Tanabe's appetite for absolute dedication seemed a little perverse. We were exhausted and overheating yet there was an hour to go and we were dressed for battle. Tanabe shouted a command "te dake". I looked around for some help in the translating. Hijikata was sat next to me and held up his fists and said "only hands". He repeated it once more and I nodded. There was to be no kicking in our fights.

"Sugimoto!" shouted Tanabe. "Hai!" came the loud response.

"Aasa!" My name shot through my nervous system like an electric current and I was up quickly after my equally loud reply. A funny thing came to mind at that moment of responding to my name being called. I was up quickly without reservation but also, I felt like I couldn't care less. Sugimoto was a decent opponent from the second-year ranks. He was fit and keen and a hard-working individual who I had noted and respected because he was friendly but earnest in his training and in his chores around the dormitory. I knew also he would give anyone a good fight and was ambitious to represent the university at some stage. But I was really past the stage of bothering too much about the opponents' form or lack of it. I was only interested in what was going to happen as the fighting started. We bowed and both uttered "onegai shimasu!" before attacking with the customary fast start. Because of the no kick rule, we engaged each other a lot quicker for there was no reason to be hanging around at too great a distance when there was work to be done with the hands. The pace was surprisingly fast and all concern about the earlier training seemed to evaporate for I was too preoccupied about the task at hand. For the first time I saw Tanabe stood behind my opponent as he gestured for me to punch with my front hand. I realized I was probably using my favoured left hand a little too often and so started to pump out the right to the face before following up with the left. It was a successful piece of advice for I connected quite easily to Sugimoto's face with not one but both punches. As usual though no sooner than a strike is made then a return smack in the face followed. I still hadn't learned to keep my hands up or to close my opponent enough to prevent the fast riposte. I swiftly moved to the side and delivered another combination to knock my adversary back against the wall where I managed to keep him pinned for some twenty seconds or so. I thought by holding him tight to the wall I could control his attacks plus minimize my movement so conserve a bit of energy. I managed also to constantly sweep his front leg, which for a southpaw fighter is relatively easy to do if the front lead leg is positioned just outside the left lead leg of the opponent giving plenty of opportunity to hook away the front foot, especially if he is leaning away from the punches to the face.

Of course, like in boxing, a southpaw fighter is more accustomed to facing an orthodox stance as opposed to the other way around. So, it can often take a little time for the orthodox fighter to adjust to the southpaw. Sometimes an inexperienced fighter won't even know the person in front is in a different stance so cannot understand why he is being taken apart by simple techniques. Quite simply they are coming from slightly different angles.

Tanabe called time and I was surprised at how strong I had felt in the fight. No sooner than I had sat down however then I felt exhausted once more. I craved a drink of water but I started to take note of the other fighters now battling it out across the floor. It was a sorry sight as the first years Tanaka and Yatabe were struggling to make any progress with the third years in front of them. One third year was Tachizawa the younger brother of one of the old boys who had accompanied Murase recently. Young Tachizawa was keen to impress, to follow in his brother's footsteps, so gave 'doctor' Tanaka a bit of a caning. It was all poor Tanaka could do but stubbornly stand his ground and take the beating. Tachizawa though for his part kept the contact mainly to the body so there wouldn't be too much obvious damage on display. Just a restless night ahead no doubt as Tanaka would try to sleep off the bruised ribs. The first years I must admit really were boys among men and I wondered if any of them would seriously be around to graduate in four years.

After we all fought once that evening, we were rested from any more sparring and finished the remainder of the session with a stretching routine. We needed it. Our limbs were aching, our morale was low and we were morosely quiet. There was never any conversation during class of course. For three hours or more there were only the instructions from the captain or instructor plus the fervent response of the students. But on this day, we were all sharing the feeling that we had been pushed to our limits, and by the look on the faces around me we were united in our contempt towards the instructor. Tanabe strolled around the dojo as we stretched giving further instructions and trying to coach retrospectively, but even though the lads of all years were shouting their responses at the right time, I knew they were not really bothered.

We filed back to our living quarters silently and shabbily. I for one wanted only to sleep but there was dinner to eat and to be honest I wasn't hungry. Before Tanabe came into the dining room there was very little conversation and I knew that there was discontent in the ranks from the highest grade down. It felt to me like a scene from 'Mutiny on the Bounty' when there was a feeling that enough was enough. But once the drinks were poured and Tanabe entered everything was back to normal and we all got stuck into the food.

I returned to my room that night and within minutes there was a letter brought in for me from a second year. It was another heart wrenching letter from my Mum. Of all the days to be reading an emotional epic this was not the day. Post training was usually an ok time but despite the excellent supper we were all tired and stretched out on our futon a full hour before lights out. After the weekend I was back to the start of a new week with a training class from hell and I felt low. Then I read from my Mum's letter;

"Now my love, is there any need to say how terribly you are missed? You are so very much. We let you go, we knew we couldn't stop you, even if we wanted, because we knew that was your dream in your life, besides, waiting to join Karate at the age of fourteen and us asking you to wait a while, who would have dreamt you would at twenty-one be where you are today? But when you went you took a part of us all with you and left such a big empty space here, our hearts and our love will be with you always. We are so very proud of you but, my love if things at any time shouldn't be right here is your home and always be a big welcome back."

My Mum could not have picked a worse time for me to read those words. I was settling in but I felt I had been here long enough. I had felt I had taken what they had to offer but there was no real reason for me to be here any longer. There was a home waiting for me and all I had to do was say 'thanks but I really ought to be on my way'. I could show them my Mum's letter and they would understand. Even Tanabe Sensei, if he could understand the emotion of my Mum's words, would insist I get the next plane home. I lay on my futon that night and while listening to some more of my tapes began to think about going home.

There was a feeling the next morning of another hard day ahead. After morning training and breakfast, I had to go to Shinjuku to change up some more money from my travellers' cheques. It was another step into the unknown as I caught the train from Hachimanyama by myself. But I had travelled this route many times now so knew the fare and there was only one destination at the end of the line so I managed that without much problem. After the half an hour or so in the bank I wandered the streets of this vibrant part of Tokyo and by chance found a large park away from the crowds of shoppers and the incessant traffic. The park wasn't crowded but there were scores of people enjoying the sunshine stretched out on the grass and under the many trees dotted around. The colours of the various trees were many and varied and there were bright green lily-covered ponds full with healthy looking colourful koi carp. I sat on a park bench and watched as happy couples paraded and canoodled. Mothers with young children excitedly running near the water's edge peering at the fish near the surface. There were some smartly dressed businessmen and women sat in a small circle eating their 'bento' boxed lunches making the most of their lunch hour.

With all that was happening around me I felt at my lowest ebb. I never anticipated a desire to go home would be this strong. Over and over, I tried to analyze the reasons for me to stay against those for going home and my head was fighting with my heart. What reason if I returned home would possibly be good enough to explain my actions? I put my hand in my pocket and pulled out the wallet containing my travellers' cheques. I thought if somehow my money was stolen or lost then there was no option for me than to return home. I looked at the fish swimming around in the clear cool waters of the pond and thought I could simply cast the wallet and its contents into the pond and it would sink without trace along with my future here in Japan. It was feasible and believable. I sat and clutched at my belongings with a mind to make up.

Those colourful fish swam around aimlessly in the pond at my feet like the emotions that were circling in my head. I had told everyone I was hoping to train for a year in Japan. I had told Shiomitsu Sensei I was here to stay and wouldn't let him down and he had promised me a knuckle burger should I do just that. But despite all those other people it was me I had to contend with. I knew that years from now these days, weeks and months would seem a drop in the ocean and that this experience given to me should not be squandered. I had made friends here and been accepted into a unique club. Ok so many people had dropped in and trained for a brief spell before swiftly moving on but what I was doing was a little more special. I knew that for the benefit of my future in Karate I had to tough it out. Those people close to me at home will always be there whenever I decide to return so there was only my own mind that I had to overhaul in its attempt to bring me down. I knelt by the water's edge and tried to coax one of the fish to the surface. They darted away quickly as if they knew at the last moment there was a ruse. That would also have been the case if I had returned home with the lame story of my money going missing. People would have detected a little lie and I couldn't have lived with that. I jammed my wallet back into my pocket left the park and all its beauty and returned to Shinjuku station. I boarded a semi express train and successfully engineered my way back to base.

I felt I had passed a grading that day when in fact I was just about to start training. I knew in my own mind that I wasn't going anywhere and that whatever training or long days alone were ahead I was in it for the long haul and I should no longer consider an alternative.

I stepped in to the dojo that day thinking it couldn't be any worse than the day before and it wasn't. In fact, Tanabe was in a far better mood and just when I was expecting to put on the mitts, we were ordered to practice some of the advanced pair work, which everyone seemed enthusiastic to take part in. It was a reflection too on their relief to avoid a fight for a day.

The next day was different however. At six o'clock we were donning our mitts for some free fighting. That phrase always makes me laugh; 'free fighting'. If it was so free, why do we always pay with a punch in the mouth I often pondered? Well, I did the rounds this afternoon with most of the third years. Nothing too serious until I had mixed it with Oshima but that was always expected. Then I faced Minamidae who had been my host on a day out sightseeing. I knew he was hard work in his communication skills and that he was a bit rough in the dojo, but I was about to see another side to my travel guide. We exchanged a customary fast start with no real superiority gained in the first exchange so I quickly went after him lifting my lead leg towards the face. It was really meant as a feint for I knew by now that my opponents in this class were more than ready for my kicks. Except one it seemed. A loud smack resonated around the dojo as my foot hit face. Minamidae then lost it. He came rushing forward with what at first seemed an attempt to punch me but in fact ended up as a mauling accompanying a temper that was well and truly lost. I backed up a little with uncertainty but my opponent was not out to score points for I realized he was out to hurt. In a moment of frenzy, he had punched me twice in the face and I was on my back foot for I had given him that initial ground between us because I was unsure of the situation. Now I knew that I had to get him off me. My eyes were watering from the punches so I even grabbed for his hair, as we were stood so close. But he probably had the shortest hair cut in the club so I grabbed in vain. He was on a roll punching me again with a free shot to my mouth. I felt my back against the wall. This infuriated me for I didn't realize he had pushed me back so far so quickly. My boxing instinct kicked in and I caught my aggressor with a sweet right hook that shook his head from right to left, but he was still not backing off. I could feel the wrath in his presence inches from me and I knew he was not going away easily. I then grabbed his throat after he had tied up my front hand by gripping onto my sleeve. We were briefly at stalemate both trying to free ourselves from our close encounter. A shout from Tanabe extricated us from the predicament.

"Minamidae!" My furious foe let go immediately and shot over to the other side of the dojo where Tanabe had been kneeling while watching the proceedings. A verbal tirade from Tanabe plus a bit of spare saliva smacked Minamidae straight in the face as he too had knelt in order to grovel in apology. He had embarrassed himself by losing his rag and was not going to get off lightly. Tanabe stood up and ranted further as Minamidae continued to look down at the floor and I could sense a verbal beheading was taking place in front of me and the rest of the class. Tanabe would walk away from him still shouting and then turn and walk back again and for a moment I thought he was lining up for a spot kick to the face. But eventually the scolding simmered down a bit and Minamidae replied "Hai, shitsurei shimashita" for the umpteenth time before standing up and coming over to where I stood and repeated the same apology. He bowed, I bowed, and that was that. I think if Minamidae had not lost his temper and had tried to give me a pasting in a disciplined way then he would only have had me to contend with. I had seen plenty of skirmishes between students up to this point but none had given way to the display of rage that I had seen that day. That was the sort of behaviour that had angered Tanabe. It took me by surprise and I wasn't impressed with my immediate response. I had dithered and although I felt I was back in the fight I felt I should have attempted to KO my aggressor, but to be honest, I wondered if that would be going too far. I knew in the future there would be other opportunities to sort out our little differences, but unlike my respect and nervous anticipation I had previously felt for Kishiyama I had no such feelings for Minamidae and almost relished the thought of a rematch with every intention of giving him some of his own medicine.

After training that day after we had proudly repeated our dojo maxims, Tanabe kept us in our kneeling position to lecture us. The lengthy address caused us to squirm a bit as time dragged on and we started to suffer. Every now and then we would shout "Hai! So!" to emphasize our understanding of the words of our leader, but I hadn't the foggiest idea of the content of his speech. Twenty minutes went by and my legs were screaming to stand. Tanabe would turn around and walk away from us as he thought of something else to say and as he did so we would all shift in our positions to ease the discomfort. But he would espy the movements in the mirror on the sliding door in front of us and wheel round quickly to reprimand us for moving. Another five minutes and my legs were numb. My head was full of Japanese words I didn't understand and lots of English words I wanted to shout out. Just before the half hour we were finally dismissed and yet nobody moved. We couldn't. Not quickly anyway, so very slowly we all unfurled our legs from beneath us and sat on our backsides to enjoy the huge relief of stretching out our legs in front of us. As Tanabe sensei left the dojo and we saw him safely out of the car park one or two senior students swore which made everyone chuckle. We pulled together for a moment when we all felt the pressure and I was glad at that moment to be among this club of characters who I was starting to identify with. I had in recent days been concerned about my own feelings away from home and understandably so for I was the other side of the world in a different culture but there were others having a tough time and I had to remember that also.

That evening after supper Fukusyo dropped in to say he and I were going out with Tanabe sensei that evening. Well of course I went to my wardrobe and surveyed the sorry spectacle of my ransacked suitcase in order to resurrect some form of suitable attire. Going out? Where? I wondered. After trying out one or two shabby tee shirts to go with my one pair of creased jeans Iidabashi came to the rescue with a rather nifty number from his collection. Well, it had a collar and all the buttons were in tact so I offered him my thanks and pulled it on. My roommates applauded me and I was ready for the night out. I felt like John Travolta and was anticipating an exciting tour of Tokyo.

"Aasa" shouted Tanabe. "Hai" I replied and stepped into the corridor to see Tanabe and Fukusyo waiting for me in their tracksuits and slippers. I felt a fool and followed them downstairs where we jumped on a bike and cycled to near the station. I wondered for a moment if we were to end up in "kaori" bar and panicked at the thought of being welcomed as a regular by the boss and having to explain that away to my sensei. It wasn't to be. We came to a stop at another small doorway with a curtain across and entered to the sound of the Japanese welcome from a middle- aged lady. A fuss was made of Tanabe sensei and he wallowed in the attention. Then I became the subject of attention and Tanabe introduced me as if to express his vast knowledge of the English language. Well, it was better than my Japanese so I sat down and let Tanabe tell her all he knew about me and I smiled and nodded at the right moments. Tanabe picked up a cigarette and the lady quickly darted forward and lit it. The drinks were ordered and before long she was pouring our cold beers for the three of us. There was nobody else in the tiny bar and to be honest there wouldn't have been much more room if there had. Tanabe started to ask me again about England and about certain landmarks he had visited. He also began to outline the successes of Nihon University telling me that always they were in the top three every year in the All-

Japan University Championships often winning the top spot. Fukusyo listened intently and topped up the beers but his English was not good so he sat quietly and got drunk. Tanabe then would ask me about certain instructors in England and commented on one who had visited Nichi Dai for a week or so but didn't do any fighting because of the exam time that I too had witnessed. When he had returned to England this instructor couldn't wait to contact a national Karate magazine to tell of his visit and relate how tough the fighting was. This had infuriated Tanabe for he couldn't understand why somebody could lie over such a matter. I could, for I knew of whom he was talking and was not surprised. Tanabe then showed me two fingers in a v sign he knew I would understand and we laughed at the rudeness of his gesture.

Tanabe sensei ordered some sake. I had previously had a sample of this traditional Japanese rice wine when in Tanabe's room one evening and found it a little sweet but with a bit more encouragement I could get to like it. The landlady started to prepare some food and Tanabe asked if I liked octopus. I replied confidently that I did, not really knowing if I had in fact tasted any since I had been here, but before long I was accepting a small glass of sake from Fukusyo while selecting my delicacy of 'tako'. There was the unmistakable look of small red tentacles on a platter with a side salad and for a moment I expected them to wriggle in front of me. Tanabe offered me some chopsticks and gestured for me to eat. Not forgetting my table manners, I said 'itadakimasu' and took the plunge. The texture was unusual, a bit chewy, but the taste was pleasant and there was also the hint of a wine vinegar type dressing which made the flavour even more appealing so I picked up slice after slice as I listened to Tanabe teach me a little about different types of sake. I assumed the octopus was cooked but after one or two beers and a mouthful of sake I was too hungry to really worry.

By ten o'clock Tanabe called it a night and stood to leave. Fukusyo tugged at my arm to leave before our instructor and we waited outside as Tanabe said his goodbyes to the landlady. Fukusyo reminded me of my etiquette and warmed me up with a few "gochisosama deshitas" in readiness for the emergence of our generous instructor. We waited in the warm evening air and I felt my head spin a little from the alcohol and I was surprised at the effect the sake was taking. Tanabe appeared from under the hanging curtain and we both bowed and said our thanks. We cycled back along the back streets and I was amused as I watched both Tanabe and Fukusyo in front of me cycling with their knees sticking out either side wandering from left to right at times narrowly missing other cyclists coming from the other direction. There were no pavements on these narrow roads that wound their way between houses and blocks of flats, in fact there were seldom any cars but mainly pedestrians and cyclists. The atmosphere at this time of night in this warm weather was pleasant with locals chatting in their doorways and groups of students sitting in one or two small parks no bigger than a large garden ordinarily used by young children during the day. There was no excessive noise however, or rowdiness, just friends congregating in the warm summer night. Their attention would be averted however as they studied the foreigner passing by. I was beginning to get accustomed to this by now so would often smile to ease their curiosity and they would respond with a victory sign of two fingers.

This evening Tanabe Sensei had been a pleasure to be with. It occurred to me that he was a bit of a Jekyll and Hyde character. He could seem intolerable in the dojo with his apparent insensitive attitude to our fatigue, discomfort or errors and he was only interested in results, improvements, and hard work. But in fact, beneath this tough outer shell was quite a shy person towards people he didn't know with a cheeky sense of humour when with people he felt more at ease with. I guess the latter would have been any of his students but an observation I had made in the first month of my being here was that he cared not in the slightest what his methods of training would have in gaining popularity among his young charges. But I had seen for myself the visits of old boys paying their respects to someone who had given them a fulfilled lifestyle as a result of their hard work under his tutelage. In a way too his little nights out with his students, and there were many occasions when he would take out a couple of first years as well as the more senior students, were in fact a bit of company for a man who was committed to his work and had little time for a social life. There was no wife in Tanabe's background waiting for his safe return so I guess his constant reference to a girlfriend was a fantasy of a woman in waiting.

THIRTEEN

The language by now was becoming a more interesting factor the longer I stayed in Japan. The use of everyday phrases was by now becoming second nature and the pronunciation was an easier proposition. The Japanese phrase book I had read before leaving England was of little use in its attempt to make the reader understand the basics of the language. The complex Japanese spoken system should always be studied with the help of a native speaker. However, learn it from the polite system of female speech or book form and you speak it at your peril. The more colloquial local Tokyo dialect is often sufficient to make yourself understood without being a laughing stock to the male population. I felt a little more confident when saying simple phrases to my seniors or contemporaries as I had heard the same expressions so many times and, in many ways, it seemed stupid to insist on speaking in English when a simple Japanese word was more appropriate.

I began to say the fundamental stuff such as goodnight see you tomorrow as a start and if there was no embarrassing feedback, I would venture to use a little more. To those I had spoken English to from the start of my visit however I was a little reluctant because I didn't want to spoil their status of being main interpreter or let Tanabe think his English was a bit lame.

The ability for me to speak a little Japanese didn't go entirely unnoticed among the Nichi Dai brethren. In fact, there was one morning when after breakfast they had decided to apply me with a little of their own humour. Knowing that I had at last taken the time out to learn from them the correct after mealtime phrase when even they spoke it in a hurried slur seemed a little ironic. Before the collective utterance, which would always be in unison, there was a lead into the phrase with a command from the captain to straighten our backs then he would say "gochiso sama deshita" after which everybody would immediately respond with the same. On this morning the captain did his bit and everybody tilted their head forward as if to speak and so I boldly spoke out the clearest "gochiso sama deshita" ever; and I was entirely on my own. They had all been primed not to speak so they could hear what I had to say. They all laughed out loud when young Kenji shouted "Aasa velly good. Queen's Japanese" and for a moment I was electrified in my chair from the shock of the ploy but I too laughed at the irony of the joke and was a little warmed to the fact they had taken time out to play a trick on me.

From the day I had arrived in Japan the weather was hot and just seemed to get hotter. I was told that the spring of this year was a little warmer than normal so I guess for me it was in at the deep end in view of the acclimatization. But every week seemed to get warmer and we weren't yet anywhere near the height of summer and its oppressive humidity. That was promised for around July to August time. I lost interest in trying to gain a tan for there was nobody around to admire it and sitting on the roof became unbearable. I mean, we spend much of our summer in Britain trying to get darker, either to impress the opposite sex or to make our mates a little jealous after we had jetted back from Majorca or somewhere. But here in the heart of Tokyo the whole concept of sunbathing became futile. I had however the need to be occupying myself during the day and I wanted either to work or study. Apart from the infrequent Japanese lessons I managed with my fellow roommates who were seldom around to help me in a consistent enough manner I was not fulfilling these long hours with any quality study. I had heard that some previous students had visited another dojo for extra training and the name of Arakawa Sensei cropped up. He was a former instructor here at the university and currently taught at his own dojo. When I raised the subject with Tanabe, he was dismissive of the idea and I was not given any encouragement to train elsewhere. Little did I know at the time there was trouble brewing in the Japan Wado Kai federation, something I would get to hear about as the summer wore on.

The weekends were a little more bearable as most of the students were around on Saturdays. One Saturday morning after training in the park we were all ordered into the kitchen where we moved away the tables and chairs and under Tanabe's watchful gaze scrubbed the dining room and kitchen floor. The wooden floor was so old that there seemed little difference after we had finished and I for one considered it a waste of a morning. But it kept us all out of mischief for a while and just as we were expecting another chore when Tanabe called us together, he made the official announcement that after evening training that we were free to go anywhere until five o'clock the next day. There was a buzz of excitement as the lads in my room hurriedly prepared some clothes ready for the off later. Fujimoto came into my room and invited me to stay at his friend’s house for the evening

We had to pay that day for our night out. Kobayashi dropped in to take the training and so we were under close scrutiny right from the start. Even in the warm up and stretch there was an intensity of sorts and I was to be the guinea pig for a variation to a routine exercise. Ordinarily after we finished our gentle but firm stretch with a partner the person sat on the floor would bend his knees and put the soles of his feet together so that the knees stuck out either side. The partner behind would then place his feet on the knees and his hands on the shoulders in order to 'encourage' the groin stretch a little more. To be honest it looked worse than it felt for the guy standing on the knees would really put most of the weight on the shoulders with the hands and then slowly release the hands to stand up straight. Done slowly it was no problem although I can't see any gym throughout the current civilized world endorsing this type of stretching. On this day, for some inexplicable reason, Kobayashi ordered two students to help with my stretch; one on each leg. The two lads stepped up and I took their weight and I was immediately in trouble. My head dropped to hide the pain and I quietly cursed as the pain grew intolerable. Kobayashi asked "Painful?" "Hai" I replied between forced lips. He repeated the question and I replied the same and I knew I couldn't hold out much longer in this position. Even Tanabe fell quiet probably not understanding the point of the exercise. Maybe he thought I was being punished for something and I was thinking the same thing as I sat on the floor waiting for my joints to snap. I thought of making a wish as the thought of a chicken wishbone came to mind but all I wanted was the two morons on my legs to get off.

Tanabe intervened. "Kobayashi!" he shouted. Kobayashi knew the tone of voice and instantly told the lads to get off. I was not amused and was surprised at the antic of this usually amiable instructor. Perhaps there was a sadistic streak to 'moon face' after all. The Shinto gods were indeed looking down on me that day however for Tanabe ordered Kobayashi to sit down with his legs wide apart and two students, under orders, grabbed a foot each and pulled in opposite directions. The lads were reluctant to be involved but there was no arguing with the main man so pulled firmly at his request. It would have been sweeter had I been allowed to grab a leg but I was just as happy to see my mentor suffer as much agony as I had earlier. In fact, Kobayashi's limbs were not as flexible as mine so the legs looked like they were going to end up at the butchers. I learned a new Japanese word that day, "ittai" meaning painful. The more Kobayashi uttered "ittai" the more Tanabe asked "ittai?" replicating the scene I had endured a little earlier. Finally, the lads let go of Kobayashi's legs and he sat still as if to count he still had both legs intact before slowly rising with an unhappy and embarrassed look across his lean face. He said nothing and simply let the captain, Tanemura, continue with the training. I never really understood the idea behind the antics of that session and never saw or experienced that sort of physical torment again so it was just a one off that just got a little out of hand.

We trained hard that day despite Kobayashi remaining a little quiet, for Tanabe wanted the best from us all as usual so we paid with buckets of sweat, fresh from our burning brows. My forehead was pouring out its usual ten litres to the minute but I managed to position myself near a window that day and felt a cool breeze start to increase as the weather outside looked to threaten with rain. As I passed that window during the combinations of linework I noticed tiny raindrops hit the small panes of glass and the sight of rain brought a modicum of relief in the arid atmosphere of that dojo.

As the heavens opened and rain fell heavily on the dojo roof Tanabe shouted even louder to drive us on as if he were in competition with the Lord himself. The rattling of the raindrops was as loud as machine gun fire and we all seemed to be united in battling with the elements as we went about our business. There was no free fighting that day but lots more of the 'line up' with wave after wave of attacks coming toward the face as we were forced once more to fight with our backs against the wall. We were told that the competition score was not the final point but that where possible we were to stay at close range once the attack had been dealt with and take our opponent down if the opportunity arose. So, a simple attack and defence drill soon developed into a sweeping and throwing frenzy. I fared well for most of the time but struggled with Kawano who should have been a candidate for a Sumo wrestling stable. He was at home grabbing and mauling so was never in any danger from anyone else in losing his feet. Minamidae and I were extra cautious with each other for the slightest spark would have resulted in another flare up but I knew eventually we were to be at each other again so we kept order for the time being. As usual I picked up a bump in the face from Oshima but I started to think that was simply his way of communicating. Kikuta spoke good English; Oshima would punch the face, and they both smiled when they did it. As this training continued, I felt the lump on my face swell and it seemed I was peering over a small hill in one eye as I now prepared to attack the lads lined up in front of me. This time we were urged to attack with only kicks. There were five lads lined across the front and after we had attacked one, we would move into the next line and briefly queue to have a go at the next. A bit like an orderly queue at the post office only this line moved a lot quicker with better service and immediate attention. However, there was no discount on offer here so no quarter was asked and none given.

After endless practice of front kicks, especially on pads, over the last five or six weeks meant my confidence in this technique had grown. I had also begun to kick like the rest, low and hard. To feel the contact in the lower abdomen and a groan as the recipient caught the technique without blocking or moving out of the way not only brought the satisfaction of a successful attack to mind but also meant that there was to be no counter punch to deal with. The harder we attacked the easier the task. If we went in half-hearted, we got thumped. That is except Minamidae, who like me was doing his best not to make excessive contact. I also felt that the first years were getting stronger and I had to remind myself that they were only eighteen. Iidabashi and Asuka were having a good day and I felt that those two and the tall figure of Enomoto were in fact causing a few problems with the seniors. Those three were probably the fitter of my roommates and so gave as good as they got unless the seniors got a bit nasty. But overall, this day was all about giving a good display so that we could earn an evening and a day away. In fact, there seemed an enjoyment to the training with the thought of clearing off later.

The shower, the bath and dinner all happened in double quick time that evening. There was a buzz of activity as all students had somewhere to go for the night. We all had to submit a contact number or an address to Tanabe sensei before departing and then all cleaned up and without a Karate gi in sight we all filtered out of the building. About a dozen of us skipped along the roadside, which would normally be taking us to the park across the road early in the mornings, and I joked with the rest that perhaps we ought to do a jog around the park before continuing to the station. Kishiyama gave me a friendly kick to the side of my head that told me the idea was out of the question. Hakoishi and Fukusyo were off to find some girls somewhere and I only hoped there were females to match their mentality for there might be a little trouble if they didn't succeed. They all had addresses to go to but I suspect there was to be some hard partying first.

We all jumped on the train towards Shinjuku and there was much mirth between us students of all ages. In fact, we all behaved like kids on a school outing, pushing, and shoving each other trying to get a place to sit down on the crowded carriage. It was Saturday evening so the train was packed with people heading into town. We couldn't contain our excitement as we all talked of meeting with a beautiful girl and not bothering to return to Tanabe. “It’s ok sensei but we would rather take orders from her instead” we joked in Japanese English.

Okano, one of the quiet third years was forever saying to me “this is a pen” for that is usually the first thing that Japanese children are taught in school. Unfortunately, Okano never seemed to make any further progress in his study so his English was limited to just this phrase and so tonight to show off in front of the carriage full of people he kept repeating “this is a pen”, as if he were talking fluently in

English. At various stations along the Keio line students from our squad would jump off and say their farewells until only a handful remained at the terminal of Shinjuku. From here Fujimoto and I split from the rest and caught a connecting train to another station about ten minutes away.

Fujimoto and I entered the small family house of his friend Nakamura who I had met before when we had taken a trip to the lake. His parents were most hospitable as I entered and were astounded when I said only one Japanese word; "konbanwa". My confidence to speak to total strangers in Japanese evaporated and I couldn't really follow up with any Japanese small talk but it broke the ice and Fujimoto filled them in on the rest. Out came the beers and snacks that accompanied the drinks. Then Nakamura announced that his sister was waiting to show me the 'tea ceremony'. His sister entered wearing a traditional kimono and I looked closely at her features for this was the first young Japanese female I had come close to. She was pleasant enough at around seventeen years old and pretty but not really my cup of tea, if you excuse the pun. But she was a smart female in traditional garb that made her look a little special. I watched closely as she went through the slow and meticulous routine of preparing a very special cup of tea. As I watched I began to melt in the presence of her femininity. I thought to myself how much I had been on my own for what seemed an eternity and for a moment she was my mother, my girlfriend and even Sheena Easton all in one and I was enveloped in her presence. After the ritual of making the tea and turning the cup and offering me the drink I was really gasping for another beer but I took the small teacup from her, enjoyed the sip, and returned the cup trying to look suitably impressed. Her parents applauded and so I joined them which made their night and so out came the sake. We had 'ebi fried' for supper, shrimp in batter, fantastic.

The three of us; Nakamura, Fujimoto and myself finally excused ourselves and retired to Nakamura's room where we drank more beer and made some audio tapes for our girlfriends. Fujimoto lived in the northern part of Honshu in Aomori so like Kikuta rarely made it home. Like me he had a girlfriend at home so we both made special messages on a tape to our ladies in waiting, Fujimoto spoke a little English "I rub you" and all that corny stuff. It is well noted that Japanese people have a problem pronouncing the 'l' and the 'r' of the English language but they also struggle big time with the letter 'v', so I rub you is not a sexual connotation but a term of endearment. In fact, I spent a good half hour that evening trying to help both lads pronounce the letter 'v'. I spoke a bit of Japanese into the tape machine like "gochisosama deshita, ittai" and another word I had used a lot recently "tsukareta" meaning tired or more appropriately 'knackered'.

The two lads laughed at the words I had strung together in a romantic 'song like' way in order to impress my girlfriend who would have no clue to the meanings. We were drunk and a little silly but Fujimoto and I were relaxed in Nakamura's household.

The three of us finally lay down in Nakamura's bedroom around three o'clock and crashed out. Almost immediately an alarm clock sounded and I jumped up looking for my tracksuit bottoms. Fujimoto and Nakamura opened their eyes and looked at me bemused. I realized then where I was, a million miles from Nichi Dai. I slumped back onto the floor and groaned; “atama ittai”; ‘my head hurts’. “Boku mo” Fujimoto concurred holding his hands to his head and shielding his eyes from the morning sun that shone through the thin curtains. The smell of stale beer filled the room and I suddenly wanted to get out of the room before I vomited. I went to the bathroom and sat on the toilet for ten minutes as well as splashed some water over my face. My companions were up when I returned to the room and so we joined the Nakamura family at the breakfast table. Out came the natto and I froze for a second for what I had to drink the previous night would not have mixed with natto. Fortunately, a very understanding Mrs. Nakamura brought out some toast and I relaxed and ate. A couple of large coffees went down well and I started to see straight.

Fujimoto's friend was off to meet his girlfriend for the day so we said our sayonaras to him and his family and thanked them heartily for their hospitality. I don't know if their small house was noisy from our drunken antics the night before, but I was invited back to stay again so we couldn't have been too bad.

The Sunday was ours to spend as we wished so we headed back to Shinjuku and went to the cinema. There was a James Caan film showing so I opted for that one as opposed to the Samurai films that were featuring on other screens. I was a little concerned that the film would be dubbed into Japanese but the film was in English with Japanese subtitles so I was able to relax and enjoy the movie. During the interval I spoke briefly to a guy from the Middle East who spoke fluent English without a hint of an accent. He was in Tokyo studying some engineering at Nissan Diesel but had in fact lived in London for a while. It struck me as we chatted briefly that this was the first natural conversation, I had enjoyed in something like six weeks and it was an absolute delight to do so.

Fujimoto and I spent another hour or so after the cinema walking around the shops. I discovered an excellent bookshop that sold English books and magazines so I picked up a small Japanese dictionary as well as a Mad magazine. The former would make sense of the things said around me; the latter would hopefully give me light relief if the first book didn't work.

Without saying too much we mutually agreed to get back to Hachimanyama and we fell silent as the train out of Shinjuku on the Keio line transported us back to a different world from the one, we had enjoyed for the last twenty-four hours. Fujimoto kindly invited me home to his place in the summer saying there were to be some summer festivals I could enjoy. I had no idea there was to be a summer break or for that matter what I would be doing in that period. I could only say to my friend that I hoped I could take him up on his offer.

I returned to my room by five o'clock, which was the deadline for us all to be back. The boys in my room were excited after their time away so the break did wonders to raise a little morale in the first-year abode. Asuka was busy sketching on a pad and showed us his unique talent of drawing caricatures of people. He hurriedly sketched a few of us in our Karate gis doing silly things you wouldn't be doing in a dojo which got us all hysterical once more. As he drew, we got on with preparing our stuff and the seniors' gis for the next day. We were more than happy to lie on our futons early ready for the day and week ahead and lights went out at ten.

At around ten thirty I heard Tanabe sensei arrive and there was some loud laughing and a little singing. I recognized the voice of Hara from the second year contingent and he was as drunk as a skunk. Along with another voice I couldn't identify they bid Tanabe goodnight and thanked him for the evening, only they were saying their thanks at the tops of their voices and then repeating it over again. Even after Tanabe had already bid goodnight, gone into his room and was probably in his bed Hara shouted again "gochisosama deshita", and again "gochisosama deshita" as if waiting for a reply. There was a loud shout from the fourth-year room "Hara!" and all went quiet. Until one more "oyasumi nasai!"

Not quite the amiable goodnight of 'The Waltons', but close.

Another Monday morning and the words from the Mamas and Papas song filled my head. "Oh Monday morning you gave me no warning what was meant to be" or something of that effect. But as I lined up along the roadside in what was another drizzly muggy morning, I penned a new song. "Oh, Monday morning you gave us no warning you'd be watching me". As we were stood with our feet apart leaning back to stretch, we spotted Tanabe sensei peering out of a window looking down. He had decided to check things were operating smoothly on our return after the weekend break. We set off along the road and as we crossed the footbridge to the park somebody caught sight of Tanabe getting a bike from the rack outside our building. The whisper of Tanabe's name went from back to front of our jogging train and back again so that everyone knew we were to be under closer scrutiny that morning.

We set off from our usual starting point in the corner of the park and kept an orderly pace with an orderly queue. Usually after the first hundred metres or so the slower or lazier runners would drop back a fair bit but not today, there were no slow or lazy runners in our club, only hard-working ones. After a lap, things were going well but no sign of our club coach and we thought perhaps he was off to the shops or back to his own apartment. Then a few of us caught sight of him through the trees on the other side of the park's surrounding border. Tanabe was cycling on a path outside the park and was watching our progress from this vantage point. Again, his name was spread through the ranks and we kept together in a perfect troop. Every now and again we caught a brief glimpse of his red top flash by through the thick green undergrowth and I wondered if he really was trying to be hidden for, he could have been a little more select in his choice of attire if he was trying to remain completely out of sight. I believed he was letting us know of his omnipresence without being too blatant. We completed seven laps and then finished the hour with a few fighting combination techniques, but Tanabe was nowhere to be seen and we returned as another closely packed line of well drilled students.

For the next couple of days after this incident our morning run was always a nervous one and as we circumnavigated the park our heads were like hungry sparrows in the garden, getting on with the job in hand but always watching for danger. That then was Tanabe's clever plan; to let us know he could always be about while he probably slept soundly through the early morning.

Kobayashi popped in during the week and suggested we perhaps go to the British Embassy in Tokyo to get further advice on staying longer on my visa. So, after breakfast one morning he drove me to Akasaka but the staff were of no real help in dealing with my trivial request. In his wisdom, Kobayashi then decided to go straight to his hometown of Uenohara. Now Kobayashi's English was pretty good but his lack of communication was even better for, apart from the clothes on my back, I had brought nothing else with me.

In Uenohara we made an impromptu visit to the high school. I had run around the grounds of the school early one morning with Kobayashi but the place looked different with cars in the car park and classroom windows with scores of youngsters peering out and craning their necks to follow the foreigner walking into their school. Some were even standing up to get a better view. We stopped at the main entrance and slipped off our shoes, placed them in a shoe rack, which resembled a large bookcase and put on some slippers. Not the soft slippers you would snuggle up by the fire with but the plastic ones that resembled the ones we wore back at Nichi Dai. Even though we were walking into a concrete building with tiled floors the custom of street shoes discarded at the door was still maintained. I was led into the main office and introduced to one of the school's principles, Mr. Tsuda. He was a barrel shaped fifty plus man with very little hair and a smile as wide as his waist. Tsuda sensei (a term for all types of teachers) made a fuss of my presence and I was brought some iced tea and cake. He could not speak any English so chatted first with my Karate instructor. I listened to their conversation trying to pick out the odd word or two but I was distracted by the awful taste of the apparently delightful looking cake that I had just put in my mouth. I had been in this situation before, on my first day in fact when I had eaten natto, when in the company of respected people, I wanted to spit out the contents of my mouth all over the floor. But I kept on chewing and swallowing with a smile that was as false as Jordan's assets and finally finished the little devil. Tsuda sensei spotted my empty plate and gestured if I wanted any more "mo kekko desu" I replied to tell him I was fine, thank you. Kobayashi said it was a bean filled cake and was 'good for health'.

Kobayashi turned to me and told me Tsuda sensei was going to Korea later in the summer and should I need to extend my visa by doing it this way then I could accompany him. On top of that he would pay for my trip. I was stunned. A man I didn't know had just offered me an all-expenses excursion to another country to help me out. I bowed deeply with "domo arigato gozaimasu" a thank you that very much came from the bottom of my heart but I wondered how many cakes I would have to eat before I got there. There was also a chance maybe to obtain a cultural visa in the Japanese Embassy in Korea, which would give me the flexibility of staying a full twelve months in Nichi Dai. Things were moving fast and I was still not certain I wanted to be here another ten months but to show uncertainty here was out of the question. So first, I was to go to the Mitsukoshi Department store later that week to get my Korean visa.

As I sat in Kobayashi's car heading back to his house my head was reeling with the contents of the last half an hour. Fortunately, we had an afternoon sleep at Kobayashi's house that cleared my head a little. At five o'clock I was roused and realized I wouldn't be getting back to Tokyo for training that evening, but we went immediately to the Uenohara dojo. As we stepped out of the car Kobayashi asked me where my Karate gi was. I told him I didn't know we were going anywhere far that day so I didn't bring it. He looked at what I was wearing, a pair of jeans and a tee shirt.

"It's ok!" He said. I was inwardly furious. "It was certainly not ok" I wanted to say. The jeans I had on were of a slim fit type and so even kneeling to bow was going to present problems. I could not imagine spending three hours teaching or training in what I was

1st Year Room

Kushanku Summer Camp

Kobayashi Sensei training Seishan on the roof top

Kawano was a handful

Makiwara Nihon University dojo

wearing. But that was exactly what I did. I helped with the kids and then joined the adults for a two-hour class in basics, kata, and sparring. The feisty judoka was present in the class and I was not in the mood for style against style today. If he so much as reaches out to grab my tee shirt I planned to knock him swiftly on his backside to stop it before it starts, Kobayashi or no Kobayashi. The denim jeans helped raise my body temperature to above danger level. I felt the two uncomfortable hours of Karate training that evening was an experience I would not want to repeat. The simplest moves were a chore and I felt a fool training in a traditional dojo dressed as an extra for Top of the Pops. The sparring was not in any way the predicament I had expected so I just moved around lightly not really interested in what was happening in front of me. I was in a foul mood all night and couldn't wait to get away from here and back to my room and the mates I had there. I couldn't even change after training so I sat in the car still sweating, without a towel, in the same clothes I had worn all day and all evening training as we joined the expressway for the hour and a half journey back to Tokyo. I looked at Kobayashi slyly at times and wondered if it was another perverse attempt to make me feel stupid. He simply reached for the radio changed the station to The Far East Network and said "Ooh good song" when The Beatles struck up 'Love Me Do'.

"Hai good song" I replied and shut my eyes.

Training the rest of the week was a mixture of tough and tougher. The tough days were when we didn't fight. The tougher days were fighting for an hour, albeit intermittently. On the days when we didn't fight, we did advanced Kata training and Tanabe started to show me a little of his knowledge in that department. He would sometimes show me Jion kata or Jitte and compare them with the way he thought Suzuki Sensei taught them in England. I was not aware of some of the more advanced Wado katas so I listened and watched intently but rather ignorantly as he demonstrated in front of me. I was however appreciative of the moments he took to help me whether it was to correct my Kata form or my fighting technique.

Friday came around and Kobayashi popped in mid-morning to first take me once more onto the roof to train for an hour with the hand weights before we showered ready to go into town. I packed my 'gi' in my bag and waited for him on the roadside. He emerged from the building and asked me what was in the bag. "Gi" I replied.

"It's ok, no need" he said. Instead of throwing it at him I threw it in the back of his car just in case.

Before long I was in the familiar district of Shinjuku and I accompanied Kobayashi into the Mitsukoshi Department store. There was the familiar "irrashaimase!" from about a dozen staff as we walked through the main doors and we caught the lift in which a well-dressed lady member of staff informed us of the content of each floor as we climbed to the fifth.

I thought it a little odd we were in a department store to sort out my visa but on the fifth floor was an airline agency where I met Mr. Suzuki the manager and the guy who could perhaps find a solution to extending my visa. The trip to Korea with Tsuda sensei was already provisionally booked for some time in July so from the airline agency Mr. Suzuki phoned the Japanese consul to enquire how long it would take for a cultural visa to be granted for Japan but in Korea. The answer was about two months. Considering we were only going to be in Seoul for two days the prospect was out of the question. My flight for Korea was cancelled and I was resolved to stay in Japan for six months maximum. I was not unhappy for I was still not sure if I wanted to be here longer but I was starting to settle in a bit more and funnily enough my little excursions away from training at Nichi Dai was sometimes becoming a little irritating, I was more relaxed around the boys in my room or even in the company of the older boys but in the company of Kobayashi sensei I could never totally be at ease.

Returning to Hachimanyama, Kobayashi did say that in the two-week summer break in July Tsuda Sensei had hoped I could teach a little English to some children in Uenohara for a chance to earn some money. So that was his way of telling me I was to be in his hometown for the vacation but I didn't mind for I certainly needed the cash. I was down to about five hundred pounds out of the seven and I could not see myself making that stretch for the six-month period. I was to go to Uenohara again soon and meet with Tsuda and a Mr. Furukawa who worked in construction. He too might be able to offer me some work. On the whole Kobayashi was pulling a few strings for me and for that I was overwhelmed.

When I returned to my room in the dormitory block there was more cleaning going on so I picked up a mop and bucket and helped in the toilets. Tanabe had made a comment that everywhere was scruffy so an extra clean was ordered. This took us until training time and we wondered if perhaps we may be cleaning instead of training that day so Hakoishi took it upon himself to knock on Tanabe's door and tell him that the cleaning was not quite done and should we continue? We stopped for a moment in anticipation. Most of us thought not a chance would Tanabe let that happen but one or two were hopeful. The loud shout from Tanabe's room made everyone jump and hurriedly put away the cleaning tools to fetch our dogi and towel. Hakoishi came out grinning stupidly as if he had tried something heroic but if there was any chance of having even a little time off training to spend cleaning then Hakoishi was the wrong person to convince the club coach.

Half way through training that day we were visited by a couple of old boys although there was a relief that 'Mighty Murase' wasn't one of them. These two didn't get involved much with the training but just seemed intent on limbering up for an hour or so, which made everyone a little nervous. However, there was no free fighting that evening so the old boys were left warmed up and frustrated. Even Tanabe paid them little attention.

The rain would still fall at odd times for a while and then the weather would return to brilliant sunshine and a damper atmosphere as the humidity started to increase. The Japanese people, like the English, spend much time discussing the weather. During these hot times people would greet each other with "atsui neh?", 'hot isn't it'. This would be a common phrase among us students and out on the street among passers-by. But sometimes I found the phrase of a foreign language seem more appropriate than the English version. Sounds funny but true. "Ima nanji" seems easier to say than 'what time is it now?' or "doko iku no" 'where are you going?'. I was quite at ease saying the small stuff, it was all the rest of the language I was struggling with. After training the word 'tsukareta' was often bandied about when we told each other how tired we felt.

The morning after my Shinjuku trip with Kobayashi we trained in the dojo because another summer downpour prevented us from going to the park. Kobayashi would often stay Friday night and so would be present for the early training. He was an early bird himself so was keen to accompany us. He decided after the jog around the confines of the dojo to put us to task on the Makiwara. While four people punched each post with solid reverse punches the rest did press-ups until our fifty punches were completed. We also did a version of the wheelbarrow walk whereby somebody carried the legs while we walked around on the hands like back in the school days. Only here we walked on the two knuckles of the fist. Once more I cursed when I took the skin off my knuckles when punching the Makiwara for I knew this would take a week or so to repair and during that time it would be a nuisance. It was a further nuisance when it came to walking on them for with every step the searing pain shot through my arms and I was eventually forced to walk on the flats of my hands. I reminded myself that from the day my knuckles repair I would be constantly doing knuckle press ups to prevent this from happening again.

Later that day was another fitness class during the final hour. We paired off and one lay down on his back while his partner stood over his head. The legs would be repeatedly raised off the floor toward the standing partner who would push them back to the floor. Whenever we did this, it was always seventy repetitions, however, today it was to be a hundred. The grunts and the groans echoed between the four walls. The groans became louder as the target number approached until finally one hundred sounded like an orgasm as each student shouted in relief and rolled over onto their side to escape from the pain of the abdominal muscles. This done we stood in a group of four with our backs to one another leaning on each other. We then started squatting deeply making sure we maintained the contact with the others. Tanabe would count and we would drop down slowly and stay still, waiting, before he counted again and we felt as if our thighs would burst trying to stand up together. This went on for what seemed an eternity until one by one each team collapsed in a heap. Tanabe cursed and then joked at our poor performance before sending us on a run around the rugby field. After a couple of laps, we did a few sprints which just about finished us for good and we were mindful that the next day was Sunday so we could rest up a bit. As we knelt in seiza back in the dojo and once more repeated our proud maxims, Tanabe informed us that there was to be extra training the next day for everyone. We slumped as he left the building.

The next day was the first Sunday I had trained. We did our run at six and we were back in the dojo for eight thirty that morning. We did basics and kata until ten thirty but without an instructor for the first hour but then Tanabe dropped in so we did kata training in earnest for another hour.

As I walked or rather shuffled back from the dojo Tanabe shouted “Aasa”. I wheeled around quickly and replied “hai!” Today Wakamei fights, we go, one hour”

"Hai wakarimashita" I further replied as I told him I understood to be ready quickly.

At eleven thirty Tanabe and I took a bike each from outside our abode and cycled to the station and then took a train journey with several changes before ending up in Yokohama. Tanabe had little to say during the journey and in fact seemed a little embarrassed in my presence and showed a slight shyness in the public domain. This was something I had also noticed with the other students for out on the streets they seemed almost innocent and inexperienced when dealing with the general public. In England the average twelve-year-old becomes street wise through a desire to be independent but the Japanese youngsters tend to develop the group mentality that is a characteristic of their society. On one hand you would see very young children journeying by train together without an adult present, which would be unheard of in England. Yet it seemed to me that the average eighteen-year-old in Japan was quite immature especially alone in public.

Wakamei sensei was taking part in a selection contest, as he had previously explained, to represent the Kanagawa Prefecture team in, I guessed, a national contest later.

I was surprised that day at the ability of my old instructor considering he had hardly trained for quite a while. He didn't show the dynamic and lightning speed attacks I had come to expect from the fighters of this nation, but what he did display was a cool measured performance, which was a credit to his experience.

Once or twice Wakamei struggled to change his pace and was blowing a bit with the younger guys but he was the only competitor that day to score with a decent kick to the head. His evasive tactics worked a treat as he moved well away from any serious attacks. It was announced shortly after the afternoon's proceedings that Wakamei qualified for the Kanagawa team.

When Tanabe left, he granted permission for me to spend the evening with Wakamei sensei, first to a restaurant where I met his old sensei, before returning home to his house. His wife and child were away for the weekend so we watched baseball on the TV until late drinking a few glasses of wine. Again, it was a relaxed atmosphere in this man's company in comparison to Kobayashi yet I didn't hold him in the same esteem as the man from Uenohara. Whether it was the training thing or not I couldn't be sure but I was more than happy to be back to basics the next day.

FOURTEEN

I realised as the weeks had turned to months the pull to return home became a little fainter. Sure, there were still things I missed in abundance, like a roast dinner, shepherd's pie, fish, and chips. A call from my mates, my girlfriend, a decent pint of proper beer and some good television programmes. But the life I lived had become more settled and I had developed a liking for much of the food, made a few friends and listened to my music every night. My training was going well and I got a buzz from the harder sessions.

One thing I was missing was a good old chat in English. The day after I had been to Wakamei sensei's house I caught the train back via Tokyo station and decided to get off here to have a look at the nation's capital district. I expected a place of similar atmosphere to that of Shinjuku but it was totally subdued and characterless. As I wandered about in the quiet streets near the station it became obvious that it was a district full of offices and banks that held no real interest to the curious visitor. When I stepped into a branch of an English bank to change a traveller's cheque however, I felt I could have been anywhere in the UK. Although the staff were Japanese while I sat waiting for my cash to be presented there were exclamations from among the customers such as, "Oh hello George haven't seen you in a while" and "You must drop by sometime" in the stiffest English accent from ex pats working in Japan. These were the first English accents I had heard in two months and I wallowed in the sounds of my native tongue. I wanted to intervene in their conversations as they spoke of the football results back home and the approaching wedding of Prince Charles and Lady Diana. I felt awkward in my jeans and tee shirt when all around me were expensive business suits and shiny shoes. I spoke to no one except the staff but for a time I was among familiar people as if they were my friends.

Wandering further in one direction past more offices, hotels, and conference centres I reached another district called Kanda, which has a reputation for its many bookshops. I spent a little time here looking for some English literature with little success although I did manage to buy a decent map of Tokyo to help me on my travels. Looking at my map I had wandered further than I had thought so I hailed a taxi, which is always a last resort for they were a luxury I could seldom afford. But stepping into the air-conditioned car out of the midday heat was a joy and for ten minutes I reclined comfortably in the back as I returned to Tokyo station for my onward journey back to Nihon University.

Throughout the journey back I thought of the selection contest I had watched at the weekend and I wondered for the first time whether I would get chance to compete in any of the tournaments that I knew were on the horizon. After all, there were a couple of hard months training behind me and I felt a desire to get out and compete, whether it would be for the club or for myself. I thought I would ask Kobayashi about that one when I see him.

My thoughts of fighting in a contest remained with me as I trained hard that week. The first two hours of each session held little diversity for us but the last hour could be the tricky bit. Sometimes we fought and fought hard like our life depended on it. Sometimes there would be kata training or kihon gumite prearranged sparring. This too would have its moments as we were warned not to take this too easily because it was 'only' prearranged. With Tanabe Sensei on the prowl our attacks to our partners had to be swift and meaningful so that the defending partner had to move correctly without hesitation. It was not uncommon for one of us to get a belt in the mouth for not moving quickly enough or not concentrating. Each move by both attacker and defender would be accompanied by a kiai to press home the spirit of our intentions.

The days off from Nichi Dai with Kobayashi became few and far between as I settled in more, but there was the odd time when he would ask for my help. One Wednesday I accompanied him to one of the high schools near Mt Fuji where I had previously visited. The students were pleased to see me and I lapped up their enthusiasm. There was to be a grading and Kobayashi asked me to help by reading out the grading syllabus to the students. This wasn't too tall an order for it was the same syllabus I had been using back home in England under Suzuki Sensei's instruction. Before the grading however I was asked by the schoolteacher to demonstrate on film some basic training and kata. It felt as if I were the one that was taking a grade as I did my best to perform for the camera under the watchful eyes of around thirty teenagers. Following my nervous exhibition, we trained for a couple of hours before I helped my instructor as he conducted the grading. As we drove away from the school Kobayashi thanked me and put an envelope in my hand. I knew it was money but I didn't look until back at his place when I was alone. I had been given five thousand yen, which was around twenty pounds. This was not going to change my lifestyle here in Tokyo but was half my monthly lodge and so was without question an unexpected and hugely generous bonus.

I had asked Kobayashi sensei about competing and he replied that it would be unlikely for I was not a true member of the university and so could not represent them. I found this hard to take for this would only amount to me being frustrated after the copious amounts of preparation for what would seem no immediate purpose.

The day after the grading at the high school and after a good night sleep in my own room at Kobayashi's house, we rose early for running and then joined the family for breakfast. Sensei's parents were both present and they smiled but said very little as they seemed to keep their distance in the activity of the busy family bustle of the morning. Kobayashi's father sat at the back of the house enjoying the serenity of the view across the river and his mother sat nearby trying to keep cool with a small hand-held fan. The rear windows were fully opened to allow what little breeze there was to venture in and swathe the occupants in the sultry morning heat. The constant din from the ringing of the cicadas was another reminder of the impending summer season.

I joined my instructor for another cleaning job at his dojo and while walking back I spotted a woman in her fifties in a wheat field scything for all she was worth. I stopped to watch her as she relentlessly swung the weapon from left to right and back again. Dressed in baggy clothing and with a wide hat to protect her from the bright sunlight she worked intensely until she noticed me watching. She smiled and offered me the scythe. I looked at Kobayashi who shrugged his shoulders so I jumped over the fence that separated the path from her field of work and took the scythe in my hand. She showed me briefly how it was done and so I copied. However, the handfuls of grass that were in my hand didn't come away as easy as I had hoped, or for that matter, as easy as this lady had demonstrated. I hacked again and brought up a few strands, which raised a smile from the lady and a laugh from Kobayashi. There was obviously a skill to this job that I hadn't anticipated so I butchered my way through a few more handfuls of wheat while under more instruction to improve my technique before eventually returning the scythe to its rightful owner. I wiped the sweat from my eyes and bid her farewell. She bowed and resumed her work with a skill and ease that I could now fully appreciate.

At Kobayashi's house my instructor insisted I write a letter to Tatsuo Suzuki to tell him how I was getting on. Kobayashi then informed me that there might be a split between Suzuki and Shiomitsu. How he knew this I couldn't tell but he thought that Shiomitsu Sensei could be leaving the UK federation, in which I was a member. This was a complete shock to me and I had no way of finding out the details of this news. Of course, Suzuki Sensei was my chief instructor, and had been for a few years, but it was Shiomitsu Sensei who had put his trust in me to allow me to train in Japan. A difficult choice should there be one to make, but already I was overwhelmed not only by Shiomitsu's faith in me but also by the many friends of his whom spoke so highly of him. It's worth mentioning here that Suzuki Sensei's time spent at Nihon University had been a lot earlier and so his fellow students of that time were a lot fewer, therefore I had very little contact with his contemporaries. I was often in the company of those who had trained with Shiomitsu so that is why his name was so often in conversation.

After lunch Kobayashi took me to a Zen Dojo. I wondered at first if this was to be a further supplement to my training, like the extra practice on the roof of Nichi Dai. The Zen Dojo was not far from Uenohara so it was considered an interesting field trip.

Our short journey took us further into the countryside where we followed a narrow track before continuing on foot for a hundred metres or so. We stopped in a clearing where there was an open circular monument of some sort in which contained tiered steps. Upon these steps were rows upon rows of little stone effigies. Each little stone statue depicted a baby that had died stillborn or shortly after birth. It was a sad place. So many little lost souls that were remembered in this way could only but have a startling effect on anyone who stood in front of these silent stone figures. A larger statue of a Buddhist monk with a small child hugging its legs stood in the centre of the steps as if to give the impression the children were now in a safe place. A few flowers surrounded this central figure and provided the only colour in this grey atmosphere of stone. I felt there were a million emotions depicted in this eerie and forlorn site of sadness.

We walked on a little further to what seemed a small temple surrounded by a well-kept garden of bushes and small trees. The front sliding door to the building was wide open so we stepped up to the entrance and Kobayashi shouted "gomen kudasai" to call for attention. There was no answer so we stayed put and admired the polished floor of the small veranda on which we stood. Sensei explained that anybody may visit this Zen Dojo for meditation but while here there was to be no food eaten, only water may be consumed. The length of stay may vary but certain times of day must be spent under strict supervision for Zen practice. This was all a bit strange to me but I was fascinated with the beauty and elegance around me. The open door beckoned so we ventured a little further inside and there were a couple of rooms off to either side of the corridor in which we crept. One room was the sleeping quarters but the beds were in the shape wooden ledges either side of the room a couple of feet off the ground.

Kobayashi explained that usually the students would rise at around four or five o'clock to begin their meditation. The Zen Master would carry with him a stout stick and put it to good use should the meditation become sloppy. I wondered if he had a cousin called Hideo.

There was no sign of life within the Zen building so we went back outside and walked around the garden to the rear. There was a man busy in the garden so we approached him and he spoke a little English. He was from Tokyo and said he had been at the retreat for eleven days. I asked him if he had eaten anything and he said he had eaten a little fruit one evening but apart from that nothing but water. I asked how he felt and he told me physically he felt a little weak but mentally very strong. I was none the wiser. He told us that the rest of the group were in the nearby village doing chores for the local people. If the lads from Nichi Dai were anything to go by then these boys were probably in the nearest Denny's Restaurant feeding their faces while this poor soul toiled in their absence. It was a fascinating trip for me that day but one that made me realize that the Zen side of Japan I would rather leave to the Japanese.

I was whisked away from the Zen Dojo that stood in the middle of nowhere to quickly return along the Chuo Expressway back to the familiar surroundings of the Hachimanyama neighbourhood. Time was tight, but I was in my gi and ready to roll for three thirty, sat among my little group just inside the dojo door. When the third years entered Oshima asked where Kobayashi was so I told him he was heading out of town, which satisfied him. Then the fourth years entered and Takahashi asked me the same question.

Training began at four as usual but without too much intensity. In fact, after the basic session, we took an early stroll to the tap outside and drank plenty. We stood around in the sun chatting nonchalantly wiping ourselves with our towels and dousing more of water over our heads. Then Tanabe cycled right in through the gates and all hell let loose. He could tell by the time that we were in the wrong place and he could also tell by our body language that we had been far from working hard enough. We sprinted back in to the dojo and tried to get our weights around our ankles as fast as we could but Tanabe was too far mad to be appeased by our efforts. He told us to forget the weights and instead lined us up at one end. I thought he was going to fight us all. We then started to perform a series of our own combinations for the full length of the dojo. 'Jiyu' as it was known or 'free'. In other words, any technique we wanted. This was normally done at the end of the second session usually around six o'clock to put all our previous kicks and punches together as a final assault. I looked at the clock as we did our first lightning-fast attack shouting as we went and it was five past five. I knew at that moment it would be a long training period. Tanabe appeared from behind the mirrored door carrying a bamboo 'shinai', the type used in Kendo. As we coursed our way up and down the training hall, he wandered behind us waving the big stick. He flicked it at our heels to speed up our movement and he prodded us around the ribs to expose our guards. There was only a moments rest as one wave of seven or eight students would reach the end and turn to wait for the others to follow quickly behind. Three lines of Karateka moved rapidly with the ferocity of advancing wild animals shouting and hollering to the response of Tanabe's angry voice. Each full length of the dojo carried perhaps a combination of about twenty moves in quick succession. It took us about ten seconds to reach the other end. We waited probably ten seconds for the other two lines to reach the end before setting off again. So that's about three combinations to the minute multiplied by the twenty techniques of course which gives us sixty to the minute. This frenetic workout lasted the full hour. I knew it would. About three and a half thousand punches and kicks later and my hamstrings were screaming for me to stop. I had never kicked so many times in one period. My feet were burning like they had on the first day. My thighs were cramping up each time I tried to lift my legs to kick and, above all I was in desperate need of a drink. Not necessarily an ice-cold beer from the bar near the station but it did cross my mind. My mind wandered to the Zen Dojo sat serenely in the middle of nowhere and the only thing that was permissible there was water they said. How ironic. I could gladly have swapped places at that moment, for the Zen life didn't seem so bad after all.

Five past six and it was over. We had our break then went straight to Kata training. Naihanchi Kata involves much movement in a sideways direction. Although this Kata contains the awkward Naihanchi stance where both feet are turned inwards on the same horizontal line with knees bent it was a relief that there were no deeper stances to drop into for my legs were shaking even standing upright. But after ten minutes or so holding various positions, this Kata became hard work particularly because we were exhausted so the mind was struggling to concentrate on the finer points of the instruction given us. Twenty minutes later and I was mentally 'in the shit'. I had not felt as bad as the way I was feeling at this moment. Whether it was fatigue, the heat or simply not enough fluid I couldn't tell but I could feel the colour drain from my face and I had the sudden compulsion to want to sit down. I took deep breaths, looked around at things to focus upon to avoid drifting off for I believed I was about to faint. I didn't want this to happen. I was not going to drop in front of these people. But I was on the verge. Instinctively I did the only alternative option and that was to drop into a deep knee bend stretch resting my hands on my knees as I did so. My feet we were still on the floor and that was all that mattered to me. I didn't know whether Tanabe had seen this for I couldn't even focus on the person in front of me. But I needed just a moment to regain my composure.

My Japanese name bounced off the four walls around me, "Aasa!" A stream of other words followed quickly that sounded none too kind and I knew my position was compromised. Of course, in retrospect it was obvious the only person to be squatting low to the floor when everybody else was stood up would easily be spotted but at the time I was desperate for the moment of salvation.

"Hai" I immediately replied as I saw Tanabe's feet in front of my eyes.

"Daijobu?" It was a question of concern as Tanabe sensed there was a problem.

"Daijobu desu" I exclaimed, assuring him I was fine. I slowly stood. I felt every student's eyes upon me but I couldn't care. My head cleared and I focused on my instructor stood right in front of me.

"Honto?" he asked.' 'Are you sure?' was the question.

"Daijobu desu" I repeated that I was ok. He walked away with a wry smile. What the smile meant I wasn't sure but I felt better and pressed on, albeit rather weakly, for the remainder of the session. But it was another training session from Hell that I wouldn't want to repeat, simply because we were out of our positions at the wrong time. I discovered later that Tanabe was supposed to have been somewhere else that day but our intelligence was misinformed and we paid the price.

The next couple of days vice-captain Fukusyo took charge of the morning runs as well as leading the training in the dojo because Tanemura was sick. Tanemura was a stern, moody fellow who rarely spoke to me except to correct my form in training but who was a responsible leader, conscientious and authoritative. Fukusyo on the other hand was a little friendlier and did not take his position quite so seriously so the morning runs were shortened to a walk after a lap or two. It delighted him further when there was a slight spitting of rain so we stood under trees to keep ourselves dry. On one occasion when both Tanabe and the captain were absent, we didn't even run at all. But if anyone were to ask, we had trained in the dojo because of rain. The effect of the daily grind of years of hard training was something I could only begin to understand even though I had only been here less than three months. So very often an easy hour here or there was a valuable moment for the seniors to savour.

Nearly three months had passed and it was time I had a haircut. There was a barber near the station shops so one morning I ventured in to get my hair chopped. To go to the barbers in England is as simple as buying a pint of milk. To explain how you want your hair styled in another language is a different proposition. I took an old photo of myself with shorter hair and went fully prepared. I had looked up the word haircut in my dictionary and I had learned "susso" or something similar, so confidently I entered the barbershop. I bid the barber good morning and said "susso onegai shimasu". Well walking into a barber asking for a haircut made me look stupid. He looked around the shop as if to say 'yes, you're in the right place so now what?' He offered me a chair and I pulled out the photograph of my shorter, previous hairstyle taken around Christmas time. He looked and replied enthusiastically "hai, hai wakarimashita" and began his work. We chatted in my limited Japanese about what I was doing in Japan and how long I had been training and the food I liked and I realised this was in fact the first time I had a lengthy conversation in Japanese. It was far from fluent and was mainly one- worded answers but I was understood and that was what counted. We didn't get round to talking about holidays and I wasn't offered 'something for the weekend' either but I came away from the barbershop happy, and with shorter hair. The cost however was one thousand eight hundred yen, about eight pounds!! The last time I had a haircut in England, which was some time ago I must admit, only cost me a fiver, some fifteen years later!

The lads in my room made a fuss of my haircut, which reminded me of school but Tanabe didn't so much as give me a second glance in the dojo, only to tell me my punches were a little sloppy. There was little fighting recently and much emphasis was on Kata and Kihon Gumite of late. Training was generally of the same intensity, which was just below very hard but a bit harder than taking things easy. Enomoto told me there was a grading approaching at the weekend so this explained the emphasis on the finer points of our Wado Ryu Karate of late. I doubted very much if I would be able to grade so soon but it did cross my mind to want to take my second dan here in Japan eventually.

I was finally settling in with most of the students of all ages. There were still the one or two who seldom spoke to me but I felt by now the majority accepted that I was here to stay a while among them. The ever-curious Kikuta came looking for me far less, which meant my roommates and I could relax more. In fact, one evening I hopped on the back of Asuka's pushbike, perched on the rack, and we cycled to the next little student village of Shimotokaido which was a bustling little place full of students out for the evening. Shops were always open until late so I browsed in a record shop and bought a tape before we stopped on the way back for a quick beer and a snack. We made it back by nine thirty and spent the evening watching another episode of

Soul Train.

We kept the television on until ten thirty because Tanabe was not around and then I settled down to listen to my new tape. A band by the name of Champagne brought out a hit single called How About Us in 1980 and I had just bought their album. Each one of those tracks even, now well over twenty years later, remind me of laying on my futon thinking of things I had done that day, thinking of home, and wondering what was in store for me.

By now of course to fill up my days I had written letters to virtually everyone back home who knew me. It took a while but the replies started to come back and it was always a thrill for me to open letters from different people. Apart from the regular stuff from my immediate family and girlfriend my dear old Nan kept in touch, as did my aunties and uncles. Mates from my hometown filled me in on the local gossip and sent me newspaper clippings from time to time. My Karate club members too sent their best wishes. Then I received a letter from Australia, it was Phil Kear who congratulated me on finally getting to Japan. He too had heard news about a possible split between Tatsuo Suzuki and Shiomitsu and of a split in the Wado organisation in Japan. He urged me to find out more. I was, however, reluctant to start poking my nose into politics that were far and above my station but I thought I would do my best with the lads around me.

Phil Kear also suggested I might avoid working for Mr. Furukawa in the summer because it is very hard work for little pay. He said I would be better off trying to teach English somewhere. Funny, I had just sent a second letter to Philip saying that I would likely be working in the summer for Mr. Furukawa. How's that for bad timing. He also suggested trying to get to Korea to extend my visa (I was one step ahead on that one) and he also asked for the date of the All-Japan Championships later that year so he could send one or two fighters. There was a postscript, "hit a few for me" he wrote. I thought about what he had written about the All-Japan Wado Championships and realised if he could submit some fighters then there should be an opportunity for me to fight. With all the training I was putting in I felt an urgency to fight sooner or later or I would start falling out big time with the people around me in frustration.

One Friday Kikuta came in and asked if I wanted to go to Akihabara. I had borrowed a personal 'Walkman' for long enough by now and I was urging Kikuta to show me the best place for me to buy a cheap one for myself. It seemed that Akihabara was the place to go for anything electrical. On this Friday there was a change in venue for training, we had to report to the headquarters in Suidobashi, normally reserved for Thursday. Akihabara is situated not far from Suidobashi by train so it was the ideal time to sort out my request.

Shinjuku was a place that had already impressed me with its shops, department stores and vibrant atmosphere. Akihabara was equally exciting in that street upon street were filled with shops selling stereos, TVs, and tons of electrical appliances for the home. I wondered how on Earth stores standing side-by-side selling the same goods possibly made a profit. Electric city was the nickname for Akihabara and it didn't disappoint. I was torn between two minds as I browsed in one shop and then another. I needed a small practical cassette player to listen to my tapes but I was also fascinated at the Hi Tec components that were on sale so I would be flitting from feeling frugal then frivolous. Common sense prevailed and I bought a Toshiba personal cassette with radio for about forty pounds. Not cheap but I was kind of banking on replacing the spent cash once I started some work. At two o'clock we left the electric city and its music blaring from the open shop windows and made our way to Suidobashi for training.

At four thirty we changed and entered the basement dojo of Nihon University's headquarters in Suidobashi. There were about a half a dozen strangers already warming up inside and they studied us as we did them. I felt a little adrenalin as I wondered what was in store. Apart from these young karate students both Tanabe brothers were present and so was Kobayashi and Furukawa whom I had met recently in Uenohara. He too was wearing his gi looking ready for action. A couple of other senior instructors were present but I didn't recognize them. Tanemura's shout started the warm up routine and we duly started training while all the other occupants stood back and watched. Fumihiro Tanabe eventually started instructing while Hideo interjected and Kobayashi and Furukawa added their coaching tips. This continued for two hours. The floor under foot was getting slippery from the humidity mixed with the sweat and I remember at one point not turning my back foot correctly when performing a roundhouse kick, for fear of losing total balance. There was a sharp pain in my left knee because it seemed the bottom half of the leg twisted to kick but the top half remained straight therefore the knee in the middle was trying to cope with both directions. I continued to train but a slow, tightening pain began to develop on the outside of the knee.

After two hours training, we began Kata training and the young students who had been watching from the side-line were then invited to join us. As we practiced Seishan kata I felt a pride and a sense of belonging as we moved as one team through the different techniques and directions of this kata. I noticed then that the movements of our newcomers were slightly different to ours and realized they were of a different style, even though their kata was very similar.

After training there was a presentation for the older instructors whom I didn't recognize, then photographs were taken of us all. Kobayashi sensei then approached me and said I was to follow him after changing for there was a small party to go to.

The visiting students were from Taiwan and were Shotokan karate practitioners. They and their instructors were invited to Japan after they had been hosts to one or two Nichi Dai visitors quite recently. So, an after-training reception was held at a nearby hotel conference room where there was free beer and a free buffet. I felt a little under dressed in my jeans and short-sleeved shirt while others wore suits but I was made to feel most welcome among the visiting Taiwanese. Hideo Tanabe was of course quick to mention the fact that his club is famous worldwide, and that he had an Englishman training with us now. So, my name was shouted across the room on more than one occasion, just as I was grabbing some food or pouring a drink from the bottles of beer that lined the table. I would quickly scurry to where Tanabe sensei was holding court and introduce myself and answer a few questions before eventually my presence would once more pale into enough significance for me to say "shitsurei shimasu", bow and get back to the table.

Finally, Furukawa collared me. Furukawa had been a resident instructor in Bristol for about a year, long before I started Karate. I never knew of him until I came to Japan so I was grateful he had offered me some work in his company. The construction company was owned by his older brother but this younger sibling worked as the foreman. He was not a big man but had the sharp- eyed gritty look of Lee van Clief, the old Western actor. Find a picture of Van Clief and you are looking into the face of Minoru Furukawa. His English was patchy but he knew what to say when it mattered and there wasn't the immediate friendliness of Kobayashi or Wakamei.

"Do you like hard work?" Furukawa asked me as I poured him a beer from the table. I replied that I could work hard but he looked at me unconvinced. "Sure?" he asked again.

"Sure" I assured him.

He let out a very long "Yeah" as if to doubt my answer. I felt a little uneasy in the presence of this man but I was at least a little grateful I was in conversation with someone at a party that I'd felt I had gate-crashed.

By ten thirty the party was over and I was to be given a lift back to base in the trusty Toyota with Tanabe sensei as passenger. While in the lobby of the hotel however when Tanabe was saying his mammoth farewells, I found a public phone and quickly rang the Karate club number and told them we were on our way. So, on our return all was in order and the boys were sleeping like babes.

The next morning my knee hurt like hell. Although I got up, I could only walk with the lads as Kobayashi led the run. I was unable to go any faster than a hobble but I was satisfied I gave what I could.

Later that day Kobayashi took me into the Shureido martial art shop in Tokyo and ordered an initialled black belt for me. Whether he felt the three months of training had earned this token or whether they all felt I was letting the club down a bit with my sad bit of cloth around my waist I never really knew but Kobayashi seemed to think it was necessary for me to wear a new belt. It would be ready in a couple of days for collecting.

The little gifts did not stop at the new belt. From the Shureido shop we went to the headquarter building at Suidobashi and this time went to see the senior Tanabe in his office. It reminded me of a few weeks earlier when I had met Tsuda sensei the schoolmaster in Uenohara. The whole office seemed to make a fuss over my presence and I was offered tea and cake, which I cleverly declined saying I had already eaten to which Kobayashi sensei looked at me in disgust.

Fumihiro Tanabe produced a red Nihon University kit bag and said I was to use this from now on as I was considered a member. I was taken aback. He also told me I was welcome to stay for as long as I wished and that I was to join the club on their annual summer camp in September. Kobayashi was grinning and I thought perhaps it was with pride on my behalf but looking back he probably thought about the summer camp and what it would entail. I, of course just assumed a summer camp was not unlike those I had attended in the UK; some good training mixed with some good times. I thanked Tanabe senior with my best Japanese and asked Kobayashi to thank him for allowing me the opportunity to train with the club in the first place. Tanabe looked at me and said one word “Shiomitsu”. The three of us then left the office to climb into Kobayashi’s car for another mystery tour.

After thirty minutes or so we stopped outside a house in a small neighbourhood, again characterised by narrow streets and tiny walled gardens surrounding houses of various shapes and sizes. Both Tanabe and Kobayashi went in the house to leave me sweltering in the afternoon sun. I wound down the windows and tuned into the American radio station and leaned back to shut my eyes. The pain in my knee would worsen the longer I sat still but I was tired and sleepy from the constant driving so couldn’t be bothered to get out for a stretch. Therefore, uncharacteristically I pushed back my seat, rested my foot on the dashboard and shut my eyes. I awoke suddenly and ashamedly when Kobayashi opened the car door. Half an hour had slipped by. I quickly sat upright. We continued our journey without Tanabe senior and I asked Kobayashi, “family, Sensei?”

“What!” He asked, or rather, stated for he never said ‘what’ with the correct intonation. It was always a flat 'what'.

"That house" I said. "Tanabe Sensei's family?" "No, no. Ohtsuka's house." I was speechless. I had been sat outside in the car while my two instructors had visited the Founder and Grandmaster of our style. In fact, I was sprawled back with my feet up, all the windows wide open and with the sound of Americas finest DJ spinning some soul as I tried to sleep. I had a vision of perhaps someone in the house looking out in order to invite the poor chap outside in for refreshment but then thinking twice when they saw me. Above all I thought about the opportunity that had passed me by, and why perhaps one of my seniors didn't give me a brief introduction. For me there were so many reasons for me to have met Hironori Ohtsuka that day but there was probably one good reason why I couldn't.

FIFTEEN

I was back for training that day but the way my knee felt I knew there was no way I could complete a three-hour stint properly. Before training I went to Fukusyo and told him my problem and I was given permission to stand in the corner of the dojo. I remember seeing the solitary figure of one of the fourth years doing this when I first arrived and also recall one day not seeing him anymore and I was hoping that this, for me, was to be very temporary. It was unusual for me to suffer any injury problems but I knew that to persevere foolishly could have made matters worse so this course of action was my best chance to let my knee heal.

I felt like a leper stood in the corner while the rest of the club worked hard. And, when Tanabe Sensei entered I felt even worse. A quick word to Tanemura and he was put in the picture so he said nothing to me and I continued with my punches in time with the rest of the boys' techniques.

I realized that the general idea of the standing in the corner was to make sure that spiritually you were still attending class. Unless there was a sickness that prevented you from getting out of bed, which happened to us all from time to time, then it was considered your duty to be in the dojo. As uncomfortable as I felt stood in one corner, I was also happy to be present while class was under way.

On the Sunday of that weekend, I did nothing but rest my knee. I was invited to go ten-pin bowling with a few of my roommates but regretfully had to turn them down in order to recuperate. I had spent quite a bit of time with senior students of the club, particularly in the evenings, so I felt I wanted to share some time with the first years. On this day there were only a few of us left in the building because the second and third years were away attending a grading. But I assured them I would join them another time and I stretched out on my futon and willed my leg to improve.

At around five o'clock as I was contemplating the situation of my knee injury and not looking forward to training the next day, I heard the familiar sound of returning students as the echoes preceded them up the stairs and along the corridor. Kikuta was first in my room and with a broad smile told me he and the rest of his year had passed second dan. The second years too had been graded which, considering they were a year behind, seemed a little odd but I was not in the know about such details but congratulated those who had passed. I didn't know where the grading had taken place or who in fact had conducted it for, I was still a little depressed at my own situation.

The next morning, I got up and again hobbled around the park with no sign of improvement. In fact, that day I didn't want to go into town to change more money so I even had to skip lunch as there was nobody about preparing anything and I had no yen to spend at the nearby shop. I felt low this day, and there was to be another three hours to follow later in the corner during training. While getting changed in my room Enomoto remarked how lucky I was to get out of training. For the first time I showed him an anger he hadn't seen before.

"But I want to fucking train!" I said "and to fight!" He perhaps meant it as a joke but could see I wasn't in the mood. The others in the room stopped what they were doing and looked at me, then looked at each other, picked up their towels and left. I followed slowly with a limp.

Halfway through training that day Murase showed up. Ordinarily I would have been pleased for him to see I was still here but I was embarrassed to be standing in the corner. He approached me and spoke, "daijobu?" he asked.

"Well, what do you think?" I thought to myself. Then put my hand to my leg and said "ashi dame" saying my leg was no good. It wasn't technical but it provided all the information I wanted to give and all that he needed to know.

"Ganbatte" he said. That cheered me up a little. Ganbatte is a word of encouragement. It means good luck in the face of adversary. It meant for me, Murase wanted me to get back training. Probably so he could give me a going over but that didn't matter I replied "hai!" in a firm voice and he walked away.

Despite Murase's appearance that day there was no fighting but he coached the class along with Tanabe during the pad work and kata. There was maturity in Murase that defied his twenty something age. I had previously only seen him show off his fighting skills but today he was as enthusiastic in his coaching as he was in his fighting. Even in kata he wasn't shy in speaking up and demonstrating his version of Naihanchi, Kushanku and Chinto. I watched Takahashi and he was lapping up the kata instruction from our 'old boy' present. In contrast to Tanabe's stern and frank teaching methods Murase seemed a little more compassionate and informative. I understood nothing of what he was saying but saw a lot of detail from his demonstrations. It was hard to believe that this was the same person I had witnessed weeks earlier serving up some 'punch pie' for anyone who stood still long enough.

That evening a letter from Dad arrived which contained a twenty-pound note. Dad said the family was discussing ways of helping me out in order to extend my stay here, which was a comfort. The money was more than welcome for it replaced a bit I had spent on my 'Walkman'. There was even a suggestion they could help with the fare to Korea but at this point I was not sure what was happening on that score.

What was clear for me now was to get to Immigration before my ninety days were up so that I could extend my stay for a further ninety. This would mean I would have to return in October. By now I was more than happy to extend my stay further if given the chance. There was the prospect of competing in the All-Japan Championships in November, a possibility of taking a grading as well as working a bit through the summer which could always lead to other avenues of employment. In short, I was settling in to the Japanese way of life and beginning to understand a little of the culture that surrounded me.

The next day I was relieved to feel an improvement in my knee. I was able to jog slowly around the park, which was a great relief, and I was relishing the thought of training in the dojo later that day. I had to get some money changed so Fujimoto offered to come with me and at Shinjuku we met up with his friend Nakamura. Together the three of us went into a basement tearoom where they were serving up free toast! The three of us ate for England, or rather Japan, for the toast was the thick 'door step' type with lashings of butter melting through the thick bread onto the plate. I wasn't going to complain about the absence of jam under the circumstances. The problem was, to qualify for the free toast we had to buy tea or coffee, so after a few mugs of beverages we were off to the toilet several times. Furthermore, in true Japanese custom the service was exemplary. Ordinarily service home in England would perhaps be a little cynical towards our intentions. But the Japanese waiter seemed to think we were simply very thirsty and thanked us for troubling ourselves for eating all the toast.

From Shinjuku, with our bellies full we travelled by subway to Kamiyacho and walked a short distance to Tokyo Tower. From the street in which we stood this iron construction rose to over three hundred metres above us. There was a similarity to the Eiffel Tower in its shape, but it had a stark orange and white colour that stood out uncharacteristically against its surroundings and the backdrop of a clear blue sky. We stepped into the elevator that took us to the observatory deck and from here I was able to see stunning views of Tokyo spread out in all directions. Within the tower there were attractions such as a wax museum, an aquarium plus the usual gift shops. We had lunch of cheap noodles during a couple of hours taking in the scenery and amusements and finally parted company with Nakamura to return for training.

More humid days followed but I was not too bothered for I lined up along with the rest of the class to get back to full strength. My knee was not one hundred per cent and in fact I asked, and was given permission, to avoid the leg weights for a day or two but things were tons better and that was what mattered. As if Tanabe was waiting for me to get back to training, we were regularly donning our mitts at the customary time of six o'clock. One evening I scrapped with the big three. Tachizawa was first and he was always a handful. Not as quick as Oshima, nor as strong as Kawano but he was somewhere between the two. He had a big jaw on which I would always seem to fix my gaze but he was an energetic second year who was more than able to give me a smack should my gaze be fixed for a bit too long. The problems with my knee seemed to evaporate as Tachizawa was giving me other things to think about. He outreached me and outweighed me so I was determined to be quicker and more tenacious. It worked, for I moved in quick with my left reverse punch feint and quickly caught him with my right lead hand. His big dark eyes opened wider as the contact was good and before he could hit back, I was away to his left and he punched thin air. My next attack was also clever for I lifted my lead leg to feint for a head kick which was so convincing he shut his eyes as he lifted his hands to block. Another free shot to his body with my left punch and I was having a 'field day'. I just wouldn't let Tachizawa settle. His front kick I stepped away from and his follow up punch I anticipated for it was a Nichi Dai trademark and I stepped underneath and hit him again with my favoured left hand. This was by far my best performance against good opposition and I felt it was another turning point during my training here.

My next fight with a very quiet and unassuming second year Ikeda went well but as can often happen the fight game can always produce an unwelcome surprise. After I had succeeded with a combination one two punch to his face Ikeda hit me back hard with a 'Haito' or inner ridge hand strike. They say the quiet ones are the worse and the strike caught me right on the ear that hurt like hell. I moved away and all but 'yelped'. I felt like a dog that had just been bitten back. Surprised. I felt like saying 'what was that for?' because a smack around the ear never seems right to me. Like I had done something wrong at school. These were the days when it was not unusual to get a clip around the ear. But I rallied my senses and picked up where I started, to give young Ikeda an unhappy time for the next two minutes or so.

As if someone were looking down on me, I faced Kawano next. I was breathing hard from two busy fights but I was not too tired to give Kawano a fight. I had only fought Kawano once before in all the time I had been here. Sure, we had faced off many times in attack and counter sessions but this was only the second time we faced each other for a match. The first time I caught him with a face kick but he made my life hard after that with a few rough assaults, which I struggled to contain. We were both pouring sweat from our heads and I could see his gi soaked through to the skin. It looked as though he too had been busy. We bowed and shouted "onegai shimasu" and he took first blood, literally, for a route one reverse punch from nowhere smacked me straight in the mouth. I ran my tongue across the front of my mouth to check my teeth were all intact for it was solid shot that rattled my front set. I didn't relish the thought of joining the handful in the club who had lost their centrepieces. I tasted the blood but steamed in to take the fight to Kawano. My front hand was way out in front to create a guard between us then I used it to smack down his front hand and give him one of my best "gyaku zukis" which came all the way from Somerset. It caught him a bit low than the intended target and my burly opponent was choking from the punch in the throat. It was an accident but for me a fortunate one for he was having a few problems catching his breath even though he was not out of commission. I kept up the pressure trying to keep my slight advantage but Kawano did what he did best and grabbed me to get in a throw. I was more than ready for this in fact I knew at some stage he would attempt this so I dropped my weight to thwart his lift. What I didn't expect was the knee that hit me straight in the groin. By dropping my weight my legs opened like the Khyber Pass. He couldn't miss. It could have been an accident but I doubted it. He let go because he knew I was hurt and I had to stop for a second to bend forward to ease the pain. Tanabe shouted so I straightened my back and put my hands up. Kawano came back in for he too would have been in trouble for not continuing but all I could do was stand still and trade a few punches.

The pain from the groin area was horrible. I had experienced this a few times before and there is no immediate antidote to the pain that passes around the whole body. I felt sick but couldn't stop. I had seen this before with the other guys and felt sorry for them for not being able to take a rest. Here I was in the same position trying in vain to put up a fight. Kawano took it easy and although he continued with his punching there was no real intent in his attacks. The fights came to an end and I was relieved to be able to sit down, but that became painful so I stood with my hands on my knees waiting as the pain slowly subsided. Nobody took any notice of my plight for they like me had seen it all before so it was a case of getting over it and getting on with it. Fortunately, we fought no more that day and we finished off with Kihon Gumite during which I craftily did a stock check of my possessions down below to make sure they were as I had last seen them. If there were any twinges left in my knee they had surely evaporated in the wake of more important issues.

It was a day that we had all fought hard. There had been no regular hard fighting recently and so we were all relieved to be in the hot tub soothing our aching bodies. There was a bit of joking about my being kicked in the groin but there was also some talk I couldn't understand as they spoke of my fight with Kawano. "Nani?"
'What' I asked Oshima.
"Fight ok today" he said. It was another little landmark for I knew I was in the mix with Kawano. Even though I came worse off after being kneed in the nuts I felt I was in a good fight and held my end up.

That evening Tanabe left to go to his own apartment. One of the second years followed him to make sure of this and then I was invited into the third-year room. One of the second years brought in some beer and crisps and so a little evening of relaxing got under way. Even the fourth years joined us. I was first under strict instructions to learn more Japanese for the benefit of guys like Hakoishi and Minamidae who couldn't communicate with me. I looked at both and thought I'd rather keep our simple conversations as they were thanks. They both looked at me and smiled. "Nihongo!" said Minamidae, urging me to speak his language. I think Kikuta and Oshima were winding them up as well as me, for they both knew I'd had problems with both these rough customers. Still, we got things going and I spoke a few new sentences therefore increasing my vocabulary.

Even though I was sipping out of one side of my mouth from the split lip I had suffered earlier the beer was going down well. Soon enough however the drink had dried up. Empty cans of Kirin beer were strewn around the room, but we still wanted more. Hijikata, who by now had been fast asleep in my room for well over an hour, was shaken awake and sent down to the shop with some money for a stock up. He arrived back panting and uttering "shitsurei shimasu" as if he were still in the dojo, apologizing for being a little slow. He was invited to stay but declined and was allowed to return to his bed. One by one the lads around us fell asleep except me, Fujimoto and Hakoishi. The latter and I just drank and looked at one another smiling. He would take a sip, so I would drink, and this continued until once more we had exhausted our second supply. But neither of us had finished. Hakoishi suggested we go to the bar near the station to resume our little 'get to know each other drink' and I quickly agreed. As Hakoishi stepped out of the room Fujimoto tried to stop me from going "Aasa, he is crazy. Don't go".

But I was up and getting into my slippers out in the corridor. Fujimoto followed when Hakoishi called him to join us. We each grabbed a bike and cycled the ten minutes or so to the cosy little pub.

Hakoishi sat opposite from me as we chinked small glasses and downed them quickly. Fujimoto poured the beer on commands from Hakoishi. "Aasa daijobu?" He asked me as we downed another. "Daijobu. Mo ippai" I replied asking for a refill. I no longer had a clear head. In fact, that deserted me back in the third-year room. I was however, in my inebriated, stubborn state determined to drink this irritating, grinning layabout under the table. Now and again Hakoishi left to use the toilet and Fujimoto would urge me to stop. I assured him I was fine. But I wasn't. Drink after stupid drink and I felt bad. I too went to the toilet but it was only to throw up some beer to make way for more. I returned after a good wash and we stared at each other across the small table and did another bottle between us.

Our drink rate had slowed to a snail's pace. Our demanding of one another to drink again altered to a pathetic "another one?" and the reply "you, another one?" It was obvious neither one of us wanted any more to continue. Eventually we shook hands mutually but I felt I had done what was necessary for Queen and country and I'm sure Hakoishi felt he had served his emperor well too. We left at two forty-five that morning. As we cycled our way back through the back streets and pathways Hakoishi suddenly shot past me at some speed so instinctively I stood up in the pedals and went after him. Picking up speed with my head low over the handlebars I started to close my target. Everything became a blur, the houses that I sailed past, Hakoishi in my sights, the crash. I landed flat on my face after sailing clean over the front wheel. The alcohol in me deadened the pain but I knew I was in a bit of a mess. Blood was pouring from my face and I was tangled in the wreckage. I remember being picked up and walking slowly back to the dormitory. The front wheel of the bike had totally collapsed and with it possibly my reputation.

Hakoishi and Fujimoto took me into the kitchen and applied some first aid. I had a nasty open cut on my chin plus gravel grazes on my right cheek, shoulder, and hip. The last two were no problem but the facial marks were a worry. How would I explain away the incident?

The next morning, I woke when the first years around me were making a fuss. "Aasa been fighting" someone said. There were bloodstains all over my pillow and my whole face ached. I started to rise but Enomoto stopped me. They had already been running and had finished breakfast while I slept soundly. I laid back and thought of what had happened and felt stupid, immature, and regretful of the whole affair. I explained to my roommates what had happened and they already started to see the funny side. Takahashi then looked in and while all the first years jumped to attention, he made a huge mocking sound as if to say 'what the hell were you playing at' but he too laughed and playfully scolded me by beating me with a towel. "Hakoishi, crazy" he said. "Aasa more crazy" and so the whole room laughed at my expense. Well, it seemed the seniors were ok about the affair for after all it involved one of them so all I had to do now was convince Tanabe that there was some sort of accident.

I spent the morning washing my clothes and pillow and hung out my futon on the roof to air. This was a regular little job anyway but I was happy to rid my belongings of any bloodstains. I sat on the rooftop and watched the traffic pass by below and pondered on how different things felt compared to a couple of months earlier. I still missed home and all its familiarities but I was now developing a lifestyle here in Japan that I was starting to enjoy. The training I was thriving on, the fighting was tough but I could cope. I could mix with students of all ages, share a mixed conversation of Anglo Japanese and above all could eat much of the food. One thing I had to remind myself was of the danger of getting too familiar and taking things for granted. I was here to train and should keep my head down and not get noticed for the wrong reasons. The previous night I promised myself was a one off and not to be repeated.

At lunchtime Fukusyo came back early from his studies and so promised to make me some rice typical of his hometown. Tanabe then appeared and immediately looked at my face. I told him I went to the shops by bike to get some batteries for my 'Walkman' and fell off. He looked at me as if to question me further but rolled his eyes as if to say how stupid and let it go at that. I sat in the dining room as Fukusyo worked in the kitchen along with young Hijikata who was preparing lunch to his senpai's orders. The television was on and I tried to make sense of the weather forecast. I didn't understand what was being said but by the numbers all over the map of Japan I knew it was going to be another hot day, thirty degrees in most places and a balmy thirty-two in Tokyo. I wished we were a lot further north for it was only twenty-eight degrees. Tanabe reappeared and he too complained at the heat when he saw the forecast. He said it would be hotter in August but he boasted that he would be off doing a swimming course somewhere on the coast. He asked me about my summer vacation plans and I said I might be working for Furukawa. He laughed out loud and said "Aasa like this" as he squeezed his cheeks in with one hand to imply, I would end up looking thin.

Fukusyo appeared from the kitchen with a large bowl of rice that was swimming in some liquid. "My home, special" he said proudly. Tanabe mocked his poor English and repeated "My home special". Fukusyo was embarrassed but gave the first serving to his instructor before serving me, then himself and finally young Hijikata. The rice was cooked with tea poured into it. A strange combination I thought as I took a mouthful. It was like eating toast after dunking it in a cup of tea or coffee. Personally, I think there are some things that are best left alone. I believe rice should stay dry and tea should be wet. But I ate or drank what was in front of me and thanked my senior for the interesting introduction to his country's special dish and I reminded myself not go there if I were to be invited. After lunch I slipped away to the cake shop and filled up with a curry doughnut and crisps.

My knee had continued to improve although still a little stiff in the mornings. But once I was up the pain eased off and I was able to work hard on it. The day after my crash on the bike we were training hard and fighting hard. Before training I not only had to wrap some tape around my toes as was customary but also stuck a plaster on my chin for it was still bleeding from time to time. The weather forecast had been spot on. It was hot and I could only guess the temperature was around the thirty-degree mark, which is about eighty degrees in old currency. I had only one Karate gi and it was not uncommon to put it on still damp from the previous day. I was also the only one to take two hand towels into training for one was simply not enough to cope with my excessive sweating. On the whole things were bearable and I took things as they came.

After training the first-year room would often be a busy little domain for us to try and relax in. Apart from the stuff the first years themselves had to get done for their studies there were always senior grades popping in to get their gi tidied up or some errand wanted. From time to time a senior would come in stretch out on the floor and command one of the juniors to massage his neck, back, head or legs, to soothe aching parts after training. This was done without reserve and without complaint. In fact, one or two of the first years were quite adept at the massage and even practised on one another. There was no inhibition over this sort of practice as there would be at home here.

The Japanese are well known to be a race with a close community spirit. Their language revolves around respectful speaking to those who are outside of their familiar group. In other words, strangers are regarded with utmost respect even though they may not be identified within their own group. However, in my case I felt there was something on offer. My hosts were curious. Bit by bit I guessed that most of the students who trained alongside me in the dojo held a curiosity over who I was and what I was about. They all had access to television and therefore American and English films that were dubbed into Japanese. I guessed there would be very little chance for many of the students around me to meet a foreign national during their industrious lifetime so it was quite a novelty to speak a little English or to simply have someone different among them. The quieter students, who had very little to say during my first weeks, became quite amicable and forward to the point of speaking as much as their English would allow them.

The night after my bike incident Tanabe sensei again returned to his apartment for the evening so all rooms were buzzing in his absence. Takahashi was doing the rounds as manager with a clipboard. "Aasa, are you coming to summer camp?" he asked. Before I had chance to answered him, he held out his hand "Go sen yen!" five thousand yen, about twenty pounds. This year's 'Gasshuku' was to be held on Oshima Island in September and so there was now no doubt I was going, for I paid him and he smiled as he looked over my scabby face.

The previous night's antics seemed to instigate an atmosphere in all the rooms on this night. More drink was brought in after ten o'clock and I for one was not going to upstage anybody this time. After eleven we ended up in the kitchen drinking and singing songs from our own childhood memories. I was surprised to even see the captain Tanemura join us although rather subdued at the rear of the pack. But as time passed even the most sombre of the ranks were happily drinking and lending their voice to song. Around midnight poor Hijikata was raised from his futon to sing us a song. He sang with his eyes closed to keep the bright lights of the kitchen from dazzling him. Once he finished his song he did more impersonations, which included the latest, the one of me happily cycling along before suddenly travelling at high speed on my face. He was funny but it was a sorry sight, for it was the second night he had been roused from his sleep for our benefit. The evening rounded off with a stunning rendition of the Nichi Dai Karate song to which Kenji stood and provided the actions. I was in a way overwhelmed to be in the presence of all senior students and enjoying their company. I felt they too were enjoying mine and it was without doubt another step of winning some acceptance among each character. As I looked around that evening, at the guys present such as Hakoishi, Minamidae, Oshima, Takahashi, Tanemura the captain and Kishiyama who gave me my first tough fight in the dojo, I had a sense that I had been partly responsible in bringing together some of the more hard headed difficult characters of this Karate club. Somehow though I don't think Tanabe sensei would be quite so keen to join our little group.

The next day was a Thursday and so a few of us travelled together in the afternoon for training at Suidobashi. Kikuta, Oshima, Okano, and myself had a little look in the shops in the Suidobashi area discussing good souvenirs for family and friends. There were a few little earthenware shops selling traditional teapots, serving dishes, sake cups and chopsticks all at reasonable prices. I made a note to return here when it was time to do my final shop before going home, whenever that would be.

We were an hour early for training so we made our way to the University common room. This was no different to the one I remember when I was at college. There were a lot of strange teenagers, listening to strange music acting a bit strange with lots of smoking. I saw Fukusyo sat among some of the longhaired teenagers and wondered if he was trying to discover himself. When he spotted me, he came over to make a fuss of the marks on my face saying that I ought to go see the college doctor. I tried to ignore his pleas but reluctantly followed him to the doctor's room where after a brief look, she gave me some cream. I looked daft enough and I didn't really need white cream to make things more obvious.

Kobayashi turned up before training and so nervously I had to explain away the facial injuries with the 'going to the shop' story. His reply "were you drunk?" just about said it all.

Half way through training that evening I was surprised to see Wakamei show up. He sat to one side to watch the training but would stand from time to time to offer his advice. Tanabe looked a little annoyed at times especially when Wakamei came over to me and spoke in good English in order to coach me on some finer points. We trained without fighting that evening but with a full hour's practice of counter punching which could often be as intense as free fighting, particularly when there was an abundance of senior instructors present to demand our full commitment in both attack and defence. Training on a Thursday finished at eight in the evening so there was often little time for us to return home. We would be given enough time to stop somewhere to eat before heading back for the hour's train ride. An hour sounds a long time but travel time in a city such as Tokyo simply involves short train journeys and changing of lines instead of one long hour ride from A to B. Often a few of us would stop off in a noodle bar or at a Yakitori chicken stall where we could have a quick scoff and one swift beer.

It was approaching mid-July and just before the weekend Kobayashi sensei stopped by and presented me with my new black belt. It was a priceless gift. My own belt with my name embroidered in English, which was my preference, but with Wado Ryu in Japanese script. Before I had time to try it on, he then took me back to the Immigration office to extend my tourist visa for the next three months. Unless there was any alternative, I would be returning home in October. Kobayashi and I returned to Nichi Dai that Friday evening for training and he then invited me for the weekend to join him on his club's children training camp. The following morning after Kobayashi led us around the park, I packed some stuff together and we were off in the car. Despite his little funny ways Kobayashi had a heart as big as his Toyota. The running around for my benefit took up much of his time and money. The time I spent with his students and his family helped in many ways towards my settling in. The belt he bought me was a symbol of his generosity and his thoughtfulness. He did everything he could to make sure I fitted in with those around me and I always felt there was someone I could talk to should it be necessary.

Saturday the eleventh of July would always be a date etched in my memory. It was a sweltering day as we crawled slowly through the weekend traffic across Tokyo. Kobayashi's car was probably the only car without air conditioning, or so it seemed, so we drove with the windows down, through which we were served the polluted air of the fume filled roads. I don't ever remember hearing any discussion on environmental issues during the eighties so the most protection available from the polluted streets was a facemask worn by pedestrians and cyclists. I felt I was qualified to wear one of those masks while I sat exposed to every dirty molecule that spewed from the high-performance cars, diesel trucks and taxis that surrounded us. To shut the windows however would have meant chronic overheating so the decision was an obvious one. Before joining the expressway to take us out of town we first drove to a district of Tokyo where my instructor's sister and her family lived. Unfortunately, only the two young children were at home which was a little strange for the oldest was only around ten years old. Kobayashi looked a little concerned but we continued our way and left the Tokyo jungle behind us to welcome the open roads and cleaner atmosphere of the Yamanashi countryside.

An hour or so later we were slowly twisting our way down the narrow lane that led to Kobayashi's house. As we approached his home Mrs. Kobayashi suddenly appeared at the open doorway and ran with a panic to our car. She said something very urgently and Kobayashi sensei sat stunned behind the wheel of his car. He said very simply "my Father, dead." Then he went into the house. I sat in the car with a feeling of great sadness for the man who was dedicated to his family and his Karate. Mrs Kobayashi came back out to the car and asked me in for lunch. I wanted to leave so they could deal with the grief without me around. But typically, they had a concern for others at a time when their own life was upside down. I ate a quick snack before Kobayashi sensei told me to return to Nichi Dai by train. He even apologized for the fact there would be no weekend camp with the kids. I could only say sorry for his loss but wanted to say so much more, like, I can get back by train ok, and the camp didn't matter and please don't apologize. But I could only say sorry once more before I left to catch the train.

My own memories of Kobayashi's Father are very faint, almost 'dream like' for he was almost anonymous as I passed in and out of the home at various times. His presence in that family house was a part of my life and I shared a little grief on my return to Tokyo.

I thought I would do the decent thing and return in time for training. With all that had happened in the last few hours I needed to get my gi on and train. My final leg of the train journey brought me back to Hachimanyama station at three fifty, so I knew I could be in the dojo for around four fifteen. As I walked the last hundred yards or so along the busy road to our dormitory and dojo, I could see a group of Karate students wearing their white uniforms approaching the bridge that would lead to the park. As they stepped onto the bridge, they spotted me and froze. I was intrigued as to what my fellow students were up to. They were worried that with me there may be a certain senior instructor not too far away. I explained what had happened and they all sat on the bridge for a moment in a sombre mood sharing among them the sad news. I had my gi with me so I followed them into the park and changed. Tanabe sensei was in Osaka with one or two seniors so the lads thought they would have a change of scenery and visit our morning venue to do a bit of outdoor training. We did a bit of light training and then Hakoishi decided that there should be a bit of humour on this sad day so Hijikata provided some more unique impersonations. I had my camera with me so there were more funny moments to be recorded for posterity. Hijikata repeated his latest impression of yours truly cycling happily on a bike before suddenly coming a cropper and travelling at high speed on the face. He was also a fish being reeled in on a line by Kikuta and friends, a baseball star and a man feeding the chickens with Enomoto as the biggest chicken on the planet scuttling around flapping his wings as he searched the ground for his dinner. The lads were roaring as the impersonations came thick and fast. It was another escape to madness for a short period when even the young first years were able to laugh at themselves while away from the severity of the dojo. We did however return to the dojo for an hour or so to finish off with some kata training as if that in some way justified our earlier antics in the park.

After training and dinner that evening most of us, except for the first years, made our way to the bar near the station but we made it a short evening and returned by nine thirty. I was ready for bed when Takahashi the manager invited me for a late supper in the shack outside on the roadside. I was always hungry enough for another meal so I had a sensible chat with a sensible guy who had a wicked sense of humour. I knew Takahashi had his head in continuing his Karate training after he would graduate from the university life, but recently he too had showed he was up for a good time between his hard training and responsible duties within the club. We sat, ate, and drank while discussing our cultures. We talked about our different countries and began to discover the similarities of our nations. Both Japan and England are surrounded by water therefore developing a lifestyle dependant on this environment. Shipbuilding, fishing, extensive naval defences all with a Royal heritage to boot made our distant lands not so unfamiliar. During their long history the Japanese had developed a respect borne out of the Samurai ethos and likewise we had our chivalrous knights to serve King and country. The more Takahashi and I compared mental notes the more we seemed convinced that we could be distantly related. I did tell him that before I came to Japan, I thought I would see a little more traditional dress and that the overall impression of the Japanese was of Samurai swords and women wearing kimonos. He laughed and told me that he thought men in England still walked about wearing bowler hats carrying walking canes.

We brought things to a close at around eleven for Tanabe had left instructions to Takahashi for us to train after breakfast. There was to be no day off while Tanabe was absent so a little extra training was meant to keep us in order.

There was no early run the next day but we did an hour's training in the dojo at nine o'clock. Nothing too severe, just routine basics and pad work. Then we were ordered out on to the football field for a game of baseball. The ground was hard and earthy so we rolled up our gi bottoms put on our training shoes and split into two teams. My cricket style wielding of the bat brought much derisory laughter from all on the pitch and no matter how my teammates tried to teach me I couldn't adopt the baseball stance so I just belted the ball anyway and ran like hell. After all, the main objective was to hit the ball and this I managed with ease, which silenced one or two opposing team members. Like the impromptu football game, a couple of months earlier the score got lost in the excitement of the match but I did end up trying to show all present the finer points of cricket. After a couple of minutes of explaining an 'over' and showing the over arm bowling action I knew from their faces I was getting nowhere so I gave up knowing cricket remained safe from being adopted by the Japanese.

The rest of the day remained uneventful. This was a Sunday of extra training followed by complete boredom, which was not a good combination among these lads for there was a restless atmosphere in and around the rooms. We knew Tanabe was returning later from Osaka so there was nothing to do but wait for his return. After dinner a couple of first years were sat at the window watching something unfold out on the busy road outside. I jostled to look over their shoulders and saw two police cars setting a speed trap for unsuspecting motorists. It wasn't long before they began their catch of the day and I smiled to myself as I realized some things never changed wherever you are.

With the return of Tanabe Sensei later in the evening I was informed that I would be attending the funeral of Kobayashi's father the next day along with several others.

There was a brief spell in the park for early training before breakfast and preparation for the funeral. I was worried for I had nothing remotely appropriate to wear for such an occasion. Then one of the third years brought in an old high school uniform that was not only in good nick but fitted me perfectly. It was a black trouser and jacket with a mandarin collar and the lads were so impressed that pictures were taken as I posed in front of the university flag held up by Kikuta and Akii.

At nine sharp Fukusyo drove us out of the gates in a mini bus. We collected Tanabe from his apartment down the road and made our way to Uenohara. By eleven we were slowly approaching Kobayashi's home. The narrow road in which we were driven was adorned either side with brightly coloured wreathes that must have exceeded ten feet high. There was a makeshift table of food and beers to the side of Kobayashi's house from which we were urged to eat and drink before the funeral ceremony. At twelve o'clock the seven of us from Nihon University lined the approach to the Kobayashi household while family and friends filed past to pay their respects. This procession lasted a full two hours and, in the midday heat wearing the black uniform I was sweltering but determined not to in any way show the discomfort on this occasion. All the while a priest wailed with a mantra that hardly gave him time to pause for breath. I was proud to be in attendance and wanted the Kobayashi family to know I was grateful for their hospitality even during their time of grief. Finally, it was our turn to approach the small shrine that was on the other side of the house. There was a picture of Kobayashi's father at the front and we each took part in the small prayer while Kobayashi looked on. We then passed over a card in which a small amount of money was placed and in return we were each given a wrapped gift. All very strange but no less dignified than any funeral I had ever been to in England.

We finally drove away from the funeral at three o'clock and after a short stop for water and the toilet we were back by five. Tanabe insisted we train so we changed and joined the rest of the class as they were racing up and down the dojo kicking in combinations of three and four techniques. It was hard to fit into the routine after the day on the road and then the atmosphere of a funeral but we adapted without question and eventually slotted into the sweaty revved up ambience of the Karate dojo. The small group of us also had to train an extra half an hour to make up for a little time lost while away.

SIXTEEN

The week following the funeral was to be the final week before the summer break. The mood of the lads was obviously influenced by the fact that soon there would be no training for nearly three weeks. Everybody was chatting about their time they would spend at home with mates or girls plus going to the beach and doing holiday things. I was excited too for a change is always as good as a rest as they say, even though I knew I had a bit of hard work to look forward to.

The hot weather was making the sleeping at night almost impossible and on more than one occasion I took a cold shower just to cool the body temperature so that I might sleep easier. Halfway through the week Tanabe caught us out again having an easy training session. He was supposed to have been up North conducting a swimming course but didn't go for some reason so dropped in to see us sat down at the wrong time. Half an hour's free fighting ensued for us all with little rest for us in between fights. He was though now spending much less time at the dormitory preferring to stay at his apartment. This meant that we would still make use of the free time in the evening to entertain ourselves although not to the extent of previous silly nights for we still had to train hard the next day.

The Thursday evening at the Suidobashi location, training took on a different meaning. Fumihiro Tanabe as always looked in but this time there was a selection to take place for a team event scheduled for the forthcoming Sunday. My mind raced at the thought of maybe getting out to fight in a contest. After a little training of basics and half an hour or so on the pads we sat around the edge with our mitts on and waited for our names to be called. Ordinarily this would be a tense wait, wondering who the opposition might be and how long we might be at it. Not to mention hoping to get it done without too much of a bashing. But on this day, I was itching to get up. Oshima, Kawano, Kishiyama, Minamidae, I didn't care I wanted to fight the best. One by one I saw these guys get up and mix it with each other. I saw Akii the skinny young looking second year split Minamidae face open with his textbook front kick head punch combination. I looked on as I saw Kishiyama knock Tanaka over with a roundhouse kick to the head. Oshima had a good tussle with Tachizawa, the other strong second year, and they had to be parted by Hideo Tanabe. Other first years got up to do battle with their senior grades with good spirit but I realized I was not going to be among the challengers for a place in any team. I sat with the feeling of not being wanted. I felt embarrassed as one or two people looked in my direction and I tried not to look bothered but that was impossible. Eventually Takahashi spoke up for me and the answer was predictable. I wasn't eligible for a place in the contest so it was pointless me fighting that evening. I said "Hai wakarimashita" but I didn't understand at all. I came here to train, to fight and compete. The first two I had endured for the past three months so surely the contest would be the chance to let loose and enjoy the results of the hard work. I was told to come along on Sunday anyway and bring my gi.

The journey home that evening was a long one. In the company of Kikuta, Fujimoto and Hijikata I remained silent as I thought about attending some tournament on Sunday without competing. Not something to look forward to. Kikuta and Fujimoto neither of whom had been selected to compete the weekend were trying to raise my spirits but I simply wasn't in the mood. I was looking forward now to resting from Nichi Dai for I felt I had had enough for a while and needed some reflection on my current status.

I didn't stop for a drink that evening so I joined the first years as they chatted in our room about their scraps with the seniors. There were three teams competing on Sunday and Enomoto along with Asuka were both in one of the teams. I congratulated them both and genuinely wished them well. By ten thirty we were ready to get to bed but there was a problem. Hijikata was missing. He had walked back from the station with me, Kikuta, and Fujimoto but I assumed he had taken a shower as we entered our building. So, all students started to call down the stairs, out of the windows and on the roof. Nothing. We then wondered if he had decided to run away. Poor Hijikata had been on the receiving end of some ridicule of late and perhaps he had taken it upon himself to escape. We split into groups and started searching around the grounds of our living quarters. As we shouted some of us became a little concerned while the seniors were getting a bit annoyed. Eleven o'clock and the search extended to the park and the route back to the station plus the shops that opened until late. Finally, he was spotted being frog marched by a couple of second years after they had found him asleep on a park bench. Whether Hijikata had decided he had had enough wasn't clear for he returned to our room and into bed without saying a word.

As the final few days before the contest wound down so too did the intensity in the dojo. Training was cut to an hour and a half and any fighting was saved until Sunday. Tanabe was around less and less as he too was winding down for the summer break. On the Friday night Kikuta along with Hakoishi, of all people, invited me out to a nightclub. By taxi we went to Akasaka and into a club called Mugen. There was an American band called Galaxy performing and so there was a good mixture of soul music from them and the DJ. We drank very little for it was an expensive club. We had already paid about six pounds to get in which included one free drink but thereafter we stayed clear of the bar and we just enjoyed the music, the atmosphere and chatting to a few locals. I had a brief conversation with Hakoishi. I knew he had developed a little more respect for me since our face off one evening, plus the drinking session we had endured. I had shown I could mix with him on equal terms and he understood that. We left around two and the three of us crept quietly back into our rooms an hour later tired but satisfied we had spent an evening without restraint but with some dignity.

Saturday was a rest day before the contest so we spent another day cooped up in our rooms after breakfast. There was a lot more cleaning to be done before the summer vacation so we got stuck into that for a couple of hours. Everybody then began packing for the contest, as well as for their return home. I still had no idea what lay ahead for me after Sunday for I hadn't heard from Kobayashi since the funeral and I certainly didn't want to become a burden for his family at this time.

I joined the club for dinner during which Tanabe made a fuss over the beefsteak that he had specifically ordered to give extra nutrition for those fighting the next day. I thought about the waste of extra energy that this food was giving me and that a simple rice meal would have been sufficient. Until I tasted the steak and I thought twice about passing it to someone else who perhaps needed the nutrition more than me.

The training contest was held at another sports hall in Suidobashi. We all set off early by train and arrived together by ten o'clock. There were a few other teams warming up and I was still feeling a little depressed at the prospect of not being involved with the fighting. Those of us not competing helped a little with marking out the fighting areas and setting out chairs for spectators and officials. However, as the Nichi Dai lads emerged from the changing rooms and began the warm up routine, I was dead keen to see who would perform well under pressure. This was the first time I had witnessed any sort of senior competition and I obviously felt an affinity to those I had trained and lived with for the past few months.

Familiar faces started to arrive. Wakamei, Furukawa, both Tanabe brothers plus many other senior people who I had never seen before but who all attracted the traditional loud overzealous greetings of 'konnichiwa' from the younger students. Finally, I was pleased to see Kobayashi turn up. He came to me and thanked me for attending the funeral and said that I would be returning to Uenohara with him after the day's events. I felt a little uneasy about this for he had only just lost his father and I was sure his family would want to be left alone to grieve for a while longer.

There were no individual events this day. It was a contest in order to gauge the progress of many of the Nichi Dai boys and to give a few other local fighters a chance to get some practice in. There was also the prospect of the All-Japan University Championships to be held in six weeks or so. Therefore, sometime in September a selection had to be made for the best seven to be put forward to represent Nihon University in perhaps the most prestigious tournament on the calendar.

The other teams at this selection tournament in Suidobashi, I had no knowledge of and I wondered if they had any idea of the strength of their opposition.

Before long the first team event got under way. I watched as our first Nichi Dai team lined up with Akii out first. He looked even younger in the larger surrounding of the sports centre but he was, as usual, first off the mark with a low front kick and head punch that snapped back the opponent's head. A little harsh I thought but a point was awarded and so the precedent was set. Akii cleaned up in just over a minute without conceding a point. Kishiyama was out second and the same score. The opposing team was not quite in the same league up to this point and they needed to rally their spirit. Oshima faced a young man who matched him in size. This proved to be a closer contest for there were good quality techniques coming back to Oshima. Once or twice, Oshima took a smack to the face but as the doctor approached to check for damage Oshima waved him away. The opposing fighter now got a little cocky and dropped his hands as if to show he was relaxed and not having a problem. Oshima shot forward with two punches that connected firmly and dropped the big guy like a stone. Oshima was disqualified and admonished by Tanabe but there were all smiles from the Nichi Dai Old Boy contingent that stood around watching the fight unfold.

Up next was Kawano and he was showing signs of impatience as he flexed in a deep knee bend and jumped high in the air before bowing to enter the area. At the present score the other team were back in the fight for a disqualification meant a win for them but I was quite confident Kawano wouldn't let the side down. Hideo Tanabe gave him some last-minute instructions from the side-line and Kawano dutifully turned to bow and shout "Hai, so!"

Kawano's opponent was slim, tall with his front arm outstretched long and probing. Kawano knocked the hand to one side once or twice and I could see he was measuring the opponent's reaction. By doing this if the opponent jumped back quickly then it could be assumed the opponent could be a little nervous, and probably fair game. However, if the reaction was a cool one or if the opponent dropped his weight in order to counter then watch out, he's probably a bit of a live one. Kawano's adversary fell into the second category, he was not going to be bullied or intimidated so held his position strong and resolute. Kawano moved in and out swiftly building up an attack that would be decisive. Tanabe was getting impatient by looking at the Old Boys watching and rolling his eyes as if to say 'I would have had it all sorted by now'. Suddenly as if he had seen Tanabe's facial expression Kawano launched forward with a reverse punch to the face that missed by a whisker but the follow up sweep that followed was the best I had ever seen. The back leg of Kawano came through and took both legs of the gangly youngster clean away from him. There were no mats on the floor so the impact as the body hit the floor took all the wind out of the poor soul's lungs. As the youngster bounced Kawano's follow up was as sweet as the take down for two punches found their way to the already crumpled body racked with pain from the sweep. The referee jumped in to call 'Yame' and Kawano smiled at his teammates as he returned to his line ready to restart. The fight was out of the prone fighter so Kawano was awarded the points and then the fight. Three to one and only Fukusyo remained to complete the job in hand. He was as confident as I had ever seen him and although he didn't strike me as a dynamic fighter, he was showing signs of an experienced campaigner with a team score to hold on to.

Fukusyo had himself an experienced fighter opposite him. Some teams put out their best fighters near the end hoping to claw back a score but Fukusyo charged in without reserve almost as a result of seeing his comrades clean up unreservedly. Fukusyo took a belt in the mouth but he too refused to be seen by the doctor which impressed me for all he wanted to do was get on with the job in hand. It was a funny sight as the doctor approached Fukusyo and was held at arm's length by the Nichi Dai vice-captain. The medic tried to walk around the obstacle but gave up when the strength in Fukusyo's grip tightened.

Years of hard training and constant rough fighting had instilled an admirable attitude among the boys of Nihon University. As I watched that day, I realized I wanted so much to be a part of this. I wanted not only to fight like these young men but to also have their attitude, their resolve, and their spirit. Today I had suffered a setback by not being selected to fight in any of the three teams that were competing yet I still had to settle for the fact I was lucky to be among this unique number of individuals. After all, comparatively speaking I had only been here five minutes so perhaps was a little presumptuous in thinking I could jump into a team and deny somebody else a place, somebody who had proved far more than I their worthiness to represent their university.

After a close fight Fukusyo won his bout and with it the team progressed to another round. I enjoyed the morning as I watched further the other two teams fight well. Without the obvious bias impairing my judgement it was crystal clear that the other teams present on this day were not of the same calibre of Tanabe's boys. There were one or two very good individuals who would give any of the Nichi Dai boys a tough fight but the strength in depth was on our side.

Kobayashi approached me at lunchtime and told me to change into my gi. For a moment I was excited until he said I was to demonstrate Seishan kata. I was nervous and excited at the same time. I wanted to fight but I also wanted to be a part of the day in some small way so readily changed and warmed up as one or two of the boys light-heartedly mocked me before my name was announced. About seven teams, twenty officials plus thirty plus spectators made my walk to the centre a nervous one. After the applause I stood and faced the main table, bowed, and completed Seishan kata in a time that passed without any recollection. I remember bowing at the end walking off the floor and Wakamei sensei shaking my hand and asking what Kata I had just performed. It took me a second before I realized he was jesting so I relaxed and watched the rest of the day's fighting unfold to see the three Nichi Dai teams clean up in the contest.

After a lengthy speech from both Fumihiro and Hideo Tanabe we were finally released for the summer break. I said my farewells to Kikuta and the rest and I was pleased that most were keen to ask what I was doing for the summer. They wished me luck and I shook the hands of two dozen students before Kobayashi said, "Shall we go?" The next time I would see the students of Nihon University would be at the summer camp in three weeks' time.

Kobayashi drove me to the dormitory so I could pick up my stuff. I had been used to being in the building when nobody was around but there was an eerie desolation about the second floor as I quickly gathered my belongings and rushed back out to the car.

SEVENTEEN

Two hours and another good sleep later I was being driven down the main street of Uenohara. Kobayashi said there was somebody who wanted to meet me and maybe help a bit during my stay in the town. We pulled up outside a modern three-storey building and I followed Kobayashi as he stooped under the traditional 'noren' curtain and then through the sliding door into an air-conditioned restaurant. To the right were some small tables on a raised floor of tatami mats much the same as I had seen in other eating-houses in Tokyo. Shoes that had been discarded before stepping up into the eating areas were lined along the floor as their owners sat cross-legged at the low tables eating and drinking. There were also a few Western type tables and chairs in the middle of the restaurant which could probably seat thirty or forty people altogether.

The customary greeting of "Irrasshaimase" came from the left as we entered and a young man in his twenties stood behind a glass counter at the front of which were half a dozen stools. I deduced that this was a 'sushi' restaurant for as we approached the counter various dishes of fish were on display behind the glass screen, sat on their little beds of rice. There were different colours and slices of fish that bore no resemblance to their former life but I did recognize the shrimps fully stretched out in pairs and already I was feeling hungry. I could tell that none of the fish on display was cooked and I knew also they would stay that way for consumption.

The man behind the counter shook my hand and introduced himself as Ando. He spoke briefly with Kobayashi then disappeared out the back. Kobayashi explained the restaurant was well known in the area for its sushi and sashimi, raw fish. Ando came back with an older chap wearing spectacles who bid Kobayashi a hearty welcome with a couple of deep bows and Kobayashi reciprocated with the same fervent greetings.

"This is Mr Sakamoto" said Kobayashi, "He is the restaurant owner and would like to speak with you"

"Pleased to meet you" said Sakamoto with a broad smile. "Are you hungry?" I realized I hadn't eaten in a few hours and said without reservation that I was. Kobayashi too joined me at the counter and Sakamoto told us to choose anything that was on display. A couple of beers were placed in front of us by an old lady who came from nowhere and so I sat and chose a couple of dishes that I liked the colour of. There was a mixture of the finest fish on display and Mr Sakamoto explained the various dishes. Tuna, mackerel, bream, cod roe, squid, and many more raw delights which his chef Mr Ando quickly scooped up at our command and expertly prepared them on a bed of rice for our consumption. Along with the sushi we were treated to some tempura and miso soup therefore giving us a full late lunch. I enjoyed every dish and finally sat back in my stool stuffed. Mr Sakamoto spoke quite good English and was keen for me to remain with him and his family for the evening while Kobayashi went off to teach. After some green tea I grabbed my suitcase from the car and walked around the side of the restaurant to a house sat back almost out of view from the road.

Mr Sakamoto took my case and urged me into his house. Mrs Sakamoto bowed at the door and I bowed back with "konnichiwa". She could speak no English but she too had a smile to match her husband's. I felt very welcome. The house was spacious and westernised with a dining room on one side that contained a large dining table. I followed Mr Sakamoto and sat in the living room on a sofa. Two small children who had been watching television now looked at me in horror as they slid slowly from their chair and hid behind their father. One was a boy about three and the other a girl a year or so younger. They looked identical with their basin hairstyles round faces and cheeky expressions. Mr Sakamoto laughed at their shyness and urged them to say hello. The boy said "herro" the girl said nothing. There was a small baby too crawling in and around our feet and Mr Sakamoto laughed as he apologized about the general disorder within his household. He shouted to his wife who came quickly running to scoop up the toddler from under my feet.

Mr. Sakamoto was fascinated with my stay in Japan. He was interested in all things English and had a curiosity to why I should want to be at Nihon University in his country. He knew well how the university system operated in Japan for he had been a graduate of Meiji University as a mountaineer. Unfortunately, a car accident after a night out left him with a serious injury and a slight permanent limp prevented him from fulfilling any further ambitions of climbing. He had however climbed with Sir Edmund Hilary as a young university student when visiting New Zealand. It was because of his command of English that allowed him to work closely with Hilary so he could communicate with the rest of his university colleagues.

Mr Sakamoto chatted with me for hours and urged me to stay with him for a few days. "I know you have Mr Kobayashi as your instructor and that is important to you," he said, "but when you are here you can relax, my home is your home. Please, don't be careful." A strange request that I took to mean don't worry.

Mr Sakamoto phoned Kobayashi sensei and told him I would be staying a little while and to me it was a fascinating insight into a restaurateur who had a large family. There was also a girl of seven who came in from school later that first day which meant Mrs Sakamoto had her work cut out for her in between helping in the restaurant. There was a feeling in the Sakamoto household that nothing was too much bother. Neighbours would walk in and out of the house without so much as a knock on the door just a shout of "gomen kudasai!" 'Sorry to bother you, but I'm coming in anyway'.

I was introduced over the next few days to all the Sakamoto family; uncles, aunties, brothers, sisters, cousins, and all were as friendly as the boss himself. Mr Sakamoto was obviously respected among the community. He was well known too for his late-night drinking bouts in the small bars around the town. Once his work in the restaurant came to an end at around ten in the evening, he would have his dinner then take a stroll around the town mixing with the locals and drinking to excess. In the days that followed I would accompany him to meet his friends and to share a bottle of sake although I was no match for his stamina with the bottle. I think he could see Hakoishi and me off at the same time. On the way home in the early hours, he would sing at the top of his voice his Meiji University song for which he was also well known, especially to those who lived enroute. His wife would wait up for her husband no matter what time he returned and happily put him to bed without a fuss.

For the first time in three months, I slept in a proper bed, in my own room with a TV. I got up when I felt like it and had a hearty breakfast ready for me; bacon, eggs, toast plus coffee. It really was home from home. I would sit in the sitting room watch TV, play with the kids, or take a stroll around the town at my leisure. Sometimes Mr Sakamoto would have his hands full in the restaurant so I would help in the kitchen with some washing up, preparing some vegetables, or peeling prawns. I would also accompany Mr Sakamoto when he had a delivery of 'bento' to make. These were lunch boxes filled with sushi and other delicacies that people would eat for lunch at home or carry with them on a day out. I learned more in a week here in Uenohara about the typical Japanese way of life than the few months I had spent in Tokyo. The close community, the excellent service industry, and the mutual respect was indeed an education in rural life of Japan. I felt also, because of the kindness that was offered me, the least I could do was put myself about when there was an extra pair of hands needed, even if I was a bit slow in the kitchen department. Mr Ando and the other chef Mr Ito were young men who seemed to enjoy having me around so we would talk about sports, girls, cars, and the like. Their English was as bad as my Japanese so we got on famously.

Kobayashi popped in after a few of days to see how I was. Mr Sakamoto insisted I was helping and that I should stay a little longer. Sakamoto was a respected member of the local community and probably a little older than Kobayashi so for the first time I saw Kobayashi having to respond courteously and respectfully to his senior. I did however insist I go training when Kobayashi was teaching at his nearby dojo. One night after training I was having some supper at Kobayashi's home when the phone rang. Sakamoto was requesting my presence after he had finished work so hurriedly, we ate our food before Kobayashi ferried me back to the restaurant. I was embarrassed and felt I was being pulled around a bit but the relaxed atmosphere of the Sakamoto household was such a relief from the stifled presence of senior Karate instructors.

While staying in Uenohara I realized who was related to who. Tsuda sensei the local school principal was brother-in-law to Mr. Sakamoto. On a couple of occasions, I would be guest of the Tsuda household for an evening before Sakamoto whisked me away to the local bar. Kobayashi Sensei was brother-in-law to Mr Furukawa, who I would be joining for work the following week. It all got a bit confusing especially when I met their wives or children in town for, I would forget who belonged to which family.

Tsuda Sensei decided that it would be a good idea if I should help some of the local kids in their study of English. So, one afternoon myself, Tsuda's two children plus four or five other youngsters and Kobayashi sat around the dining table in Sakamoto's house and, with the help of a tape recorder and some printed cards, began an English lesson. Although my Japanese was very limited the tape was in Japanese and English so it helped to get things under way and I would help with the pronunciation and encouragement. We did the self-introductory stuff and then began to work through the course and it became an enjoyable couple of hours for us all. Tsuda later said I would be paid for the English instruction and that the parents of the children wished for me to continue for the remainder of the duration of my stay in Japan. That meant I would be returning at the weekends after training so that I would work on the Sunday afternoon for a couple hours to earn about forty pounds. That was great news for it meant not only I would have a little regular income coming in but that I had also somewhere to escape from the often-desolate atmosphere of the university, just one day where I could relax and recharge the batteries so to speak.

The weekend approached and I was a guest of the Sakamoto family when they drove to Chiba prefecture for a couple of days at the beach. Mr Sakamoto's brother and his wife and two children, plus Mrs Sakamoto's father also accompanied us and I was relaxed as ever as I swam with the children and sunbathed. We played on the sands of the beach before eating from a barbecue and drinking by the water's edge. We stayed in a chalet type hut that reminded me of my own childhood waking up to the sounds of the ocean during my summer holidays. This was an unexpected bonus in the middle of the summer and I was a million miles from Nichi Dai and the constant pressure of its environment. Even knowing that I would return in a couple of weeks to join up on the Summer Gasshuku it was, for the time being, a long way off.

However, if this easy going and relaxed atmosphere of the week in Uenohara had rested me from the training it in no way prepared me for the week's work that lay ahead of me.

On the Sunday evening after returning from Chiba I was to stay with Kobayashi again before reporting for work the next day. I said farewell to the Sakamoto household for a short while and took some of my belongings in my sports bag.

I don't recall the name of the suburb of Tokyo to which I travelled on the Sunday evening but I was introduced to Mr Furukawa senior and his wife at his house where I ate dinner with them and their two children. It was another long evening of weary conversation and English phrase books, plus the usual excellent Japanese hospitality. At around eleven o'clock Kobayashi left and Mr Furukawa walked me down the road to the office of his company where a futon was laid out for me to sleep. The next morning his brother who was the foreman and former Karate instructor in the UK would collect me for work.

I stretched out in the tiny office squeezed between a desk and a litterbin. The latter served as a reminder of my sleeping arrangements at the dormitory of the Karate club. This was a little step back from the previous week of luxury and I smiled as I wondered how the week ahead would pan out for me.

I was roused sharply at six o'clock with the sound of boots clumping through the office, or rather my bedroom. "Ohayo! Ohayo!" Furukawa shouted as he and a workmate entered. I jumped up and hurriedly dressed. It had been another sweltering night and there were no air conditioning facilities in this makeshift motel so I had nothing on but my underpants to save my embarrassment. I pulled on a tee shirt and a pair of shorts. I was fitted out with some 'tabi' socks, and shoes to match. These resembled a ninja's footwear. These were soft shoes that had a split for the big toe that made me look like I had the feet of a giant pigeon. These were supposed to be sensible footwear for the building site. I couldn't think of anything more laughable unless I was to try and climb the buildings with a black mask and a dagger in my mouth. I was also issued some work trousers that were one size too big but all in all I was ready for the pantomime. I had a quick cup of green tea, a piece of toast from the toaster that had been installed especially for my benefit and we were off.

I sat in the front of the pickup truck along with my two workmates and answered a few of the same questions that by now were standard. Again, Furukawa asked if I liked hard work and I said I didn't mind. "Sure?" he asked. We had been down this track before with these questions so I answered in Japanese "honto". His workmate laughed which embarrassed Furukawa a little and so they continued to teach me a little more of their language as we crawled slowly along in the early morning traffic.

From a suburb of Tokyo, we drove to a suburb of Yokohama. In miles this was probably only twenty odd but after leaving the office at six thirty it took until eight due to the sheer volume of cars and trucks on the road.

The place of work was a brand-new housing estate. Many of the houses were virtually finished but there were one or two still at the foundation stage. My initial job was quite simple. I had to take a shovel and clean up any excess cement from around the foundations plus clean up the paths that led into or away from the estate. There was plenty of shovel work to do and by nine o'clock I had a raging thirst on what must have been the hottest day of the year so far. At ten thirty I was told to go and fetch some juice from a vending machine situated at the side of the site. So, with coins in hand, I found the oasis and spent a good five minutes satisfying my own thirst before carrying back the rest. No sooner had I returned to hand out the drinks to the four or five workmen when I was off again to get another.

"Don't drink too much," shouted Furukawa. "No good if too much" he said. But I went anyway.

The day was broken up at lunchtime when we jumped into the truck and went to a nearby 'café'. There were simple meals on offer like noodles or 'tonkatsu', a favourite of mine; breaded pork on a bowl of rice. We sat and ate for half an hour then returned to the site where we all found a place to stretch out and sleep for twenty minutes or so. This was a nice time of the day. I had always enjoyed an afternoon nap even when coming home from school as a teenager before going training in the evening. It continued when I started work, home at five thirty, tea, sleep then training. I was adjusting my sleep time to the middle of the day, which suited me fine.

The remainder of the day took us to five o'clock when we would clean the tools before setting off back on the road to Tokyo. Once back at around six thirty just as I was looking forward to another sleep after my first exhausting day on the building in the sun, we went straight to a pub. This was, to tell the truth, the last place I wanted to be. I wanted to shower and go to sleep. But I was in Japan and after work most of the male population join their colleagues in the bar. Here I would share a five-minute conversation with the men before they found more important things to talk about among themselves so I would drift into obscurity for another couple of hours before it was time to go home.

I was dropped off at Mr Furukawa's house at around nine so that I could have a bath then dinner while I entertained the family with my English. Eleven o'clock and I walked the fifty yards back to the office where I would get my head down before it all started again.

Philip Kear's letter reared up in my mind as I lay on the office floor struggling to sleep in the heat. "Try not to work for Furukawa for it's very hard work for little pay" he had written. Well at least I could write back and agree with him and as yet I had no idea what I would be paid.

The first day of work with the Furukawa Company was no different than the rest of the week. Up early, on the road, lots of manual labour in temperatures that I had never witnessed before, lunch in the same eating house, a sleep, more work until five, lots more sun. The only difference was in the variation of manual jobs that were on offer. Apart from the shovelling there were plenty of blocks to shift by hand and a bit of digging to be done and all the time I was suffering in the heat. I noticed the foreman Mr Furukawa junior always had a tin hat that seemed too small for him perched right on the top of his head and that one or two of the others wore bandanas to cover their heads. I wore nothing but just got on with the job in hand.

I would wander around the site sometimes with my shovel in hand and look at the fine new buildings that were on display. A few houses were already occupied and one fine detached house at the back of the site would have its windows wide open so that all around the site could hear the piano playing from within. I wondered if this family were in any way related to the one that owned the house outside the Nichi Dai Karate dojo. Despite the warnings from Mr Furukawa not to drink too much I often slipped away to get to the vending machine that served up ice cold drinks. I was unaccustomed to working in such temperatures so I felt I needed to get some fluid into my body regularly. The site was an arid expanse of half-finished roads and dusty tracks on which heavy goods vehicles, diggers and dumpers thundered through kicking up the dust and mixing it with their fumes to give off a throat burning cocktail.

The long day on the building site I could handle, even the long journey home was a relief to be sat down when I could also grab a snooze in between the jibes of the one or two workmen in the cabin.

But the hardest part of the day was the two hours spent in the pub. This may sound strange for after training back at Nichi Dai I would always welcome a beer from the local shop or even better in the bar near the station. But the time was quite limited after training until lights out so we simply made the most of it. Also, with boys from the Karate club there was a mutual conversation such as how the training had been and how much Tanabe had pushed us that day. Sitting in a bar with workmen twenty years older than me who were just delaying their return to their families was hard work. However, they were friendly, generous, and overall funny so I mixed the best I could knowing they were doing their level best to make my short spell with them bearable.

The senior Furukawa I saw only in the evenings when he returned from another site of work to join his family. His wife spoke no English but made the most of my presence by urging her two young children to speak with me even though they knew no more than she. I must have often seemed a little tired but to tell the truth I was exhausted by the time I sat down to dinner at around nine o'clock. My usual enthusiasm for making conversation was jaded by the urge to want to go to bed and by the time Mr Furukawa said "yosh, nemui" 'right, I'm tired' I had to be careful I didn't jump up and clap my hands.

I worked the full week and on the Saturday morning did a little overtime with the boss as he built a wall in the local neighbourhood. This was a little more laid back and we were finished up at lunchtime. I was given a lift to the station so I could return to Uenohara until Monday.

I spent the evening with Kobayashi sensei until Mr Sakamoto phoned. Again, I was ferried up to the restaurant where I spent an evening with him and his wife. In fact, his wife would simply pour the drinks while the two of us spoke at length. I enjoyed Sakamoto's company immensely. He was always interested in my progress in everything I did and was also concerned that I should enjoy as much as possible my stay in Japan. The evening continued when the two of us walked up the road and into a bar but by midnight I left my host and made my own way back. Mrs Sakamoto was waiting for her husband, but I came back 'empty handed,' bade her goodnight and went happily to my room that contained my own bed. I awoke in the night with the sound of "Oh Meiji!" as Mr Sakamoto came down the street singing at the top of his voice. He was a one-off character was Mr Sakamoto. I felt very much at home in his company. In fact, he would always remind me "my house is your house, don't be careful". Even leaving him in the bar during the evening I did not feel rude for it was my wish and it didn't bother him. No matter how late home the boss returned he was always up by six thirty the following morning to be on hand for the start of the day. He ran a successful business and the drinking was always done after the work was finished and for that I admired him.

The Sunday of that weekend I taught English to the six local children. This time we had the privacy of the second floor of the restaurant, which was an impressive layout of several rooms with sliding doors to separate them. There was no help from Kobayashi this time so I took it upon myself to make up a few scenarios for the kids to enact. Before long they were walking up to one another shaking hands and saying "how do you do? I'm John, here's my card", and "oh thank you I'm Peter, here is mine". They laughed a lot as they went through these roles but it worked, for when we finished, they would walk down the high street greeting people in English, much to the amusement of the locals.

In towns all over Japan the summer is festival time. Uenohara was no exception and there was to be a summer festival the following weekend. Mr Sakamoto asked if I could help him out during the week in preparation for the increase workload in his restaurant. I was more than happy to oblige to pay my way for the board and lodge. In his usual generous style, he promised me a trip to Kyoto too for an educational visit to the old capital. He insisted I see as much of his culture as possible before I went back to the daily schedule of the Karate club.

Uenohara was a small town that only contained one main street for shopping. Its size therefore made the community a lot closer knit and within a short spell I could walk down the street and greet people who I had only briefly met. Sakamoto's brother had a fish shop a hundred yards down the road from the restaurant so I couldn't pass there without him or his wife shouting out "Aasa konnichiwa" to which I would wave or drop in for a chat. These family run businesses were almost always at the front of their family house so they lived at work, or rather worked where they lived. Many of the shops would be open late into the evening and it was not unusual to wander into a chemist for example and find nobody behind the counter. But with a polite "sumimasen" (excuse me) the occupants would shout "hai!" from their living room at the back and rush to be with you straight away only to finish what they were doing later. The honesty among the community was of course as natural as the surrounding countryside but I for one, conditioned to locking up after anything was done with, found the trust quite exceptional. But I had seen it for myself and felt humbled by the whole experience.

I was due back for work on the Monday morning so Sunday evening Mr Sakamoto drove me the two hours to the suburb of Tokyo and to Furukawa's house. This was not entirely for the benefit of saving me a train trip for he wanted permission for me to come back on the Wednesday evening so that I would help for the 'Matsuri' or festival. It wasn't the first time I was a little embarrassed for I felt I wanted to help him but Mr Furukawa had given me a job and I felt indebted to him for that. Sakamoto however was a persuasive man and after a brief encounter with the family and some of his good humour it was settled, I would catch a train out to Uenohara on the Wednesday evening and join up with Furukawa's gang the week after.

EIGHTEEN

The three days on the road to Yokohama and back again with all the building site work in between seemed longer than the previous five-day week. The sun was never off duty from morning until late evening and the long days seemed even longer. The final day of my week was the Wednesday and I knew this time there was to be no pub visit but straight back to Uenohara. I was given a lift to the station and was on my way by seven o'clock.

The journey to Uenohara took a couple of hours and during this time I started to feel unwell. Once I arrived at Uenohara station I felt worse. What the problem was I couldn't tell but I was in desperate need of a drink. I bought a can of orange from a machine before catching the bus to the town centre and to tell the truth I was dreading speaking or mixing with anyone. Once I was at Sakamoto's place his wife was in the kitchen cooking me a steak while her husband finished up in the restaurant. The sight of the steak in the pan made me feel sick. I needed to lie down and without taking the customary bath I made my excuses went straight to bed. I opened the window of my room, stripped down to my underpants, and lay on top of the bed. It was another warm evening but I felt hotter than normal. Mr Sakamoto came in a little while later but all I wanted was a drink so he brought me some iced tea and with that I slept.

The next day I felt no better so I stayed in bed. I had a severe headache to go with my feeling unwell. I wondered if perhaps I had eaten something that didn't agree with my system but I really couldn't tell. All I wanted to do was drink and sleep. Both Mr and Mrs Sakamoto came in to see how I was doing and their young boy Takeshi would come in early and say "good morning! Aasa good morning!" while shaking my arm to get me up. But as much as I wanted to get up and join the family I couldn't. After talking with Mr. Sakamoto whose wife's father owned the chemist around the corner we deduced I was suffering from sunstroke. All the days I had been out on the building site without protection to the head had finally taken its toll. Philip Kear's words came back to haunt me as he warned me about working for Furukawa.

Three days I spent in bed with nothing to eat. When the summer festival hit town, I was moved to Kobayashi's house on the outskirts so that I could sleep peacefully away from the din of the banging drums and shouting revellers. Even there in the serenity of a house on the edge of town I could hear folk laughing and enjoying music down by the river. It kept me awake until late into the night and I was wishing I were home with my own family for there's no better place when you're ill than with mum. Your own mum that is, and not someone else's.

Finally, after three bedridden days I was up on my feet and with that I was summoned once more to the Sakamoto household to witness the last day of the festival in the centre of town.

It seemed that every one of the town's population was dressed for the celebrations this evening. The men wore the summer 'yukata', a light loose kimono type robe, along with headbands and sandals. Many of the women were dressed in beautiful silk kimonos that were patterned with flowers that shone in a night sky illuminated by the hundreds of lanterns that hung either side of the road, around the shops, and from the houses. Festivals in Japan can last from a few days to a couple of weeks and are an ancient tradition of praying to the gods for good fortune in the household, commercial prosperity and for peace for their ancestors.

The 'main event' in Uenohara on this Saturday evening was the carrying of a huge shrine around the town. This shrine needed no less than twenty men to hold it aloft and every male over the age of fourteen seemed to want to get involved. As the shrine slowly weaved itself through the crowds of people along the main street the bearers would be chanting in unison to give each other encouragement under its enormous weight. Every now and again an over exuberant male would jump up onto the shrine and you could hear the extra groans from underneath as the sudden addition in weight would catch the tired souls by surprise. Women too would join in the parade carrying sun hats held aloft and dancing traditional steps often forming a large circle as they too followed the procession as if they were in some way assisting their male counterparts in struggling with their task. Throughout the evening drums were beaten and other various musical instruments plucked or blown providing a melodic rhythm to the carnival type atmosphere. It seemed to me that the whole population of Uenohara was on the streets in celebration of the summer of '81.

Across the road from Sakamoto's restaurant set back from the road and hidden behind shops and houses was a Shinto shrine with a small park in front. This too was a setting for locals to provide some entertainment. On a temporary stage a few youngsters played in a band after which a kimono-clad lady sang some traditional folk songs to a taped orchestral background. While the entertainment was in full swing people mingled in and out of side stalls set up around the edge of the park. These were no different to the ones you see at fun fairs on England, tempting a few coins from your pocket with tacky but sometimes innovative games. Food and drink were on sale in abundance from all corners of the park setting an aromatic atmosphere to match the sights and sounds of a unique seasonal celebration that never seemed to end.

I wandered around the festival with Mr Tsuda's two sons who were also my English students. They were keen to show me everything they could to give me a good time and I felt I was getting over my recent bout of sickness when I happily tasted some of the food on sale. I was not ready for the beer or sake yet so I cleverly stayed away from my host Mr. Sakamoto when he shut his restaurant. No doubt after a bumper evening in his shop he would be in the mood for a bumper session in the bars.

As I wandered from place to place on this warm vibrant evening I couldn't help thinking if this were a similar occasion in England, of the same magnitude, by ten o'clock the fights would have got under way among men or women who couldn't control their liquor. The place would be swarming with police and every point of sale of alcohol would be a magnet for youngsters too young to smoke let alone drink beer. Instead, there was a carefree but orderly revelry throughout the evening that was as refreshing as the late breeze that blew in to from the surrounding countryside

Wherever the shrine was carried that evening I could hear its trail of chanting and cheering off in the distance but I decided to return to Sakamoto's house just after midnight. Mrs Sakamoto had been busy early in the evening with her eldest daughter who had joined in the procession but now she had put all four little ones to bed and waited patiently for her husband. She urged me to take my bath before I made my way to my room at the back of the house. The town's celebrations went on through the night but I was more than ready for sleep after the previous couple of rough nights with sunstroke.

I must have slept well for I didn't hear Mr Sakamoto's university song nor his drunken entrance to the house which could sound quite comical while his wife urged him to be silent for fear of waking the children. The first I knew was the tug on my arm as the four-year-old Takeshi pulled on my arm "good morning, Aasa, good morning". This time I was more than ready to rise and join the family for breakfast. Mr. Sakamoto sat at the breakfast table with the sorry look of one too many. He asked if I was ok and I assured him I was fine. "Please explain fine", he asked. I told him it meant ok. "I wish I am fine", he said. Despite his pretty good command of English, he was always trying to improve. "A little too much drink last night, what do you say, overhang?" I laughed and corrected him. "I have hangover" he said with pride. "Oi!" he shouted to his wife. She came quickly "Nani?" she asked. "I have hangover" to which she would want to know its translation. His wife was a hard-working lady but often sat in on our conversation to glean what she could from her husband as we spoke of various topics in English. I was more than relaxed in their household and felt part of the family.

This day was Sunday, which meant another English class in the afternoon. Until then I offered my help in the restaurant in the wake of the previous busy night. I washed up, carried out refuse, washed vegetables, moved some furniture all the while chatting to the young chefs as well as the older ladies of the kitchen. They taught me as much as possible the Japanese words for the contents of their workplace and I strung the new vocabulary together with my basic knowledge to make some conversation. I also went out on delivery with Mr Sakamoto in his tiny van that was perfectly built to weave its way in and around the tiny back streets of this rural town. While chatting to Sakamoto he asked how much I was being paid for my work with Furukawa. I was honest in saying I had no idea. He said he had a friend not too far away who needed a bit of help in moving his factory contents to another location. I didn't want to create problems with those who had been so kind to have already found me employment but once Sakamoto had an idea he was like a dog with a bone, or a piece of sushi. When back at his house he made a few phone calls and came back with a few answers. Apparently, I was to be paid just over thirty thousand yen for the eight days working with Furukawa. This was after some money was subtracted for my having dinner at the boss's house and no doubt wear and tear on the office carpet. So, in pounds I was owed in the region of ninety-six. It worked out at four thousand yen per day. Sakamoto was not impressed. He then phoned his friend who said he could pay me eight thousand yen per day, which was double to what Furukawa was paying me. I had a further seven days remaining before returning to Nichi Dai and the summer camp so it made sense to earn as much as I could in that short time. Sakamoto phoned Furukawa and thanked him but told him I wouldn't be returning the next day. Ouch! I could feel the Nichi Dai old boy cracking his knuckles as he looked forward to meeting me in the dojo later.

It was settled. The next day I would catch a train to Hachioji, twenty minutes from Uenohara and Sakamoto's friend Mr Chujo would collect me from the station and take me to work. I must admit the thought of earning double wages put me in an enthusiastic mood so I was ready for anything. The bonus of this new job of course was that I could return every evening to Uenohara and to a relaxed comfortable surrounding. I was a bit concerned with what Kobayashi would have to say about the change in plans, for it was he who had originally negotiated some work for me with Furukawa. I could be heading for the biggest bashing in the dojo if they all decided I had been disrespectful. I was however powerless in stopping Sakamoto's wheels of motion but truly grateful that I couldn't anyway.

Another couple of hours was spent that day teaching English to the half a dozen local children during which they learned different ways of saying sorry and excuse me. I had them bumping into each other or stepping on one another's foot and saying "Ooh excuse me I am sorry". They loved the acting bits and were sometimes a little too energetic so I took a leaf out of Tanabe's book of fearful scowls and short reprimands and that soon restored order.

The next day Sakamoto gave me a lift to the station at eight and I was in Hachioji by eight forty-five. Mr Chujo, a little guy with a big car greeted me and took me to his house with his office at the front. Mr Chujo owned an interior decorating company and showed the signs of an enterprising businessman. He was a smiley; cheerful character and I could see why he made good friends with Sakamoto. I met one or two of his employees in the office that morning. They were sat in his office drinking tea and eating biscuits from his kitchen. One of them was amusing himself with the luxury chair that reclined and massaged the back at the same time. There seemed no real urgency to get started until Chujo issued directions for the day.

I was introduced to Tanaka San who was a few years older than me and spoke little English. He was to drive the pickup that was a cross between a van and a lorry. It was the shape of a lorry but no bigger than a van. Our job was to load up advertising hoardings on the pickup, strap them down and transport them a few miles up the road to another location, then unload them in a new warehouse that was under construction. We worked well together and we got to know each other with our limited English/ Japanese. Tanaka had previously worked in a bank but was disillusioned with his position so came to work for Chujo. He displayed the usual fascination over my presence in Japan and couldn't understand why I would want to travel so far to train at such a place. In the same way I couldn't understand the reason for his change of employment and so we left things at that. He probably thought I was on the run from the English police and I wondered about his goings on at the bank.

The loading of the lorry, the little drive and the unloading meant we probably managed four trips in a day. Our work rate was constant but we didn't break our backs. The freedom of the job was pure relief in comparison to the Yokohama building site and I was grateful to both Sakamoto and Chujo for their generosity. At the end of the day, I would be back at the office for around four thirty and wait for Chujo to return and give me a lift to the station. I would then be back at Uenohara before six and have some dinner with the family in the evening. As usual Mr Sakamoto would later join me at the dinner table to pick my brains about some English topics, over a beer or two.

Tanaka and I worked well together. There was no seniority as I had experienced on the building site, we just got on with the job and enjoyed the fact that we were from different nations. For us, working together was an education not a hardship.

The advertising hoardings we were transporting were approximately two metres high by one metre in width and made of wood so were hefty to shift. In our enthusiasm to get the job done we piled the boards as high as possible on the back of our little truck. One afternoon we were racing against time so that I could get to the station in time for my return to Uenohara. In his wisdom Tanaka took a short cut enroute to the new warehouse location. What he didn't anticipate was the steep hill that stood in our way on this narrow country road. Tanaka dropped down through the gears as we crawled slowly at a painfully slow pace up the hill. Behind us a trail of cars followed patiently in our wake. Suddenly I noticed in the wing mirror of my side a car swerve violently towards the hedge. I looked back through the cabin window and was horrified to see our load sliding off the back of our neat pile, like playing cards being dealt from their pack. As our load left our truck one by one the following cars swerved left and right to avoid collision. Our brightly coloured adverts, featuring attractive women and hunky guys, wearing new style jeans and trendy tops, along with seductive smiles were scattering in all directions skimming across the tarmac like pebbles across a pond. They seemed to stare up at the terrified drivers like discarded corpses from a hearse and if I had stood back and watched the scene unfold from a neutral position, I would have fell about laughing. But I was the cause of this debacle and appalled at the prospect of the carnage that was unfolding in front of me. Tanaka hit the brakes as I shouted and so the remaining pile at the back shunted forward hit the cabin and then flew off the back for a second wave of collateral damage. The narrow road was a minefield of angry drivers, colourful pictures and a young Japanese man with an even younger foreigner dodging cars and insults trying to clear the debris from the road. Fortunately, there was no real damage done and the drivers were on their way as soon as they were able for fear of being held up any longer.

Our short cut added another hour to our journey so I ended up catching a later train back to Uenohara and on the way home I wondered if Mr Chujo had regretted taking on an ex-bank clerk and an English Karate student on summer release from Nichi Dai.

With the change in my schedule, I managed to train for a

couple of evenings of the week with Kobayashi at his dojo. He didn't seem at all bothered about my working for a different company. On the contrary he was genuinely pleased I was finding my way around without too much trouble and I realized too I was becoming a little more independent while living and working out in the country.

Towards the end of the week my workmate Tanaka promised me a night out with him and his wife before we were to say our farewells and this would be the last time out before a return to the Spartan life of a Karate disciple. Tanaka and I seemed to be destined for ill luck. Nearing the end of the week Mr. Chujo asked whether Tanaka and I could drive over to a recently built block of flats, which the Japanese called a 'penshon'. This, I deduced could be a combination of two English words; penthouse and mansion. However, there was no similarity to either. We were given a roll of wallpaper and instructed to go to a certain flat that had just been decorated by his company and replace a strip of paper that was not up to his normal high standard. We thought this was a simple operation and looked forward to a change of scenery. Arriving at the 'penshon' we let ourselves in to the empty flat with a set of keys and looked for the dodgy wallpaper. We soon spotted a strip of paper that had a few bubbles running down its narrow length so stripped it away from the wall and began our decorating. It was my first ever attempt at papering a wall and Tanaka the banker too had little experience in this department. After an hour and a half and three attempts of measuring, cutting, and sticking a strip no larger than a door we had to be satisfied we had done the job. To be honest it looked no better than the original piece we had stripped from the wall in the first place but we were sure we had done our best. We then wandered around the rest of the apartment to admire its freshness and layout of the new rooms. As we entered one of the bedrooms there was a strip of wallpaper that had a big cross pencilled through its centre indicating it was to be replaced. We stood in horror at what we had done and the fact we had no paper left to complete the task after our bungled previous attempts had all but used up the roll we had took. We returned to the office with our tails between our legs and apologized to Mr. Chujo who had to return to the apartment the next day and put things right for himself.

Overall, we had worked conscientiously for our boss that week and he was genuinely pleased with our efforts. Tanaka and I decided to celebrate after work with a drink in Hachioji where his wife would join us in a bar. I asked Tanaka to check the time of the last train back to Uenohara and he said he had it covered. The weather that evening turned nasty and although the humidity was high there was also some heavy winds but this didn't bother us too much as we left the car and entered the local bar.

Tanaka and I enjoyed a couple of beers and played a game of pool in this small cosy bar. His wife showed up and they ordered a simple meal of burger and chips for us all. The bar was of an American type sixty's theme, which made a change from the tiny Japanese drinking houses I had become accustomed. The music from the jukebox varied from Elvis to Buddy Holly and this was also a welcome break from the sad heart-breaking Japanese ballads that were a common trait of the Japanese bars. The odd thing in this place were the staff, for they tried their best to look like rockers but it didn't quite work, they were too nice and stood too politely. An American bar must have a bit of attitude and I'm afraid the average Japanese person is a bit short in that department. Still, they served us our beer and food in the usual snappy efficient way so there were no complaints. The time moved fast as we enjoyed our pool and conversation. We laughed at the antics of our working week and Mrs Tanaka quietly and politely laughed along with us.

The last train to Uenohara was around eleven that evening and I constantly checked with my workmate the time. He was not too bothered about how time was progressing but I on the other hand became a little concerned as the time went well past ten. Just one more drink he urged so I relented but insisted we make it a quick one so that we would have plenty of time to get to the station. At ten thirty after I stood up in a hint to be on our way, we finally left the bar. The weather by now was a storm and we quickly rushed to the car as winds and rain lashed us. Mrs Tanaka drove us but she was looking more than a little nervous as the visibility reduced dramatically as the rain belted against the windscreen. The car was a little two-door affair and so its stability came into question as we challenged the high winds that were now picking up speed. The more nervous Mrs Tanaka became the more I feared we wouldn't get to the station on time.

It became apparent to me this was no ordinary storm when I saw anything about floor level swaying violently in the strong winds. Our car slowed to a pedestrian pace and I saw a line of cars ahead at a standstill. I looked back through the rain lashed rear window and could just make out the headlights of another queue of cars behind us. We had now stopped and Tanaka switched on the radio flicking through the channels. There was obviously a problem up ahead and so we considered turning around. Between the surges of rain lashing our precarious position I could just make out the circular top of a huge bridge ahead. Then I saw a figure leaning forward in defiance of the wind hugging a raincoat that was tightly wrapped around his body. With the torch that was in hand he tapped on the driver's window. It was a policeman and he gave us the information that we dreaded. This was no ordinary storm, but a typhoon and despite not being right in the middle of it there was a need to close the bridge ahead until the winds abated. On top of that there had been an accident a little way behind us so that direction too was now closed. He ran off quickly to stop the car behind from turning around.

We were well and truly stuffed and I was quietly annoyed. Had we left a little earlier we could possibly have avoided this sorry predicament. The storm raged even more angrily around us and any idea of it soon abating became a lost hope so we eventually settled to get some sleep. If I were in Mr Chujo's luxury Nissan there wouldn't have been too much problem stretching out in the back but in this matchbox replica of a motor vehicle I had to curl up like a cat in order to be able to try for some sleep.

The night lasted an agonizing five hours and I slept in small doses as I turned incessantly to avoid seizing up. I had to wake my friend Tanaka a few times to let me out so I could relieve myself on the roadside verge after the previous consumption of beer had passed through my system.

Finally, as daylight broke, we made our way forward across the bridge and drove to the station where I said my final farewells to Tanaka san and his lady, thanked them for their kindness and caught the six o'clock train back to Uenohara.

There were a couple of days left before returning to Tokyo and the regimen of Nihon University so I enjoyed a relaxing evening or two in Sakamoto's company and during the day visited friends to thank them for making my stay so enjoyable. I had eaten so many meals, drank beer and sake in many different sitting rooms and sat through many hours of ineligible conversations. I felt though I had been adopted by a town and all its inhabitants.

On the last evening at around seven thirty while I soaked in the bath Mr Sakamoto rushed to tell me my older brother was on the phone. My sister-in-law had just given birth to a baby son so Mr Sakamoto thought we should celebrate and typically held up a huge bottle of sake from beside his dining room chair. I was a little apprehensive for we had not yet had word from Kobayashi about the details of the next day. I had a few small glasses with my host but remained sensible in preparation for what lay ahead.

At eleven thirty Kobayashi Sensei phoned from Mr Furukawa's house to inform me I was to be at Nichi Dai the next morning for nine o'clock sharp ready for the trip to the summer camp. Then he said there was someone with him who wished to speak with me. The unmistakeable voice of Tatsuo Suzuki pierced the short silence;

"Hi how is Japan?"

I replied coyly that I was enjoying my stay. I was taken aback for I had no idea that Suzuki Sensei was even in the country.

"How about Japanese girls?" he asked. I said they were ok which sounded a bit dim but it was all I could think of at the time so late at night. We spoke briefly for a minute or two before he wished me luck for the remainder of my stay. With that bit of encouragement ringing in my ears I bid Sakamoto goodnight and turned in.

NINETEEN

I was on the early train from Uenohara and managed to be back at the Hachimanyama dormitory by eight forty-five to find the bus with all Karate students and Tanabe Sensei already on board waiting for just one straggler. I was flustered for I still needed to dump my suitcase and collect one or two more things from my room. I ran into the building with Tanabe sensei shouting after me to hurry up.

"Aasa! Hayaku! Hayaku!" I smiled in my panic as I ran up the stairs and thought how nice it was for Tanabe to welcome me back so affectionately.

I was on the coach before a full two minutes had ticked by and as I made my way to a seat at the back, I greeted the familiar faces that playfully chided me on being the last to board. Just as we pulled away from the kerbside I glanced out of the window in the direction of the dojo and was stunned to see just an empty space. I had to look again to see if I was mistaken. Enomoto saw my startled look and explained that the dojo where I had trained for the past three months had been pulled down and was to be replaced with a brand-new construction over the next year or so. He had no idea of where we would be training once we returned from our summer camp.

The coach took us to Atami, a small port a couple of hours drive South West of Tokyo and from there we boarded a ferry for a further couple of hours to Oshima Island. The trip over was pleasant with everybody in good spirits looking forward to a change of scenery. It reminded me of a school trip to France when I and my schoolmates enjoyed standing on deck in the warm sunshine with the wind and sea spray licking our faces as we leaned as far as possible over the side. We took pictures and Tanabe joined us, along with a couple of old boys who had met us at Atami, and cheered us with his satire. Some little kids were running around so they too jumped in our photos.

The sound of the Orient attracted my attention and I saw an old man with a flute playing a tune as he looked out over the water. I quietly joined him and enjoyed his music while I watched the distant island of Oshima gradually close us down. After a while Tanabe called me away and we lined up ready to disembark. I saw a beach, a little resort with some shops and a few boats bobbing in the small bay and everything looked as welcoming as we could have possibly hoped for. However, we were quickly herded on to a couple of mini buses that took us away from a scene of 'Wish you were here'. The minibus took us out into the country, along quiet narrow tree lined roads surrounded by fields that stretched out as far as the eye could see. Finally, after twenty minutes we pulled up outside a hostel. Here we were put into rooms half the size of those at Nichi Dai but with the same number of personnel in each. My six first year roommates and I attempted to make our room fit around us. Whichever way we turned it wouldn't quite work. Finally, once the futons were out of the cupboard, we found a place to put Enomoto. He was not too keen at the idea but saw the funny side when we pointed out he had his own private room.

We looked around the hostel and familiarized ourselves with the dining room, the washroom and showers etc. A few yards to the side of the hostel was a sports hall of some considerable size, which no doubt we would soon be putting to good use.

At five o'clock we had dinner and then four more old boys plus four high school students joined us. The latter were probably contemplating joining the ranks of Nihon University Karate Club and decided to have a look at how we spent the summer. There was a meeting at nine to outline our schedule for the week and Enomoto filled me in later on the details. Daily training would be from six to eight in the morning, then nine thirty to eleven thirty and finally two in the afternoon until five. I wondered what we were going to do with so much spare time on our hands. At ten o'clock lights were out for our customary early night.

Our alarms, or should I say everybody else's alarms, went off at five forty the next morning and our training was back with a vengeance. Unusually our morning training was to be in our Karate Do gi rather than jogging bottoms and we lined up outside as the second, third and fourth years joined us on the tarmac. We had already placed shoes for the instructors and old boys in a neat line just outside the doorway and eventually they appeared and stepped neatly into the waiting footwear. Among us first and second year ranks we were given various things to carry such as iron geta (clogs) and makiwara before setting set off for the run. We ran in a neat line of twos, the captain Tanemura would shout every ten yards or so and we would reply with a loud kiai or yell. Even at six o'clock the temperature was close to roasting and the familiar feeling of sweat and fatigue started to close in on me.

We had set off in our clean white gis on our morning run that took us probably a mile and a half to a sandy, grassy field. There were some lorry tyres already half buried in the ground and we hammered the four wooden punching posts into their positions. We were then separated into groups and put through our different forms of training. We did sprint, leapfrog jumping over the tyres, makiwara punching and wore the iron geta which we strapped to our feet by a belt that lashed around our ankles. We punched the posts until our knuckles bled and we did knee raises up and down the field with the heavy geta before moving on to front kicks. As we went through the various training programmes instructors and old boys would scream at us to improve our speed, power, and overall performance. The pleasantries of the ferry trip over quickly evaporated as we were brought back down to reality with a huge bump. After an hour and a half of going round and round the field we jogged slowly back to the hostel with more shouts to match our sorry steps. The fatigue of our bodies was reflected in our weak, strangled kiais. We were in the middle of nowhere as we followed the lanes back and I thought to myself if our shouts were for help nobody could hear us. Now and again as we ran along the narrow roads a scream from the back would break our rhythm,

"Kuruma desu!" to warn of a car approaching from behind so we would all squeeze to one side to allow the vehicle to go by. Even though I like running there was a huge temptation to stop one of those cars and hitch a lift. A three-week summer break had been the worse preparation for a summer camp and now I wished I had trained more in Uenohara. That place was just a distant memory as I ran back in the searing sun in a grubby sweat-soaked Karate gi.

We were back at the hostel by eight and the shock of the intensity of our first morning had silenced every one of us. We returned to our rooms and changed out of our uniforms before making our way to the dining room for breakfast. The room was set up on traditional tatami mats with tables at knee height so we all sat cross-legged and waited for our first meal of the day. Out came a bowl of rice with some dried seaweed in a packet and a raw egg. We mixed the egg with the rice and seaweed and some soy sauce stirred it all up furiously and ate heartily. That, with a cup of green tea, was breakfast. I did consider asking for an upgrade but settled for a visit to yet another vending machine stood conveniently outside the front door that offered ice cold drinks.

We returned to our rooms and stretched out on our warm tatami floor and dozed before the shout went up to get ready for our next session. Our gis were still damp from the morning run even though we had hung them around the room in a vain attempt to dry them.

We filed into the sports hall next door and set to work with cleaning the floor with our little cloths. The hall was much larger than our own dojo and had sliding windows all around that stretched from head height up to near the ceiling, which gave an impression of a large airy training venue. But as the sun began to find its way through the surrounding trees, I had the feeling that we were going to feel like fresh tomatoes ripening in a greenhouse. The large floor area was of a parquet tile type and took some cleaning. In fact, when the second years entered, they too had to jump to our assistance to get the job done before training. We also had the responsibility of carrying in a barrel of pocari sweat, which we placed on a table in one corner along with one glass. Naturally we had a sneaky drink or two before the seniors arrived, and so did they before their seniors showed up and so on.

We began our training at nine thirty prompts with both Tanabe Senseis present plus the old boys who varied in ages from thirty to forty. The four young high school students tagged along on the end of our line and looked petrified. We spent the first hour after our warmup running through our basic techniques before moving on to 'keri waza' or kicks. This was a small marathon up and down the full length of our dojo that must have measured about thirty metres by ten. I had taped my feet before training but the burning sensation from the repeated kicks on the less forgiving floor made for an uncomfortable second hour. We finished at eleven thirty and I wondered about the barrel of drink in the corner. We hadn't touched it so perhaps it was one of those Tanabe mind games.

We stripped once more in our room that had now become a little hotter than earlier and quickly showered before returning to the dining room for lunch. Here we were served some fish with rice, miso soup and pickles. This went down well but I couldn't wait to get to the vending machine outside and then to the floor of our room where we all flopped and slept again to the raucous tune of the insects outside. No sooner than our eyes had closed when it seemed we were up again for our afternoon training. I was already physically drained from the two morning sessions and the heat that went with them. Nevertheless, I duly changed into my Karate gi and silently followed the rest of my first-year colleagues. Looking at their faces they were clearly having no more fun than me.

At two thirty prompt we began our third session for the day. Starting with the traditional basic training for fifty minutes or so then a five-minute rest before lining up to begin a lengthy duration of various punching combinations. By now the sun was high in the sky and my mind drifted to the sensation of drinking ice-cold lager in one of the pubs back home. It was a reminder of my thoughts and feelings when I first began my training here in Japan and now, they flooded back to me as I struggled to cope with the intensity of the training and the temperature.

Our punching training session was of the relay type that was already familiar, but the extra length of our dojo threw us out of our stride a little. The tops of my legs were burning from the morning exercises so the constant driving forward to produce quick punches made them hell to cope with. The harder floor was not of the sprung type so was unforgiving on the joints of the body, especially the lower back.

We rested after a further half an hour or so then miraculously we were given permission to take a drink from the barrel in the corner. As I stood in the queue waiting my turn I watched as each student took the glass and filled it once with the lemon-coloured liquid and throw back their head to quickly satisfy their thirst. I thought perhaps when it came to my turn, I would take smaller sips and swill the fluid around to enjoy the moment a little longer, but no sooner was the glass in my hand I filled it and buried the contents as quickly as I could so the smack of a cold drink at the back of my throat was at its most effective. However once that quick action was over, I wished I had taken things a little slower and as I pondered the empty glass in my hand, I felt Enomoto breathing down my neck urging me to step aside.

The remaining hour and a half began with the five Pinan katas, but at a quick pace. Mistakes were punishable by press-ups plus the accompanying shout of apology. After the Pinans were finally completed we moved on to Kushanku. This too was done at speed. Before long we were all dropping and shouting "shitsurei shimashita!" as our tired bodies and the quick time practice were catching us all out.

Seishan kata followed our Kushanku. This was a welcome change, for the opening moves are performed slowly so gave us the opportunity to rest our legs a bit and to concentrate a little more on our technique. That sounds funny, for very often the thoughts in the head were about getting through the tough bits and getting finished, regardless of style or form and yet, when given the chance, there were times when we all persevered to learn and improve our technique.

Both Hideo and Fumihiro Tanabe taught for the duration of Seishan. From time to time they demonstrated various applications of our kata moves as we stood to attention and responded with loud "hai! so!" for every explanation. The other old boys wandered around but hardly said much and I think their presence was just a matter of keeping us on our toes when perhaps we might be slacking.

Our first day of the summer camp or 'gasshuku' finished at five thirty. I was glad to get out of my gi and into the cool shower. We had dinner at six and we were all relieved to be in our rooms for a lie down. The first years around me were complaining about the intensity of the first day and I could only say "I wanna go home". Enomoto was having his say but little Hijikata was in better spirits and seemed to mock the bigger man for his weakness. They said a few words that could have resulted in a more serious argument but Asuka intervened with words to the effect of "we're all in it so let's get on with it".

I looked at the thin guy Tanaka and the fatter boy Yatabe and I wondered how long they would last. They both seemed unusually quiet and were in no mood for joining in the conversations that went on around them.

We set out our futons ready for the night and to give Enomoto his bit of space in the cupboard. Our windows were wide open to try and let some air in while a mesh screen was pulled across the window to prevent the mosquitoes from having us for supper. There was little to do but lie around and sweat.

We were summoned to the dining room at nine o'clock for a meeting where I sat at the back and tried to look interested. The three fourth years Tanemura, Fukusyo and Takahashi conducted the meeting while their colleague Hakoishi sat to one side showing a complete lack of interest.

I knew nothing of the meeting or its contents and the rest of the first years didn't bother to fill me in on the details. We were just happy to get to bed.

Just as we were about to turn in for the night the second year Sugimoto came into our room carrying a futon. Everyone but me jumped up and made a fuss over his presence. It seemed another old boy had turned up and there was very little room available so everyone had to shove along a bit ending up with one more in our already cramped room.

Although I was shattered from the day's events getting to sleep was not easy. The warmth of a tropical type summer added to that of the sweaty bodies in close proximity made for an uncomfortable night. When I did finally manage to drop off there were some nasty looking crawling bugs that would often find their way across my chest or legs causing me to jump up quickly in a panic. They were somewhere between a large beetle and a small scorpion in size and black with pincers. Fortunately, these bugs were not poisonous but ugly enough to cause a little concern. This caused me to scratch incessantly and once I was awake it took another half an hour at least before I would get back to sleep. All the while I was counting down the minutes before I was up again for early training.

When the alarm clocks sounded, we all groaned. We sat up and looked at each other before the rest of my room mates realised, we had a second year in our midst and quickly jumped up to dress.

Sugimoto sat up and told his kohais to hurry up. I think he felt it his duty to say something of authority and no doubt he was none too happy to be among inferior lowlife.

As we stepped outside, we were surprised to see the ground wet from an overnight rainfall. When the instructors emerged from the hostel, they discussed the ground situation and decided it would be too mucky on the field for training so set us our tasks in the dojo next door and on the road that ran past our camp. We still set off on the run but our route led us back to our starting point. I was in the first group to strap on the iron geta and while the rest of the happy campers went inside the dojo I lined up with a few others and started the knee raises up and down the tarmac road. The four high school students were also training with us but they were saved the trouble of wearing the heavy shoes. Although I was a little more accustomed to the geta than the day before there was the added problem of a wet road surface. After the knee raises came the front kicks and this was where the slippery surface made speed an enemy. The one or two old boys who were assigned to babysit us were not fully aware of the precarious ground underfoot. They just bawled and shouted like they were instructed and before long it was no surprise that someone hit the deck. Yatabe, the larger of the first years, crashed to the floor with a loud smack and one of the old boys quickly ran to his aid. Yatabe was down and didn't look like he could get up. As we kept on training, I felt like a guilty driver passing a crash victim on the road not bothering to stop. But I also enjoyed seeing the panic of the old boy as he tried to return young Yatabe to his feet. Yatabe held his back with a grimace of pain across his face and so was led away from the rest of us into the hostel.

After fifteen minutes outside we changed places with another group in the training hall. When we entered, we were greeted with the sight of a mass of tired young people doing various painful looking exercises across the width of the floor. We took up our positions to one side and started 'duckwalking' down on our haunches forwards to the opposite wall and then backwards again. The more tired we became the more we had to lean from side to side to bring our legs through the next step. Hence, we waddled rather than walked. We tried to rest our arms on our legs but Tanabe was having none of it shouting from his vantage point up on a balcony overlooking us all. We then moved on to walking the length of the dojo and back on our hands with a partner holding the legs. A cluster of press ups were next, plus sit ups, squat thrusts, star jumps and finally everybody was back together again for some light sparring. Another run with the accompanying kiais followed before the morning session was complete. I was done. It crossed my mind to go to one of the Tanabe brothers and tell them I wasn't well or something. I thought I had done about everything there was to be done here in Japan until this course was served up.

The most demoralizing aspect of the morning training was the fact that there were still another five hours of training ahead. I knew in my mind that if I were to get through this week, I had to take each session as it came and try not looking ahead to the rest of the day, or the remainder of the week.

As we finished the morning training, I couldn't help but savour the irony of our predicament as the instructors would sit out in the sun and drink ice cold tea, one or two enjoyed a cigarette and they all talked loudly with much laughter. They would appear to be enjoying their trip away from home and even chastised us for having dirty gis while they paraded in their still white, creaseless uniforms. In the style of the day before we trouped quietly into our room and stripped off our wet and grubby outfits, before having a quick wash before breakfast. We only had an hour after breakfast before training so there was little time to do anything but stretch out and groan. Yatabe had been carted off to a makeshift sickbay so we soon made use of the extra room he had left behind to stretch out and doze.

The following two hours training took much the same routine as on the first day; an hour of basic training plus combinations of kicks. This passed relatively quickly and we were soon back in our shack waiting for lunch. As we sat sweating in the dining room two familiar faces peered around the doorway. We all stood quickly to welcome Kobayashi and Wakamei and I felt almost relieved to see these two characters among us in our wilderness. But as uplifted as I felt to see their arrival it would not be long before I would be glad to see the back of them.

The afternoon session got under way and for some reason I pondered on the fact that it was a Saturday. At home I would be having a day off from work and wandering nonchalantly around town perhaps buying something to wear as I looked forward to a night out. I thought about the typical unpredictable British summer that would often bring an unwelcome patch of dull weather with rain, wind, and cold spells. As I glimpsed out of the windows that surrounded us in our training ranks all I could see was clear blue skies and a sun that shone incessantly. I wouldn't have minded just one of those miserable English summer days on the island of Oshima.

TWENTY

There was now a total of two instructors and six old boys parading around the dojo as we trained, and their presence seemed to have us more on edge. There seemed to be someone on my shoulder every second so I tried to give my training as much application as possible under the tired circumstances. I felt that if this Gasshuku had taken place before the summer break I would have been more physically prepared for its intensity. But it was like starting all over again for my body and feet ached and my mind was subsisting on the commands of Hideo Tanabe who, undeterred from the look of our sorry faces, continued his demands for more effort.

Our last hour of practice concluded with Seishan kata and it became clear to me that few of the students were very competent with this kata. Apart from Takahashi, who seemed to make every kata look his favourite, and one or two others we all had problems in matching our interpretation of what was being taught in comparison to that of our instructors. After the physical exploits of the previous few hours, I enjoyed this lesson and tried my best to understand what was being taught. This kata begins slowly with every move performed with a modicum of tension as the Seishan stance is held firmly with both feet turned in and knees as bent as possible to lower the centre of gravity. Then suddenly the kata moves into a series of quick combination of punches and turns. The contrast between the two halves of the Seishan bring with its practice a unique mental and physical challenge for the concentration needed at the beginning is matched only with the speed of movement for the latter part.

After nearly seven hours training when thoughts are of resting up for the evening the last thing, I wanted to hear was the command for putting on our mitts. Even the most proficient and competent among us like Oshima, Kawano, Kishiyama seemed a little annoyed at the prospect. We sat and wiped our faces with our towels before we took to the floor with various opponents. As I sparred with the different opposition, I cared less for a winning attitude preferring to opt for the economy of movement and less energetic techniques. Not that I was trying to perfect what Grandmaster Ohtsuka had in mind when developing our style but I was frankly doing my best not to work any harder than was necessary. I kept my feet on the ground as much as possible for lifting them proved hard work. I was 'spent' and wanted only to rest.

I traded comfortably with my hands plus threw the odd low front kick. Kobayashi quickly rounded on me and served me a mouthful of Japanese expletives. He sensed what I was doing and didn't like it. I had it in my mind to speak up and say 'well how would you feel after what we've just been through?' But he knew perfectly well how I felt for he had done this summer camp four times as a student and had proved his worth many years before me. I replied with a strong "Hai! So!" and steamed into my opponent with a combination of punches and kicks matched with a loud kiai for good measure.

"Yame!" was finally called and we sat in the kneeling 'seiza' position for another lengthy period after we had repeated our dojo maxims. Fumihiro Tanabe had a few words to say before Hideo took over and decided to give us his interpretation of the Queen's speech. The sweat from my head found its way to the front of my face and finally to my chin from where a constant dribble would hit my chest just above where my gi jacket crossed over. As I sat tired and thirsty, despite the one glass of pocari sweat that I had drunk quicker than a tequila slammer, I suddenly realized why I had a few spots on my chest. The constant sweat that dripped from my face was the cause of my body acne. I nearly bust out laughing at my discovery. Then I wondered what reaction I would get if I did just that. As Tanabe continued to speak and I continued to not understand my mind was racing in all directions trying to take the thoughts away from the pain in my knees and ankles. Finally, we were dismissed and we rose slowly to our feet and shuffled out into the sunlight.

Outside sat on a little patch of grass were two old boys who had left the training hall a little early. There was a wooden bench on which were slices from a huge melon. We were each handed a fat juicy slice and the old boys smiled with their offering. We tucked in and slobbered away burying our faces into the red inner fruit leaving tidemarks around our faces like babies at the dinner table. We laughed at each other as the juices ran amok and we helped ourselves to more servings that were sliced up and offered us. Two days done, three to go. That didn't sound too bad.

The extra talk that Tanabe had given was to urge us on during this difficult week. He said there were a few contests approaching in the next few months and that everybody had to pull together in order to be in top shape. In effect then this was like a pre-season training for the coming contest period. Enomoto told me that on the last day of the summer camp there would be a club contest. I asked him if that meant everybody and he assured me that nobody would be excluded. My mind did somersaults at the thought of my first chance to fight in a competitive environment. My fellow students were to be my opponents and my heart lurched with excitement at the prospect of fighting some of the handy opponents in the club.

After dinner that evening, we returned as weary and sleepy as the previous night knowing we still had most of the week ahead, but I for one had something else in mind to spur me on a little.

Unlike the atmosphere at Nichi Dai this summer training camp held no social interest between training times. For example, back in Tokyo after training a few of us would get together and go for a beer, have some fun, compare notes of our cultures, and generally get along as best as we could before it was time to get serious again. Here, on this Godforsaken Island we trained ate and slept.

The next morning the sun shone no less fierce as we jogged our way to the field of morning exercise. Our legs were sore from the first two days training and the simple task of getting up off the floor from our futons had been painful enough. After we had run for about twenty minutes carrying all the stuff and shouting all the way I was intrigued to know how the instructors always seemed to be at the training ground about the same time as us and in no way the worse for wear like we were. I guess we ran the long way round and they just hopped over a couple of hedges. This morning's training was no different although now we had half as many instructors and old boys in charge as there were students training. The four high school students were down to two and the remainder seemed ready to throw their hand in at any time. If the truth were known that probably reflected the feeling throughout the rest of the camp.

This day I had a hard time with the iron geta. In fact, Wakamei stood in front of me while I marched up and down the field lifting my legs as high as I could. My senior's response to my efforts was, "Arthur, your kicks are not so good. Look at him his kicks are far better than yours". I looked at 'him'. It was Iidabashi of my first-year group and I swear he was doing no better than I. His face was twisted with effort as he tried to kick. We were then both told to snap back the kicks rather than let them just drop to the floor. The pull of natural gravity became stronger than the pull of my leg muscles so I was fighting a losing battle with old Isaac Newton himself. Then Kobayashi decided to visit me in my anguish. His little habit of mimicking me in a sorry state only made me grimace in anger instead of effort, but thankfully he knew not the difference. As he stood next to me urging me on, I wondered if this was like the good cop bad cop scenario. First Wakamei had come along to soften me up before Kobayashi stopped by to finish me off.

The rest of that early morning training seemed harder than the previous two days. We did more of everything. We couldn't punch the makiwara at all by now for our knuckles were red raw so we just belted it with our elbows. The sprinting and hopping over tyres slowed to a pathetic pace for there was nothing left to give in these routines. In fact, we ended up just stepping over the tyres such was the strain. I looked at the faces of the likes of Kikuta, Fujimoto, and little Hara as they passed me and they were not coping any better. In fact, we were all simply mindlessly moving forward to the tune of "hayaku hayaku", and "osoi osoi" as we were told to hurry up and not be so slow. Our jog back to the hostel was the slowest yet and the shouting the weakest.

Back in our room Enomoto said when this week was over, he was going home. I sympathized with those words entirely. I knew if I got through this without quitting then I too would probably think about returning home. After all, this was the worse week I had ever spent with a Karate gi on so there wasn't much point in staying any longer to prove anything to anyone. On top of our hard training schedule, we had the filthiest Karate uniforms to put on each day, which didn't feel at all inspiring. We decided to get them washed that evening and wear them the next day no matter how wet they would be. The senior grades and instructors came fully prepared with a second or even a third gi. We were not at all so well informed and had only the same wretched piece of cotton to put on each day.

Another sparse breakfast, another catnap and back in the dojo for our elevenses. I mentally prepared to go through the same routine of basics for an hour but was surprised when we started a little differently. Basic training, we did, but a shortened version, followed by Bassai kata. What a welcome change this was. For one thing it was a relief for the tired limbs but it gave me chance to develop further the technical side of our Wado style. I mean I would have felt a fool if after training in Japan for a while I returned to England fit and razor sharp but unable to remember kata moves fundamental for a dan grade. The mid-morning training with its concentrated practice of Bassai seemed to fly by. The afternoon session however was the complete opposite. Just when I thought that perhaps we had worked so hard for the first half of the week that things would start to slow up then I was hit by a rough three hours training with so many kicks, many more punches and then a marathon free fighting period. I fought no less than ten opponents in the space of ten minutes when one after one we were summoned to the middle of the floor and attacked from all different angles. This I had done before at my old club as a brown belt and found it a lot of fun. Stood in the middle of the dojo the instructor called out a person's name and they would quickly shoot forward to catch you off guard from an unsuspecting direction. It was a little rougher on this our third day of this summer camp compared to the fun I'd had at home. There was no laughter in the sudden shock of being punched from behind and as one would expect the man in the middle became a little enthusiastic in his attempt to defend himself from the onrushing attacker. In a panic to avoid an attack he would lash out a bit indiscriminately creating a somewhat chaotic free for all as the opponent retaliated with the same. The order of the day was to take the man down rather than simply score points. I sometimes came off worse against one or two of the bigger boys for once I was held, I struggled to remain on my feet. But on a good few occasions my mitted fist and bare instep found their target with a satisfactory smack and one or two wobbled with a mild concussion as I gave out what was asked of Tanabe and the rest of the coaching staff. Each one of us took up this challenge as best as our tired bodies would manage.

I looked around at the faces of those waiting to be summoned to the middle and there were a few looks of anguish from the younger lads as the action heated up in front of them. But when their names were called, they shouted "Hai!" and shot forward without hesitation.

I watched Wakamei Sensei coaching and grilling students and I thought of the first summer camp I had attended in England in 1976 in Southport when I trained, as a white belt, under his instruction. He had taught us in a clinical, meticulous fashion with patience and a sense of humour. Here he was pushing for more effort and not looking quite so friendly. The instructors on this camp had been well schooled in looking grumpy and dissatisfied with our progress.

I also remembered that by this time of the day the summer course in England would be over and we would probably be in the pub or on the beach enjoying the rest of our free time after the four hours training. Yet here I was in the seventh hour with mitts on waiting to step forward for a fight.

After training that day I watched from the window of our room as Wakamei and one or two other old boys plus the high school kids said their farewells to both Tanabe Senseis. I felt a little envious as they departed from sight. Despite my previous friendly outings with Wakamei he had not spoken to me once in a familiar manner and by now I fully understood this mentality. He and the rest were not there to party or enjoy a break of any sort, only to assist in the developing of our spirit.

My third day here had ended and so psychologically another milestone had passed, two thirds done. Apart from Yatabe of our room who had hurt his back there were one or two more that had bowed out of training through injury or illness. This spurred me on for I was now determined to see out this week no matter what.

A few of us from our room stuffed our dirty gis into a couple of washing machines at the back of the hostel and sat by closely while they went through their cycle of grime to shine. We were fearful a senior student would take over and discard our uniforms so Enomoto, Hijikata and I stood guard hoping for a quiet evening in the launderette. Kikuta showed up with his typical curiosity but played no part in poking any fun at the first years. None of us were in the mood for it and he knew it. Eventually we recovered our gis from the wash and hung them up, still dripping, in our rooms.

After dinner and yet another meeting we returned to our room for more rest and quiet conversation before finally one by one we fell asleep.

Putting the gi on the next morning was a shock for it was still wet, but a clean wet. The yellow tint of mould around the collar was now only faintly visible but the stiffness of the jacket made for uncomfortable running. This made the armpits rub a little and create a little soreness by the time we had reached the field of morning training. Overall, however I felt less tired than the previous days and although the dreaded jumps over the tyres and the iron geta drained me of energy I seemed to recover a little quicker. Punching the makiwara was impossible as my knuckles were already skinned so once more, I resorted to the elbow as a replacement.

The dampness of my freshly washed gi picked up every speck of dirt from the ground as I trained that morning so the futility of trying to stay clean only attracted unwanted attention. Tanabe in his quest to make light of the odd situation found the spectacle a little comical, which in fact lifted my spirits a little as I laughed with him at me. I had almost forgotten what it was like to laugh and it felt good. The rest of the morning passed slowly because I knew there were only two days remaining, but the intense aching in the legs from the first day's training had thankfully evaporated and my body generally felt in better shape.

The two-hour training period after breakfast began in earnest and after the customary basic training we were on the striking pads. We did no punching for the duration of the pad work, just hundreds of front kicks as we moved from one line to another to attack the various targets lined up across the width of the dojo. My toes stung when I failed to catch the target cleanly with the ball of the foot. As loose as I was in the hips and legs, I was never blessed with supple toes so my ball of foot was a lot less accessible than most and I was glad when we eventually moved on to the roundhouse and side kick. It was always a relief to finally hold the pads for the others and this day was no exception. We had no five-minute break this morning and psychologically this knocked me back a bit. It's stupid when you think about it. After basic training we would always have a little sit down. The mind would look forward to this period of respite, a small moment to sit and rest up a little and to prepare for the next bit of training. Today we went without and we all looked a little perturbed when "Yame!" was called after basics and we were ordered to line up straight away with the command of "Keri!"

Hideo Tanabe had that little knack of annoying the hell out of us. Like the omission of our break, or the extra few minutes he would add on to a two-hour training session. At times we thought we were over the worse before he would up the intensity. He seemed to sense our mood so would therefore set the tempo for training accordingly.

Fumihiro Tanabe could be little more discerning when it came to injury problems and would often stop the class to check on someone's condition. His trademark hand on the shoulder seemed to have an uplifting effect on many an individual, and they would insist on continuing as if Jesus himself had healed them.

The hiatus between lunch and afternoon training on this day held only one topic of conversation in our room, and that was, the next day was the last. Which also meant contest day. Sugimoto had returned to his own room when the numbers had thinned out a bit so my fellow roommates were openly planning on taking a scalp or two from the seniors during the competition. They then discussed my chances and all concurred that I would finish in the top five. Our spirits were up as the end of the week was in sight. I promised all the first years a drink when we returned to our dormitory in Tokyo. They thought this was fantastic.

There was another three-hour training stint awaiting us on this penultimate day and there was to be no let up on the week's intensity. Our basic training for the first hour was a drag for we had to double and then triple our punches. This tightened up my shoulders as I tried my best to inject some speed in the combinations. Kobayashi was still roaming around like 'Hawkeye' so gave us as much scrutiny as he was able. There were about four old boys left as well as both Tanabes so we were still monitored closely like close circuit television. Just when you thought you had escaped detection of a minor mistake your name was broadcast loud and clear and you picked up the tempo to appease the senior grades.

Many times, throughout this week-long training course I asked myself what on Earth I was doing here. The answer was simple enough; I had no idea it would be like this. The training back at Nichi Dai had been tough for the past three months and I had persevered to the point of thriving on a diet of daily Karate. The cultural differences and the frequent loneliness had brought about other issues which I had not anticipated but eventually with the help of many around me I sought to overcome those problems and deal with them. Here on this summer camp, I was shocked at the intensity, the duration, and the overall frugality of our surroundings. But with the end of the camp in sight there was an overwhelming satisfaction that I had not quit even though the first two days were close to forcing the issue.

I sat after basic training on the second from last day and looked at the faces opposite me. The third and fourth years were weary like me and yet had experienced all this before, and were still here. I admired them. Takahashi caught my gaze across the dojo smiled and nodded. I felt it was a little nod of praise and I soaked it up.

We continued the day's training with more punching combinations, up and down, back, and forth, with pads and then without, an hour's worth before lining up for our counter punch training. This would no doubt prepare us mentally for the fighting the next day.

I was determined to put in some good work during this session so I would go into the next day with confidence. When the likes of Oshima, Kawano Tachizawa faced me as I stood in the line-up I refused to back off and did my best to counter as early as possible to get my punch in before I received a smack. I did all right, only once or twice falling for a cheeky feint from Oshima before he let go with the real punch. I took this as a compliment for he needed to resort to a feint before catching me out knowing I was perhaps giving him a problem in the speed department. It didn't make the punch in the mouth any less sore but I was on to him and looked forward to the next day. I also think he sensed my ambition and held his stare for a little longer as we maintained our awareness after each exchange. Despite him being a junior to the fourth years Oshima was probably top dog and carried an air of confidence that he felt was justified. He could be a humorous individual but with a ruthless streak, not a good combination from a close friend's point of view. But there were one or two who saw him as a scalp to take and I felt to be in the running.

Kihon Gumite prearranged sparring was the final training of the day and we carried our fighting demeanour into this routine. Every attack and counter were at full speed and with a loud kiai to match every move. Our fitness was returning and with it the atmosphere of a well drilled army outfit.

The evening before the final day was a treat for us all. A barbecue was set up on the grass outside the training hall. There were small steaks, sausages, and bread rolls. Where they managed to get this stuff was a mystery but it was as if the Red Cross had flown a special mission to come to our aid. There were various fish steaks wrapped in foil but I was only interested in the meat and bread plus lashings of ketchup. I looked for the barrel of lager that must be tucked away under the table somewhere but I searched in vain and settled for the cold juices. Our spirits were lifted as we gorged on the ample food and there was the feeling that things were getting back to normal as we wandered around freely, even chatting and joking with our seniors. A taxi drew up and out stepped Murase senpai. He greeted his seniors with sincerity before he too tucked in to the food. His presence among us made us a little uneasy. It was late in the week and the dreaded thought struck us that he may be along for the contest. I had heard that he liked to fight as regularly as possible and what better practice than with a bunch of tired individuals who had stuffed themselves silly the first chance they saw a plate of meat. I figured I'd had enough to eat anyway and placed my plate on the table.

The evening fizzled out by ten but generally we had enjoyed a relaxing time for perhaps the first time since we arrived here. We were still in good spirits when we returned to our room and the thought of early morning training didn't bother us so much as we continued to wonder about Murase's appearance among us. Asuka was an expert on Karate competitions and knew that Murase had won the All-Japan Student Championships in both '75 and '76, the only Nichi Dai student to win it twice since its inauguration in 1957. We listened and replied with a 'waw', (Japanese for wow), "sugoi", (great). He was also listed in the 1977 American magazine Black Belt Hall of Fame, fourth in their Top Ten Japanese Karateka at the age of twenty-two. He then went on to win the All Japan all styles contest and would be defending the title later this year.

TWENTY-ONE

September 1st 1981 and we were up for our final day of the gasshuku on Oshima. There had been a little rain during the night but not enough to avoid running to the field. The thought of a drop of rain during the run was wishful thinking for the cloudless sky held no hint of anything but another hot day ahead as we ran along the country roads bordered by hedgerows that were no more than five feet high. Birds sang only intermittently no doubt shocked by the sudden shouting emanating from the line of white figures that otherwise quietly padded by. There was not the intensity on the field this morning. Although we went through the same training routines but most of the seniors took little notice of us preferring to chat among themselves only looking up now and again to shout someone's name as a matter of habit. I had the impression they had stayed up far later than the rest of us the previous night so felt a little delicate in the brightness of the early morning sunlight. Only Kobayashi and Murase roamed around the field, the latter demonstrating his ability to leapfrog the tyres and then punch the makiwara with considerable force. He gave the iron geta a wide berth which I thought was a little inconsiderate but instead he did a few free fighting combinations bringing his legs into action. He was impressive in all departments and was showing an irritability to fight, like he had an itch that needed scratching.

Murase oversaw training after breakfast. He took us through our basics and then treated us to a technical fighting lesson, which, judging by the level of attentiveness from my fellow students was well appreciated. It was a fitting last lesson before the afternoon contest.

After lunch I found it hard to rest. I was restless with the thought of fighting later. I stretched in our room hoping to be as loose as possible before my first fight. I was a couple of hours away from my first competition in many months and the first against a depth of field that had so much to offer. There were talented fighters among us in every year and there was so much pride at stake especially with the more senior boys who had so much to lose. I felt I had to make the most of my kicking ability as well as to stand strong to counter. Scoring on the way back would not be tolerated particularly as Hideo Tanabe had attempted to instil this into us all week, all year in fact.

The first years and I made our way to the hall at two o'clock as normal carrying the barrel of refreshment. There were two areas crudely marked out with white tape. On the wall near the entrance was a piece of paper with our names written on. It was the draw. We checked first whether Murase's name was on it and we were relieved to see that he would not be entering this tournament. We joked that perhaps the opposition looked a little stiff for him especially with the prospect of him losing to a foreigner. Then they looked for their own names and the names of whom they would be fighting. I stood looking perplexed. I knew my name in Japanese katakana script but I had no idea what name was next to mine for my first fight.

"Aah Aasa" said Iidabashi "you fight Ikeda." A second year who I felt was not a genuine threat, but an excited shout from Asuka interrupted my thoughts. "Aasa if win, you fight Minamidae in next round if he wins first fight too." They thought the prospect of me and my old adversary Minamidae was to be the highlight of the day knowing there could be a repeat of our dojo encounter of several weeks earlier. My friends started taking bets and I wandered off to mentally prepare for the afternoon ahead.

I stood opposite Ikeda after I had waited some thirty minutes as others had begun their first round. Two areas were in action at the same time but I felt the eyes on me as I stepped up to fight. Kobayashi was refereeing on the other area with one of the old boys while Murase was the man in charge of my fight, along with another senior. The two Tanabe instructors sat to one side to watch the proceedings unfold.

Ikeda was a second year and quite anonymous to me. Steady in training but not particularly strong but I was not going to underestimate this young, fit, hungry fighter who stood with no emotion as we waited for the off. Murase shouted "shobu sanbon" (three-point match) and then "hajime" and I shot forward but quickly moved off to one side. His one two punches missed by a mile and I hit him straight away with my own counter punch to the face. I was awarded the point but straight away as the fight resumed, I got tangled in a scrappy encounter as Ikeda decided to try and rough me up a little. My legs felt heavy as I tried to kick and I realised I was far too close to try such a move and I felt his punch connect with a wallop. Ikeda's tactics had succeeded because I had not read the fight and tried to just resort to instinct and kick. We were level and I was blowing a bit from the extra spurt of adrenaline that my opponent had suddenly ignited inside me with his stronger determined attitude. I had to be strong in this fight, that was for sure, but stubbornness was not the answer. When we resumed after his score was awarded, I moved forward quickly and then out again and I felt this was the answer to his tactics. As I moved out, he was already punching thin air much the same as in the first ten seconds of our fight. This time I saw clearly my target and caught my opponent with a clean roundhouse kick off my leading right leg that staggered him. The fight was stopped momentarily as Murase held onto Ikeda for a second. He was ok and I was given the 'ippon' score. There was a little time remaining and I put it to good use by combining the kicks with the punches to score a couple more points. I was through to fight Minamidae who had also won earlier against one of the first years.

Minamidae would be my bogeyman on this day of competition. I watched as one or two more interesting fights unfolded between Kishiyama and Kawano, Oshima with Tachizawa, little Akii with Fujimoto, who surprised me with his strength. My first-year friend Enomoto had a blinder of a scrap with the fourth year Hakoishi to pull off a fine win. The others were busy fighting when I was up so I missed a lot more of the action.

I knew if I tried to fight with Minamidae by standing in front of him for too long I could lose and get hurt in the process. Nagashi zuki was to be the principal weapon for I anticipated he would come looking for me in his brash bullish way. My heart raced as I stood opposite the one man who had tried to bash me in the dojo when things got a little out of hand. He knew full well that he had backed me up against the wall in our previous encounter and perhaps he thought that psychologically he was slightly ahead. I knew I had the speed and superior technique over his limited fighting ability and that would have to do the job.

I looked at the face of my opponent and he looked a little scary, which was fine because he normally looked a lot worse. Minamidae would often bolster up the front of his mouth as if chewing on something distasteful, but I think it was his way of mustering up his courage. I leaned slightly forward in my ready posture, for I was eager to get off my line as quick as possible. At the sound of 'hajime' we both raced forward. I was quicker but my pre-fight plan hit a snag as I met my opponent head on. My reverse punch connected to his body a split second before his front kick hit mine. But I was away before his follow up punch came anywhere near me and so I had scored first, but his front kick did some damage for I was winded and had to breathe out with a silent groan to hide the discomfort. While Murase scored my point I messed around with my gi a little, pretending to straighten it up, all the while trying to catch my breath. The few extra seconds paid off and I stepped forward in left stance for the next encounter and as my aggressive adversary came hunting for me, I hit him with a left hand Nagashi zuki that snapped back his head and that stopped him from advancing any further. Another point awarded and I was now getting the measure of this thick-skinned angry individual. Minamidae by now was showing some reluctance in his advancement so I polished up with a face kick that reminded him of why he had lost his temper in the first place many weeks ago. The fight was in the bag and my opponent came forward after the bow and shook my hand with sincerity, he had lost but was gracious in the defeat.

I had no idea who would be my next opponent so I watched the other fights and tried to work out who could possibly be next. I knew there weren't many left in the frame so I sat and waited for my name to be called. There was a huge trophy placed on the table in the corner where the barrel of fluid normally sat and I was dreaming of lifting that prize when I heard "Aasa!" then "Kawano!" To have any chance of winning today I had to beat this opponent. I knew Kawano and I knew his ability and I wanted so much to beat him. This time Kobayashi had moved across to referee this fight and I realised we were down to one area which meant possibly the last four fighters.

Kawano was strong but I was confident I had the speed to get my points before he came too close. Kobayashi set us going and we raced off our line to get an early grip on the fight. Our punches were stifled in our impetuousness to score first and as Kawano grabbed me for the inevitable pick up, I smacked him with a 'Haito' which although is a Karate technique I had modified it like a short boxing hook. It worked, for he let go and continued to trade punches before Kobayashi separated us. No score was given. Our techniques were a bit untidy but I didn't mind for I felt I had to stand toe to toe for a while to hold my ground. The next encounter saw Kawano try to continue where he had left off, he rushed in and I sidestepped with another Nagashi punch that connected cleanly to his face. Kobayashi quickly jumped in to break us up and awarded me the point. What I didn't expect from Kawano was a good kick and he let go with a roundhouse as soon as we resumed the fight. As I stepped in to punch, I walked into the low kick and it was too late to prevent it from catching me clean in the lower belly. We were level, but I was as excited as I had ever been in any competition. I knew I was fighting one of the best in the club and I was pushing him all the way. I wasn't even breathing hard as we resumed our next engagement for I had settled down and any nerves I had were replaced with pure emotion of wanting to win. I feinted with a front kick and hoped to catch Kawano with the follow up roundhouse to the head but he was too smart for such a move and moved off to one side instead of trying to deal with the obvious dummy. I was moving in and out making the most of the fact that he was thinking his way through the next phase of the fight. As he thought for a moment too long, I virtually ran forward and hit Kawano's face with the crudest of reverse punches that knocked the stout fellow back a bit. He was caught cold and I was two one up. I knew then that there wasn't much time left and that my determined opponent would not hang about any longer. Inevitably when Kobayashi resumed the fight Kawano came off the line in a flash and I was sure I had got to him first with my left reverse punch to the body. At the same time his punch to my nose made my eyes water a little but after we were separated, I looked at Kobayashi and he was adamant in his decision that Kawano had scored not one but two punches quickly in succession and so awarded the two points. I lost when I thought I had won.

I was disappointed and embarrassed. Even though I had shown proper etiquette at the end of the fight I was reluctant for a moment to step away from the area. It was as if I had enjoyed the occasion so much, I wanted to do it again. I was still convinced in my own my mind that I was the faster in the last exchange of techniques and wanted to do a re-run. I knew better than to show any more dissent than I had already.

I thought that was it. My day was over and I would be getting changed without a result. But as I sat mulling over what could have been Tanabe shouted, "Aasa!" then "Fujimoto!" I jumped up and faced my friend who stood emotionless across the fighting area. I was wondering why I should be fighting again and how I was going to resurrect my motivation after such an encounter with Kawano.

Murase's shout of 'hajime' startled me into gear and automatically I started to 'rev' up my movement in a build up to attack. Fujimoto had been fighting well during this afternoon and had pulled off one or two victories much to the surprise of those watching and competing with him. Fujimoto was not particularly quick but he had a keen eye and his experience counted for much. He would not waste time moving excessively and to be honest I don't think his fitness was good enough for that anyway but he was a little like the old sixties fighters who never moved about much but were like a storm waiting to happen. As I feinted to attack, he didn't flinch but simply crossed his arms over as if to cover any target that may be exposed. Even though we were the same age he was like the proverbial old fox and I felt like the young jack rabbit.

I had fought Fujimoto many times before in the dojo and the fights always seemed to go my way. Or so I had thought. Those encounters in training probably meant nothing to Fujimoto, they were more important to me at the time and it didn't occur to me that he could do any better.

I attacked quickly with a razor-sharp front kick but his front hand intercepted the technique and his deft body movement kept him out of the way of my follow up punch. I pressed again with a one two punch combination and he calmly moved away to my right. From that moment he quickly let go with a low right roundhouse kick that caught me low near the groin. I saw it coming but couldn't get out of the way. It was a good point scored and a disaster for me for I was losing patience with him and with myself. Fujimoto wasn't going to attack; he was relying on me to make the mistakes so that he could clean up after. I had to make him believe I was about to attack but then draw out his counter. I pressed with as much commitment as I dared without getting too close. With a few quick hand movements plus a swivel of the hips I finally forced a reaction from Fujimoto and he leaned back to avoid the punch that never came. Instead, I followed through with a sweep off my rear leg that scythed away his front leg and caused him to turn a half circle that left his unguarded back exposed long enough for me to punch and get my reward. Fujimoto smiled at the deceit of my move but there was still time left for him to win the match. I felt however that the momentum was now with me and I repeated the front feint to roundhouse that caught him in the face with a slap. He reeled away in agony but I felt I hadn't made that much contact. I knew also he would not be shamming an injury to gain any sympathy. When he turned back to face me, he held his left hand under his right arm and I realised his pain was not from the kick to the face. My leg had caught his thumb enroute to his head and he was in no condition to carry on. Following an inspection from Tanabe it was probably broken and needed patching up immediately.

As I walked away from the fighting area one or two students approached me and congratulated me. "Sain" they said, third place. I had no idea how the draw was made or who had won overall but suddenly I felt a thrill of a sense of achievement. Not least in finishing a week-long training course from hell but also knowing that for a day I was a major player among a group of skilled fighters.

We lined up to finish the day's proceedings and the presentation was made. Oshima was overall winner after he had earlier beaten Kawano. Kawano was second with me in third. Oshima claimed the trophy that had stood regally in the corner of the dojo. Kawano was summoned forward to receive a small gift and next I stepped up to be given mine. Customarily, gifts no matter how small are always meticulously wrapped in Japan and so I held it proud as I bowed to the senior instructors not knowing what memento of my efforts were hidden under the wrapping. It is usual not to open the gift until later and I didn't want to spoil ceremony by tearing apart the paper like a kid on Xmas morning so I waited until I was outside the dojo before I succumbed to temptation. Under the pretty paper was a slender box that was of a size to hold a watch or maybe a bracelet. I removed the lid and there it was, a tube of toothpaste. I didn't know whether to raise it aloft or hang it around my neck. I was disappointed for a moment but then I felt stupid. After all, I hadn't won but I had done enough to be applauded by my fellow club members and that made the day a memorable one. Mind you, with what I had won I would have been a little sick had I lost my front teeth during the contest.

The reception in my room on my return was resounding. There was a lot of backslapping and adulation from the youngsters who had silently urged me to win after they had been eliminated from the tournament. Even though I wasn't technically a first year it was a result from our humble ranks that made them feel as happy as Larry so I jostled with them as we recreated a fight or two from the day's events. I showed them how my roundhouse kick had connected to the face of one or two of my opponents and young Hijikata hopped around swearing with his hand tucked under his other arm imitating the agony of Fujimoto's injury. A cruel way to celebrate but nobody could stop themselves from enjoying one of Hijikata's finest creations.

The week was over and with it the celebrations were soon under way. We were summoned to the dining room that evening where a spread of food to feed an army was already prepared for our arrival and standing like toy soldiers between the dishes were bottles of beer that glistened with the cold chill of the refrigerator.

We began the evening with the usual reserve while the instructors were present but gradually the atmosphere relaxed as the drinks flowed and the conversations lightened up. There was a call for each student in turn to stand at the front and sing a song, another one of those annoying Japanese customs especially for the non-melodic among us. But I duly followed suit and sang a simple song that had recently been in the charts before I had left England. I made a few slip ups but nobody noticed, which was hardly surprising for they knew not the song or what I was singing about. There were no musicians for me to keep time with so I made the best of my first ever attempt of acapella.

Murase stood and impressed us all with a song from his 'country'. He strolled among us like a seasoned cabaret performer. In his hand was a bowl of sake that he offered us to sip from time to time as part of his act. When Hijikata was called upon to sing, the fourth year Fukusyo, in a moment of spontaneous compassion, joined him with one arm around the shoulders and they were a fine double act. The performances were concluded when Kenji led us through the Nichi Dai song that told of rallying the spirit and fighting with unparalleled bravery.

It wasn't long before we were drunk and both Tanabes along with Kobayashi and one or two of the remaining instructors left us to wallow in our immature celebrations. After an hour of more singing and watching Asuka do a strip tease show Takahashi beckoned for me to join him and the other fourth years to a small bar five minutes walk along the dark country lanes. Inside the bar senior instructors were sat enjoying their own version of the week's climax although a little more subdued than the party I had just left. I sat stiffly and respectfully while Hideo Tanabe coached me retrospectively on my performance in the contest saying I should have done this and I didn't do that but I was only half listening for I didn't really care less at that moment of merriment. Fumihiro Tanabe interjected with his own few words and congratulated me on my fighting spirit and result. That went down a bit better and before long I was talking nonsense to the other instructors about England, movies, and pop music. It felt good to talk about something I knew was of great wonderment to my senior listeners. I chatted about the Beatles, The Rolling Stones and Sheena Easton almost as if I knew them personally. I kept their fascination and enjoyed keeping their wide-eyed open-mouthed attention.

The next morning came round with very little recollection of the previous night ending. I woke in a sorry state but thankful there was no training to look forward to. The bright sunshine half blinded me as I tried to focus on the activity around me. The rest of my roommates were already up and folding away their futons into what was Enomoto's sleeping space. I wearily stood and joined them in preparing to clear out.

The final day on Oshima Island was as pleasurable as the previous week had been unsavoury. We were summoned to the breakfast room for our last meagre meal. There was a silence among the ranks as the previous night's celebrations muted even the instructors this morning. Kawano displayed a lump under his eye, from the contest scrap with Oshima, that matched the raw egg on his plate and Oshima sat smirking as he quietly enjoyed the silent boast of his handiwork. Kawano remained quiet and reminded me of an animal licking the wounds of battle as he ate the raw egg from his bowl of rice that was held in his paw like hands.

Our day began with a visit to some botanical gardens. No doubt our learned instructors felt it necessary for us to be educated in the wildlife of our host island. To tell the truth I think most of us were looking forward to seeing the back of it. While we queued outside the garden entrance Murase gave us an impromptu warm up, no doubt a little frustrated after watching the previous day's contest. I was impressed with the kicking ability of Murase as he ran through a combination of powerful front, round, and sidekicks in his khaki shorts. His face displayed an emotion that was as ruthless as the heavy boots that swung through the air missing the heads of the first years Tanaka and Yatabe by the width of the shoelaces. Murase's performance was watched by us all but was only let down by his dress sense that was almost comical. Considering we were to look at a few plants it seemed he was dressed for a safari. All he needed was a wide brimmed hat with corks hanging from it.

Our day continued with a visit to a dairy farm. As a West Country lad this was as exciting as watching milk pasteurise, but most of both students and instructors insisted on having their picture taken while stood next to a black and white cow. Even Murase and Kobayashi posed with one arm around the cow's neck as if Marilyn Monroe herself were snuggling up.

Things improved somewhat with a visit to the beach. We had a sumo wrestling contest on the volcanic sand that was as black as coal and the swim that followed lasted much of the afternoon, only to be interrupted by having lunch from the little bento boxes that we ate while sat on the rocks in and around the water.

This final day spent relaxing and swimming did much for the mood of those who were perhaps coming to the end of their tether from the week's training and for those who had not performed well in the competition. The previous days' toil and turbulence were quickly forgotten in just a few hours of fun and frolics. We were paid off cheaply I thought for our diligent efforts and the senior instructors acted like they had given us a weekend in Disneyland. It didn't matter for we were soon on the mini bus and returned to port in fine fettle ready to cross back to the mainland.

The return to the Nichi Dai dormitory after the previous week's quite inhospitable, cramped conditions was a relief. 'There's no place like home' was the overall feeling as we slung our bags across the tatami floor and pulled out our musky futons from behind the sliding doors.

I looked around the room as each individual set about settling back into a familiar routine and prepared for the following day. The week -long summer camp on Oshima Island had been a shock not only to me but also to all my roommates in their first year here. However, like me they had come through the other side in one piece and so quietly carried a little more confidence in their mannerisms.

Enomoto sat tall next to me munching on some dried squid out of a packet not worrying about the salty smell that wafted across my sleeping space, in fact he didn't seem to be worrying about anything else for that matter, which made a change.

Towards the far end of the room Hijikata, Asuka and Iidabashi sat together near the open window near one another chatting excitedly about the events of the summer gasshuku that had now become a subject of 'we were there and we did that'.

Tanaka and Yatabe were a little more subdued as they sat

cross- legged repairing their frayed dogi while watching a samurai series unfold on the telly with its usual inevitable climax of tedious violence. These two first years did not fare too well on the summer camp and were perhaps a little embarrassed to be wholly proud at its conclusion but would somehow work towards an earnest resumption of training.

Resuming training however brought us all together as we wondered where our training would take place in view of the fact our dojo was no longer standing proud and erect in the car park adjacent to the motor club next door. We didn't have to wonder too long for the captain Tanemura, who rarely lowered himself by entering our room, appeared at the doorway. We all stood and the confidence I had just witnessed among the first years was clearly limited to our own company. I understood " ashita" and "renshu" as the information that was conveyed was about the following day's training but I had to wait for Tanemura's departure before I was filled in on the rest. It seemed we would be training for the next few days in the fencing dojo at the basement of our dormitory while the fencers were still away on vacation. After that it was to be on the roof!

There was still a week or so before all students from all the different clubs of our dormitory would be back from their own various summer vacations and gasshuku training camps. For a few days then there was no hot water for us because the boilers were not yet switched on so we washed in cold water or on a few occasions visited the public baths that were in the vicinity of the station.

There were no classes either yet for the students to attend during the day which meant an extra two hours training at eleven o' clock to fill the hiatus. So, with the relief of having completed a week-long course of seven hours a day came the news we would be resuming with six. On top of that there was the All-Japan University Championships on the horizon at the end of September so we were getting back to the old routine of plenty of fighting.

The two-hour mid-morning session was a mixture of basic training and fitness work through repetition of combination techniques. The old fencing dojo was a little longer than our former training place but it made no difference in our efforts to get to the other end at top speed. Tanabe did not always attend these morning classes but was inevitably at the evening training when there was fighting to be done. The oncoming tournament meant a daily dose of the rough stuff and it was all systems go for the ambitious ones to make their mark in order to be selected.

One afternoon however it seemed one of the younger among us overstepped the mark in his zealousness to match his skills with a senior. As I sat waiting for my turn to fight, I saw out of the corner of my eye Hijikata wheel suddenly and uncharacteristically away from Oshima and bend over with his hands on his knees. I thought for a moment he was going to be sick until I saw a tooth drop to the floor, followed by some blood and then another tooth. Oshima stood over Hijikata with a scowl, his eyebrows knitted together in anger. He shouted at his kohai to clean up the mess that was forming on the floor, the floor of the fencing club that we were only temporarily using. I wondered at the time whether any blood was ever spilt during fencing classes and I wondered further if they had characters such as Oshima allowed to wield an epee or a foil. Tanabe viewed the scene from the other end of the dojo and shouted to a couple of the other first years to help clean up the unsightly remnants of Hijikata's front row.

I felt sick to the stomach that Oshima should deem it necessary to hit Hijikata hard enough to produce such a devastating result. The size between them, not to mention the vast experience, did in no way leave any room for mitigation on Oshima's part and I think his anger after the fact was an attempt to cover up this oversight of his. Only it had the opposite effect. His own third year colleagues said nothing but looked on with disdain and I think Oshima lost a little respect that evening. The dojo was silent as Hijikata went about cleaning up the last of the blood-spattered remnants of the incident and the last he would ever see of his two front teeth.

Hijikata was a forlorn figure for a few days after the Oshima incident. If anything were to test his mettle and resolve to continue training at this Karate club then no doubt this period was it. Even those of us around him were bitter and a little dismayed that Tanabe who, though present at the time, had not in any way admonished Oshima for his handiwork. We were part of an institution that was self-sufficient, the buck stopped with Tanabe and so it was not as if anyone could go anywhere to make a complaint. But who would want to if there were? I'm sure throughout the time Hijikata sat alone by the window watching the traffic sail by he wrestled with his thoughts of returning home and for a while our attempts to cheer him up seemed to go wide of the mark. But the best place for Hijikata the next few days was the dojo. The daily routine of Karate, sleeping, eating and more Karate had the simple effect of slotting him back into the familiar, young, not quite so funny, first year.

After a week or so of training in the fencing dojo morning, noon, and night we were pushed up onto the roof. This was fine until about six o'clock when daylight dimmed. The lights that surrounded us were not state of the art 'flood' types so the fighting that followed this time was more than risky, it was nothing but stupid. I thought a good idea would have been for us to fight in the first or even second hour of training when there was plenty to see and not even a shadowy light descending. But as routine would have it, we were reduced to sparring, albeit a little lighter, by virtual candlelight.

The floor of the roof was made of rough bitumen so our already hardened feet had to be protected with more tape particularly around the smaller toes to prevent what I could only imagine could be diagnosed as 'tarmac feet'. Our routine was the same three hours only the scenery was different, which did make a change. The one good thing of course with the open-air training was the relief from the heat and I noticed for the first time as training came to an end at seven o'clock there was a coolness under the darkened skies that I had not enjoyed since the first few days of my arrival.

TWENTY-TWO

During mealtimes my ability to use chopsticks had inevitably improved somewhat since the early days among the Japanese, but there were times I still struggled a bit. When there was a large fish for example to be dissected on the plate in front of me it was a case of trying to separate the meat of the fish from the backbone within, without resorting to fingers. This meant using the chopsticks in a different manner. Instead of squeezing the two sticks together to pick something up they would be speared into the flesh together then separated to tear away the fish meat. That's how my colleagues around me demonstrated so swiftly and easily. I did a rough version of this but only succeeded making a mess in comparison. I would tear away small bones together with the meat that came away and did my best to eat what was on the end of my sticks. When those around me had finished their meal there was a perfect skeleton of fish left on their plate and nothing else. My plate looked like the fish had been dropped from a great height and died a horrible slow death from scavengers. I would walk away from the table less than full and sweating from my efforts.

After one such meal I ended up with a huge fish bone stuck in my throat. That evening Enomoto suggested I "'dwink' wice", that is, to eat rice without chewing. I remembered hearing the same back home about 'drinking' bread. Enomoto's advice unfortunately failed to work and for two days I carried this bone of what felt like a killer whale at the back of my throat. As I gagged one evening on the roof during training little Takahashi asked my problem. He took me over to one of the spotlights that dimly lit our open-air dojo and held my head back to take a closer look. Takahashi's sudden laughter startled me and attracted further attention from the other seniors. They all took it in turns to see the bone lodged below my tonsils before Hijikata was ordered to fetch some tweezers from the first aid box. I felt a little worried when the tweezers were handed to Minamidae of all people, but he passed them over to Takahashi who quickly extracted the offending sliver of bone.

It was one of those sultry afternoons in mid-September when the prospect of training on the roof looked in doubt when the heaviest rain in two weeks fell from the skies. Ordinarily this would not have meant anything unusual but with the fencing dojo no longer free suddenly we seemed dojo-less. We thought that possibly training might be cancelled but we sat anyway at three thirty in our rooms waiting for further instructions. Tanabe sensei in all his wisdom shouted from his room for us to don our karate gis and wait outside our rooms in the narrow corridor. My roommates and I stood opposite the fourth years while the second and third years stood just as quietly further along. There were whispers and shoulder shrugs indicating no knowledge of our destination. Surely, we weren't going to train in the rain! We could hear it lashing the windows of our rooms.

"Tanemura!" shouted Tanabe still from the confines of his room.

"Hai!" replied the captain who was embarrassed for not knowing the answer to Tanabe's empty command. There was silence, but a pregnant one as we all investigated the worried face of Tanemura. Suddenly the door to Tanabe's room swung open and our head coach peered from around the narrow opening,

"Taiso!" he commanded.

"Hai!" came the response. Our stiff shoulders dropped in recognition of that one word. "Warm up!" We were to train where we were. Even though the corridor leading from our rooms opened by the top of the stairs there was hardly enough room to swing a first year, yet we trained. We adapted by doing our basics on the spot before taking our turn on the pads in the space near the stairs. We had the ankle weights that we put to good use as well as the small dumbbells. It was a ridiculous circumstance and some of the training that day seemed futile. While some did the attack and defence training the others had to stand tight against the wall to wait their turn. We didn't really get a lot done under the circumstances but we filled the three hours without Tanabe bothering to show his face again until suppertime.

After ten days of training six hours a day since the end of the summer camp the university dormitory returned to normal and the students resumed their college work during the day. This meant the cessation of the eleven o'clock training and more free time for me to do not very much. In a way I was sorry not to be occupying those two hours with some familiar company even though it meant extra dojo time.

I had seen very little of Kobayashi sensei since the gasshuku, but I was not surprised when he dropped in one Friday night to take me to Uenohara. Typically, he wanted to ensure I thanked those who had helped me throughout the summer vacation. I had bought a couple of bottles of 'Shochu' (fortified sake) and some candy at the shop in Oshima port prior to boarding the return ferry trip. It is a Japanese custom to bring a small gift with you when visiting someone's home and so for the first time I was able to hand out gifts to Mrs Kobayashi, Mr Sakamoto, and his wife, who all showed great delight in accepting my presents. That weekend I was herded around the town of Uenohara and thanked various people for their generous hospitality. I visited the home of Mr Tsuda, one of the principles of the local high school and he was adamant that I continue with the teaching of the six schoolboys that I had helped through the summer vacation. It was agreed that I could teach for a couple of hours every Sunday at the Sakamoto restaurant, as long as Tanabe Sensei would give his consent.

That Sunday afternoon while I relaxed at Kobayashi's house my host came in waving a letter. "From Shiomitsu Sensei" he said. He sat across from me and read the symbols that were scattered across the page. I was eager to hear what words of encouragement Shiomitsu would have for me particularly now I had been here a while. After reading the letter Kobayashi pointed to some letters "Look! Your name" he said. "Shiomitsu sensei said "how is Arthur getting on?" I smiled at the mention of my name. "If he's not training hard send him home!" My smile dropped. Was that it? There was a silence. "Come," said Kobayashi "we go running". As if the letter was a reminder to my host that I was not a tourist we went running to the dojo and trained for an hour before I was driven back to Hachimanyama.

With the approach of the All-Japan University championships at the end of September the need for a decent training venue was paramount. Tuesdays were still allocated for Suidobashi at Nihon University headquarters and this also became our training venue on Saturdays. Throughout the rest of the week, we travelled alternately between two other places. A high school gymnasium and a Kendojo, both in Medaimae, a few stops along the track from Hachimanyama. Training at these different training venues each afternoon subliminally became a bit of a social occasion as the various age groups of the Karate club travelled together. We would walk in uniform of Karate club t-shirts and tracksuit bottoms carrying with us our Karate club bags slung over our shoulders. The first years would chat and joke quietly among themselves while the older boys would be more vociferous often aiming funny or derogatory comments to the junior kohais.

Apart from carrying bags filled with mitts and focus pads it was not unusual to see the first-year group carrying more than one kit bag. I saw on one occasion four bags draped across the shoulders of Enomoto so that the senpais could travel light. All in all, it brought the students closer together and the return journey would often be significantly better. We were given extra time to allow for the train journey. This meant slipping away for a quick beer enroute before supper. It was quite usual for me to leave for training with the first years but return in the company of the third or fourth-year group.

As if the approaching contest was not enough to intensify our training there was also the odd time when we would be paid a visit by one or two spectators. During these visits, Tanabe, as if to prove a point, would see to it that we impressed our spectators. One such visitor was the young seventeen-year-old, Masuda, who months earlier I had witnessed win a high school tournament. He sat quietly while we did all the shouting and hollering. He was obviously considering joining the Nichi Dai contingent and I remember thinking as we went through a fierce session on the pads that Tanabe was supposed to be impressing the young lad not frightening him.

Then one evening half way through our training two Europeans walked in and stood nervously in the corner. At the break Tanabe summoned me to speak with the two strangers. They were from Italy and were Shotokan practitioners on the way to the Japan Karate Federation Headquarters. They were also writing for a martial arts magazine and wanted permission from Tanabe to stay and train for a week at Nihon University. Tanabe sensei stood up and made a fuss of looking them over which made them shrink with nervousness.

"One week ok," said Tanabe. The promise of magazine coverage obviously too tempting to resist. Then Tanabe looked at me and said, "Aasa, onegai shimasu!" I was to look after our guests for their short stay.

We trained hard and fast the remainder of that evening while the two guests watched, but Tanabe left a little earlier than usual so the fighting was left for another day. I made small talk with the two Italians as we returned to our dormitory and I found it refreshing to have some different company around. They unloaded their belongings all over the place so they could make room for some place to sleep. It was a bit of a squeeze when I had first moved in so now, we were like sardines as we all pushed up further towards the window. Still, no one complained, it was important they were made welcome.

The following day I roused our visitors for the run and no doubt due to fatigue of their travelling they were reluctant to rise but followed us to the park where they ran slowly and wearily. Still, the rest of the day was full of excitement as the three of us spoke of many things and they were thrilled at the prospect of training in Japan.

That evening training was at the Kendojo and this gave our two visitors a further treat. Often, we would have to wait for the high school students to finish their Kendo practice before vacating the dojo. The atmosphere of the Kendo club was not unlike our own Karate environment. Lines of young men dressed in traditional flowing Kendogi with their bamboo shinai held in both hands outstretched covering the length of the dojo in quick steps as they shouted fervently and furiously at their imaginary attackers. Then with their head protectors on they would perform fast and aggressive attack and counter techniques with their partners producing loud smacks from their weapons on the hard protective head gear. These smacks mingled with the kiais produced a deafening sound that carried much farther than the four walls.

Our own training that evening started with the usual slow build-up of a lengthy stretching routine and a 'loosening' basic training hour. Then Tanabe sensei turned up and the fun started. We started with the usual repetition of hundreds of kicks, on the spot and then up and down the full length of the dojo. Without rest we continued with the pad work and rattled off the one two combinations hitting the pads as we went across the width of the dojo performing a couple of hundred repetitions before handing the pads to our partners. I took the pads from Enomoto when "Yame!" and "gotai!" for a changeover was ordered. While I rested, I looked across at the two visitors and they were clearly having a tough time. Their movement was not good as they tried to keep up their movements in time with the shouts from one to ten. They were losing time with those around them and with it their concentration. To be fair Tanabe paid them little heed but that did not excuse them from the pressure of the pace that was set for them.

After a short break we put on our mitts and six of us lined up at one end of the dojo. The rest of the class lined up in front of those waiting and proceeded to attack with a kick. With our backs to the wall, we side stepped and countered the oncoming technique as best as possible moving as quick as we could to avoid contact. Sometimes it was possible to step forward and thwart the kick altogether to deliver the perfect counter. Other times we would side step a little too early and the oncoming kick would change its course and find its new target easily. These were times when Tanabe stood over us urging us to be strong and resolute. I would often finish this type of training with bruises the full length of my forearms as the kicks were blocked or swept aside to prevent them slamming into my body.

This evening with our roving reporters in our midst it seemed Tanabe wanted to give them something to write about. They had taken a few pictures the day before while we were training. Now I wished I had the chance to stop and take their picture as they were clearly at the mercy of intense fatigue and dehydration. We stopped for another break and our visitors quickly took off their mitts to which Tanabe shouted at me as if it were my fault. I told them we hadn't finished but to sit quietly before our final hour. They sat glumly, their spirit on the verge of breaking. Before setting out from home they clearly hadn't prepared for what might come and now wished that perhaps they had trained a bit harder.

We were up and fighting after five minutes rest and to be honest I didn't see much of how the two Italians fared, for I was too busy with my own opponents. Each one of us had to work hard in our fighting. There were those who wanted to be selected for the All-Japan Championships and there were those who were perhaps weren't bothered but had to fight hard with the former. Which made the fighting an interesting merry-go-round. I had my fair share of competition from Tachizawa, Oshima, AND Kawano one after the other. I was hoping after that maybe Tanabe was considering putting me in the team as some sort of wild card so was giving me tough opposition to see how I would cope. Bring it on I thought even though I felt I had lost heavily to Oshima without giving much in return.

The end of training that evening was memorable. I remember asking the two visitors from Italy how they were, which brought back memories of when Kikuta came to me after my first three hours in the dojo. They were clearly exhausted and said "ok". I remember saying the same thing but I too probably didn't convince Kikuta that I was ok. The two visitors changed quietly while all around them there was the usual banter of seniors winding each other up, going through the motions of successful scoring techniques and mimicking the poorer movements of their kohais. This was usual, for it reflected the relief that another three-hour training stint was at an end.

That evening I shared a beer with the Italians and Kikuta, who was his usual curious self. The visitors to Nichi Dai said they had not expected such arduous training. I smiled at the reminder of my first time here and told them to make the most of their week for it would soon be gone.

That night after supper they were sleeping soundly long before lights out at ten.

The next morning at five forty I roused them for the morning run. They sat up but couldn't move very easily. "Come on" I repeated.

"Ok" one of them replied while looking for his socks among clothes scattered around him. As we did our warm up on the street below, I watched the doorway but nobody else came out. I considered dashing up the stairs to hurry them up but I jogged along the path to the park with the rest not wishing to get left behind. At seven when we returned to our room, I expected to see the Italians fast asleep on their futons. However, I was shocked to see the empty spaces that had once been two people. They and their belongings were gone. They hadn't even folded away their futons. Not a thank you or a bye your leave. The first years ran around kicking and punching celebrating that their room was back to normal. I folded away the two extra futons before we all went out and cleaned the toilets.

TWENTY-THREE

The All-Japan University Championships was the most important contest of that year. University club teams from all over Japan, from all styles, assembled at the Budokan in Tokyo for the chance to win top honours. The week leading up to the competition our training schedule gradually wound down so that we barely did an hour for the last couple of days. This ensured that each competitor was injury free for one thing and in top shape. Also, the previous months' hard preparation followed by a lull in training produces a fervent hunger to get out on the mats and get stuck in. Alas, I was not to be included in any of the fighting so my frustrated body would only be put to good use carrying the `bento` lunches to the tournament, along with all the others who hadn't been selected. We were, in short, official cheerleaders.

The Budokan main auditorium was an impressive expanse of polished wood probably the size of a football pitch. On this day there were three green tatami fighting mats with markings ready for the contestants to take their places. This floor space was sunk a good ten feet below the tiered seating that surrounded the whole area and so this gave a superlative viewpoint of all the proceedings.

The Japanese love their ceremonies and so before the contest started there was an impressive parade of all teams wearing their Karategi before lining up and listening to the official opening. University flags of all colours and designs were draped from the seating areas above down over the edge of the balcony and all around the perimeter.

I sat with the rest of my club mates above the teams behind our own University club flag waiting in anticipation at what I hoped would be a memorable day for Nichi Dai. The teams broke from their neat lines and I watched jealously as seven of my colleagues warmed up intently led by Oshima. Enomoto, Kishiyama, Sugimoto, Akii, Kawano, Tachizawa, a team that was a mixture of youth and experience. I felt confident on their behalf.

There was further ceremony when five members of the Nichi Dai team demonstrated Seishan kata together while the rest of the Budokan fell silent. Once that was completed a round of applause signified the start of the early rounds of fighting.

Nichi Dai stood patiently to one side of the contest area waiting for the teams ahead of them to finish their matches. Soon enough Akii, Oshima, Kawano, Tachizawa and Kishiyama lined up ready to go. Akii always went out first. His lightning-fast start and fearless attitude often took opponents by surprise so Tanabe would rely on him to get the first win. This worked. But it was the only thing that went to plan that day. Oshima won his fight, although after some close encounters for too much contact and penalty points awarded to the other side that saw Tanabe shouting from his coaching seat. Then disastrously Kawano could only draw and Tachizawa and Kishiyama both lost. I didn't even know the team that faced them and perhaps the five Nichi Dai boys were not taking them too seriously either and maybe had their eye on the later rounds. The wins were even but the number of points scored went to the other side. Nichi Dai was out.

Hideo Tanabe walked away from the area in disgust. We were all summoned to meet outside the Budokan immediately. It wasn't yet lunchtime so the bento boxes of rice, fish and pickles were still in our bags unopened. Outside in the warm sunshine the sombre mood of the team's performance hung like a black cloud over our heads. We waited. An hour passed and there was no sign of Tanabe, Hideo or Fumihiro for that matter who had been watching the fighting from the head table. Another thirty minutes saw the emergence of Kobayashi sensei from the building so we straightened up. He said nothing and simply stood with us as if he too were to blame for the frightful result. I guess he felt partly responsible that his young charges were in this predicament.

Finally, after nearly two hours spent waiting for the inevitable both Tanabe brothers strode towards us. Fumihiro Tanabe, Kantoku coach stood in front of us and ripped into us all. His fury was startling and I was under the impression that this was not a team rollicking but a club one. The admonishment continued for a full ten minutes or so with every pause filled with our replies of "hai" and "hai so!" Finally, we were dismissed and I turned to Enomoto to ask what was said.

"No Sunday off for a month." I knew this day would be a memorable one. I thought about the implication for me while we all made our way back to Hachimanyama. I was due to start teaching on Sundays from that weekend in Uenohara and was worried my chance to earn some more yen was compromised. As if my thoughts had been read Kobayashi sensei turned up at the dormitory early that evening to tell me that Tsuda sensei of Uenohara wanted to see me. We were in the car within twenty minutes and on the way, I was put at ease with the knowledge that my Sundays for teaching English were safe.

That evening I was entertained at the Tsuda household and

fussed over by his charming wife, Sakamoto's sister-in-law. It seemed that Tsuda sensei had some business to attend to in Korea the following week and wondered if I would want to join him in order to sort out my visa. Although it wouldn't be possible to officially change the visa status I could, however, take a chance to re-enter Japan with a new tourist one. Since my six months were coming to an end, I had to take the opportunity without hesitation.

On top of this Tsuda sensei insisted on paying for the flight and hotel to save on my limited resources. I was overwhelmed and felt deeply indebted to this schoolteacher who barely knew me. It meant I was possibly going to remain in Japan the full twelve months, which was my original ambition. Furthermore, it also suddenly dawned on me that should my extension succeed, I could fight in the All-Japan Wado Tournament that was scheduled for December. Now that was a result!

Things moved fast that weekend. I spent that night at the Sakamoto household then helped him in the kitchen of the restaurant the following morning. In the afternoon I resumed the teaching of English to the six boys I had taught during the vacation. The evening was filled with more conversation at the family table with Mr and Mrs Sakamoto after the kids were finally put to bed. I declined the offer to go to a bar for I wanted an early night to get back to Nichi Dai the following Monday morning.

Training for the next few days was miserable. Tanabe sensei was grumpy for obvious reasons and he felt it was his duty that we should be too. In the dojo he asked about my trip to Korea and asked me to bring back some decent fighters because his lot were useless. I couldn't help but smile at his cruel joke and I said I would do my best. He looked around quickly at Oshima who dropped his head to stare at the floor.

"Baka" said Tanabe "Minna baka da na!" 'These are all a bunch of fools' were his words.

Despite his deep disappointment and no doubt embarrassment at the recent early exit of his team Tanabe sensei couldn't totally hide his fondness for the students he coached. He was in it as much as they were and he could have easily had a few days off to wallow in his own misery but it was his duty to straighten them out and return them to a winning attitude.

My head was in getting ready to fly to another country and on Wednesday I was packed for the next morning early start. I was taken to Narita airport by Kobayashi sensei where I met Tsuda sensei. From there we flew by Japan Airlines to Seoul, capital of South Korea.

Arriving in Seoul that Thursday morning was an experience. Unlike the neat, orderly disciplined country I had just left, South

Korea seemed a country trying to play catch up with its neighbours. There was pandemonium in the airport with crowds of passengers not knowing where to go for their bags. When we finally emerged from the terminal building, we stood in a queue at a taxi rank. There was a line of cars that seemed to have been supplied by a second hand car salesman. We jumped in a cab that was either an old Toyota or Datsun. It was the next in line on the rank so we had no choice on the matter anyway. As we sped along the potholed highway there was a constant thumping coming from beneath our feet. Eventually our driver stopped at the roadside without indicating, much to the annoyance of the cars behind and we all got out to kneel and peer underneath. Half his exhaust pipe had been dragging the ground. I helped him by lying underneath to hold it up so he could tie it up with some parcel string. Tsuda sensei found it all very amusing as we continued our way only to be held up by a sudden traffic problem. As we slowly inched forward, we saw two cars had pulled to one side and the two drivers were having a fight. I had been in Japan nearly six months and didn't so much as see a row (dojo excluded of course). I was in Korea on day one and it was all kicking off. Tsuda sensei said Koreans liked a fight and they were good at head butts. I thought I would bear that in mind.

Although Japan and Korea are neighbouring countries, I sensed that there was no love lost between the two. They traded with each other, exploited what there was of interest from one another and did their level best to smile in passing through gritted teeth. A bit like the English and the French, I guess.

As we neared the city centre there was a strange contrast of modern high- rise buildings alongside run down scruffy wooden shacks. It was almost like somebody had decided to put a farm here and there in London's Dockside development. Very similar to the mixture of old and new cars I had witnessed on the roads. I saw some banners stretched across the road above our heads that celebrated the Seoul Olympics in 1988. I remembered then that they had just been awarded the Olympics for seven years' time so there were these posters and banners everywhere in an effort to convince their own people that they were now global. I felt all they had to do now was convince the rest of the world.

The few days I spent in Seoul were limited in activity. My sightseeing was restricted to the route between my hotel and the Sheraton where Mr Tsuda was staying and where there was a casino. Gambling in Japan is forbidden so a trip to Seoul gives the Japanese an opportunity to exploit that little area of interest. I guess the Japanese smile on their way into Korea looking forward to winning some won (the Korean currency) and the Koreans smile back as they fill up with yen. Perfect.

I was not going to be tempted to offload any of my hard-earned cash so I watched as Mr Tsuda worked hard at the roulette wheel. Instead of taking things slow he piled on large amounts of chips on any one number and got excited as the silver ball whizzed around the wheel. He almost seemed to enjoy losing for he smiled widely at the female croupier each time she raked in his used chips. Then Mr Tsuda gave me a handful of chips and told me to go and play. I sat across from my smiling friend and strategically placed chips across various numbers, on corners etc, reducing the odds but increasing my chances. I started to win a little so I became a little more adventurous as my confidence, and luck, increased. Gradually over the period of a couple of hours my starting stake of around twenty quid had grown to about one hundred and seventy. By this time Tsuda sensei was broke for the day and was now standing over my shoulder enjoying my little success. It didn't occur to me at the time that maybe he was waiting for me to throw a few chips his way so that he could restart his lost game. I was protecting my winnings at all cost and was too focussed on what was happening in front of me to think of anything else. However, inevitably I started to lose my luck so I called it a day and cashed in my chips at around one hundred- and fifty-pounds worth. I was elated.

On my return to my hotel that evening I ordered a steak meal and a bottle of wine to my room and rang my mum, no expense spared.

Looking out over Seoul city that evening was a strange experience. At that time South Korea was still under martial law so there was a curfew from midnight until four in the morning. Nobody but the military was allowed on the streets during those hours. From my tenth floor I studied intently the eerie criss-cross of empty streets down below waiting, almost hoping, to see if anybody dared to venture out. Nothing. Now and again headlights caught my attention but they were from the army vehicles patrolling what seemed a deserted city.

The three days in Korea swiftly passed by and the long hot summer that seemed to have gone on forever was finally coming to an end. For the first time in nearly six months, I wore a jacket when I boarded the plane to return to Japan. I looked forward to getting back to a more familiar environment and returning to training.

At Narita airport Tsuda sensei and I both collected our bags and queued for immigration. Tsuda sensei went quickly on through the 'Japanese only' gate and I stood waiting behind some other foreign nationals in the 'alien' line. When it was my turn to pass through the immigration officer studied my passport closely then asked me "Why are you coming back to Japan?"

I was a little taken aback at both the question and the sternness of my interrogator.

"I like it here" was my only feeble reply.

"But you have only just left" he stated.

I realised that this was no ordinary routine question, answer and have a nice day conversation. He stood up and summoned another official who also studied my passport. I looked over their shoulders to search for my friend but he had happily strolled on through without looking back. I was then ordered to join these two officers in a nearby office.

"You have been in Japan six months already! You should go home now."

The seriousness of that statement must have registered in my face. I was worried.

"Where do you stay in Japan?"

I was told beforehand not to mention Nihon University because other foreign nationals had created problems and brought some unwanted attention to the Karate club. I told them about Kobayashi sensei but I couldn't produce his address or even his telephone number. I managed to find Sakamoto's number at the restaurant, which they rang. In that serious moment I thought how odd that they should be ordering a sushi takeaway from such a distance. There was some conversation with Mr Sakamoto's wife and they hung up.

"How much money do you have?"

"About two thousand pounds in Uenohara" I lied. I knew they were worried that I may be looking for illegal employment so I tried to convince them that I was simply here to enjoy their culture and practice Karate in their wonderful country.

"What grade are you?" That seemed like a question of interest rather than for further background information and I sensed the conversation was turning my way a little. I told them of my instructors back home, who had graduated from Nihon University and they immediately recognized the name.

"You should try to go there, if possible," said one of them. "Very hard training," I smiled at the irony of the situation. They talked among themselves for a couple of minutes and finally one of them opened my passport and said,

"Ok final extension, then you must go home!" and stamped it. I thanked them and quickly left the office feeling like a fugitive as a small crowd watched me go through the gate.

Tsuda sensei was anxiously waiting for me in the terminal. I opened my passport and saw they had given me ninety days. That meant I was staying until the sixth of January 1982. I felt the luck of the casino had followed me that day for I was nearly at the mercy of Japanese deportation.

There was a small ounce of regret that I wouldn't be returning home sooner. When I returned to Nichi Dai that day from the airport another three months suddenly seemed a long time when I looked at the calendar hanging in our room. Still, my first-year colleagues welcomed me back and we busily prepared ourselves for the off to go training.

There was a newfound impetus in my training, which was accredited to the approaching All Japan Wado Ryu Championships. Initially they were to be held in November but they would later be put back to December due to some unforeseen problems within the Wado Kai association. With the dismal result our club had suffered in the September contest our training became a fierce and determined undertaking in order to succeed in all departments in Ohtsuka Sensei's own tournament.

This meant the return visits of some old boys who would also be competing in the senior section. Tachizawa older brother of our third year, Murase, who would soon be competing in the All Japan All Style tournament and Aikawa a slightly built, nervous looking character but who had the smoothest of movements that typified our brand of Karate.

It was one evening, in the dojo belonging to the Kendo club, that Murase shared with us his full fight philosophy. After instructing us through the hour of focus pad training he had us mitted up and ready to go. He explained that the fight in the dojo should not always end with a point scored but that there should be a further element of reality. In other words, takedowns, knee, and elbow strikes and anything else that should come to mind in the 'mix up'. He explained all this with the help of Kawano whom he slung around like a rag doll while demonstrating the takedown and the other strikes not ordinarily found on the contest area.

We sat in a line while Murase matched up a couple of fighters. Then he decided on an opponent for himself. His outstretched finger ran along our line and stopped at me. "Aasa" he beckoned.

"Hai!" I jumped up and eagerly stood opposite him. My heart was pounding unlike I had felt for a while. I had become accustomed to the fight patterns of all my fellow students so this was a new experience. I also knew of this man's capabilities but was keen to impress. I knew he had seen me fight on the summer course and I guessed he saw a modicum of opposition in this twenty-one-year-old 'gaijin'.

From the command 'hajime' I shot forward to get in an early attack, just the way we had often trained, hoping to unsettle my opponent. My ploy might have worked had it not been for the fact I was up against the most successful fighter ever to graduate from Nihon University. Murase pounded me with a perfect Nagashi zuki that hit me on the right side of my head and halted my quick advancement. I had not been hit so hard since my days in the boxing ring. That fuzzy, ringing sensation went through my skull and I had to briefly move away to clear my head but I immediately stepped back in and threw my favoured lead leg reverse roundhouse kick. It found its mark perfectly and smacked Murase flush in the mouth. There was a groan from the ranks behind me as if they sensed the inevitable consequences from my impertinence. Murase rushed in grabbed and swept me but I hung on to his jacket and so we became entangled and both crashed to the floor. Immediately Murase butted me with his head and I returned the same. He smiled and let me up and we resumed our scrap. I tried to get my hands working in the fight but a perfect front kick from my adversary hit me in my leading right hip that stopped me dead. Then another hit the same place as I failed to anticipate this man's forte. I then attempted to feint with my legs to unsettle Murase but he was not the unsettling type. His fast one two punch both found their marks on my ill guarded face and all I could do was grab and wrestle in vain. I could taste the blood that pooled in my mouth from my split lip and tongue, but I was not done. At the break I shouted to muster some spirit. Then another front kick hit me again in the same place as before and I was fast running out of ideas. My mind was racing yet my opponent appeared calm and had hardly broke sweat. His general movement seemed almost casual yet he seemed to be everywhere. He could read the fight easily as he stood with his front arm outstretched majestically controlling the distance between us. Even though I was outclassed I kept at him throwing single punches or kicks that whistled past their intended target while he leaned or sidestepped away to counter with ease.

Finally, Murase called time. We bowed and both thanked one another.

My fights that followed that evening with one or two of the first and second years were tougher for I was tired after the Murase experience which had probably lasted around five or six minutes. I was glad to finish that evening and when I pulled off my Karate gi trousers some of the skin covering my right hipbone came away with the material indicating direct hits from Murase. Although it was sore as hell it created a tumultuous laugh from my club mates. Kikuta shouted to everyone to come and have a look so I told him he should stop looking down men's trousers, which embarrassed him when the others teased him. Kawano celebrated the finish of training with his backward somersault from a standing position. For a big man he was as agile as a cat.

I walked back with Murase Senpai that evening towards the train station and he was as gentlemanly out of the dojo as he was ferocious within it. Nothing was said about our sparring match. It was history, as if it was now unimportant. We spotted Fukusyo and Hakoishi in a small bar near the Medaimae station so joined them for a swift beer. Murase spoke of his desire to go to England to learn English to which Fukusyo also expressed the same. Hakoishi looked at me as if to say 'not interested'. Then suddenly realising Murase's presence among us blurted out, 'hai, watashi mo'. "Me too!"

TWENTY-FOUR

It's funny how songs reflect so vividly an era, or a time of a certain emotion. For example, when I first arrived in Japan I went through a tough period when I could think only of home. I would hear songs and sing along to the ones that were so appropriate at the time. 'Tie a yellow ribbon round the old oak tree' was one. "It's been three long years do you still want me?" and all that. Then there was 'Mr Postman' by the Carpenters when I would be waiting to hear of any news from friends or family. And the list would go on. Of course, in the evenings when the intensity of training was over there were other songs to listen to which reflected a happier mood. Often our room, which slept seven people, would be a tatami dance floor when Michael Jackson or Kool and the Gang were playing on the TV or portable stereo. However, there was another reason for me to become a little more literate in song singing, the Japanese love to sing and often implore their guests to do the same. This I first discovered on the summer course, and it became apparent to me that everybody seemed to have a song ready to belt out.

At the time Karaoke was unheard of in England, so it was a surprise to me when I visited one of the small bars in Uenohara with Mr Sakamoto. In the small, but often cramped, bars that you really couldn't call a pub there was often a machine that seemed far too conspicuous to be part of the traditional décor. But it was no ordinary music machine, for there was an intrusive microphone attached that could reach any corner of the bar and therefore gave any unsuspected foreigner a fright if he thought he was to sit out of the way and have a quiet pint. Once the introduction got under way a screen would light up and the words would be displayed to a poorly produced video that in no way resembled the emotion of the song. Fortunately for the proprietor and unfortunately for me many of the songs were English, and so were the words that rolled across the screen. I must have murdered "Hey Jude" on more than a few occasions. There was no getting out of singing in Japan.

However, singing to a screen in a small bar is one thing but giving an impromptu performance in front of a crowd is another. Kobayashi one day asked whether I could help him do a Karate display at a wedding one weekend. I was more than happy to help so at the last minute we worked on some 'ohyo gumite' pair work that Suzuki Sensei back home in England had put together. There were some interesting fighting techniques and a few throws that seemed made to impress both Karateka and lay person alike.

The demonstration was on behalf of the bridegroom who was a former Nihon University Karateka and who also lived in the Yamanashi prefecture. The wedding was a mixture of Eastern and Western customs. It took place in a hotel where there was an 'in house' Shinto shrine and a priest to go with it. The priest blessed the pair with some chanting that sounded a lot like the chanting I had previously heard at a funeral. The mood was very sombre and there was complete silence from the eighty or so guests. We were then moved to a much larger brighter room where long tables were set out for the afternoon banquet. On entering the dining room all the guests handed over envelopes containing money. I had no idea of these customs so I had no envelope. But as always Kobayashi had it covered. Sitting at our place where our names were displayed on a card there were two meticulously wrapped presents for each guest.

Apart from the presents there were dishes of brightly coloured fish, some whole and staring up wide eyed at the guests, some finely sliced in the style of sashimi; raw meat glistening under the bright lights. As usual bottles of cold beer were huddled together in groups the whole length of the table. The beer was tempting but instead I opted for the fruit juice not wanting to allow my thinking to be impaired when Kobayashi Sensei started to set about me in our demonstration. I ate sparingly too for I didn't want to risk bringing anything up either. I sat picking and sipping resisting the temptation to open a present in front of me.

My presence at the wedding created a lot of interest around me and so I chatted half in English, and the other half in ropey Japanese. This caused some excited reaction from the guests especially when their normal inhibition weakened under the influence of the alcohol. The previous mood of the ceremony had gradually changed to a good old-fashioned piss up. Kobayashi sat next to me and seemed only too pleased to let things develop naturally.

Throughout the afternoon there were various lengthy speeches, some serious, some with wit that caused a few titters around the room. Finally, Kobayashi prodded me for us to get changed and warm up. We disappeared behind a curtain that hid a small stage and as I changed, I realized just how limited our space was. The beautifully polished flooring under our feet reminded me of the old Nichi Dai floor so my calloused feet felt at home on the familiar surface; only there wasn't the room to swing a 'neko'. There was no point in saying anything about it, we simply warmed up and slowly went through our routine before an announcement was made and the curtains went back. The auditorium fell deathly silent as we stood solemnly on the edge of our dais looking quite out of place as two spare karateka at a wedding. We bowed forward, then to each other and began the pre-arranged pair work in a slow deliberate motion giving our audience a chance to see our techniques clearly but also to give them a sense of antiçipation. As we performed our routine only the sound of the air conditioning humming above could be heard over the rustle of our uniforms. Then suddenly our kiais broke the silence and we repeated the same routine only this time with speed and intent. There were about eight attack and defence routines and the fifth and the sixth included a couple of takedown throws that when done slowly can be executed on the spot. At speed however momentum and adrenaline take over and the space around me closed in. I attacked my instructor with the verve and speed he wanted and he deftly sidestepped, parried my final kick, hit me with a haito (ridge hand) technique in the floating ribs, grabbed at my collar and swept away my leading leg. My left arm was outstretched in anticipation of the breakfall but it wasn't needed because my head was first to stop my momentum as it crashed into the wall at the back of the stage. There was an "oooh" from the horrified wedding guests. I was stunned as I crumpled to the floor where Kobayashi finished me with a final well-controlled 'shuto' knife hand to my face. Despite the mild concussion I scrambled to my feet to take 'kamae' (fighting stance) and looked into Kobayashi's face. There was no emotion, instead just a desire to get on with the final set sequence. I wanted to put my hand to my head to check for blood but something held me back from doing so, possibly the thought of Tanabe sensei scolding me even though he was not even in the same county.

Our bow to finish was met with a resounding applause and the curtain passed across the front of us. "Daijobu?" Kobayashi asked with a thin smile.

"Hai, daijobu desu!" I smiled back. Sensei thanked me for helping him and urged me to get a drink.

Returning to our seats there was more fuss made as the folk around us showed excited gratitude over our demonstration. I felt a little like Clark Kent after the fact that I had quickly changed and resumed a quiet foreigner's existence among people who had just witnessed a spectacle, at an event you wouldn't have expected, from two people who perhaps didn't seem capable.

But my day of entertaining the folks was not yet over. While we ate and drank there had been several guests who had stood before the rows of tables and sung a song or two and I thought, like us with our display, they had been invited to do so beforehand. Then Kobayashi turned to me and said "Aasa sing a song?" The fact that he made it a question gave me hope that I could decline the offer. I declined but he insisted. Again, I tried to put him off the idea but my sensei was adamant and I began to sweat profusely when I realised there was no getting out of this one. Not only can I not sing but also, I knew very few songs. This was not a funny situation and I was genuinely unhappy with having to stand up and be introduced as a "singer from England".

A polite round of applause found me stepping out in front of what seemed the whole Japanese nation. If I had an hour to think of something to sing, I would have come up with a blank yet here I was with a thirty second cue and about to let rip.

Now in my younger adolescent days I had sung along to one or two mindless rugby songs and suddenly one of these flashed into my brain. For fear of breaching political and moral correctness I don't think it appropriate to go into details of the song but I thought the crudeness of the words and their meanings would be lost in my poor rendition. So, I began. I first started my guests clapping along to a funky rhythm before I cut in with my vocals. As I waded through the song, I watched Kobayashi's face gradually alter from a happy serene look to one of concern. I think he got the gist of what I was singing about or perhaps knew well the song I was singing from his six years living in England. He was now looking around nervously at the guests to see if they too were catching on. Fortunately for him, and for me, they continued with their clapping and smiling to indicate that no damage was being done. My sensei said nothing when I sat in my place and I thought to myself perhaps he would think twice before setting me up again. I smiled to those around me and continued with a beer.

Coming from England there is little doubt that our climate is as confusing to the English as it is to the visitor. In Japan however you could almost set your clock to the change of season. There are two phenomena that are a little more difficult to judge however; one is the unpredictable rain showers that fall during June and the other are the typhoons. But as October made way for November so the temperature dropped considerably. There was a beauty however to the autumn and winter months that could not go unnoticed. When I had travelled with Kobayashi to and from Uenohara for the wedding demonstration I saw the clear blue skies and the change in leaf colours of the forests that emblazoned the mountainsides, like flags of different nationalities. My mind took me back several months when I saw the same beauty of spring, but the cheerfulness of that season had been overlooked in my vulnerable mental state as I struggled with my new environment and daily regime. Now however I was much settled and more than ready to take on the final couple of months that lay ahead.

My official visa expiry date was January 6th 1982 but I

decided I would take my family by surprise and be home for Christmas day. Anyway, there is only one Christmas dinner in twelve months and I wasn't going to miss that for the sake of six days training. Besides, many of the students would be going home for New Year so it would be pointless staying on, therefore my open ticket was confirmed for December 24th.

There was no such thing as central heating in the Nichi Dai dormitory but we were privy to the 'kotatsu'; a small table that had a heater underneath plugged into a wall socket. The table was then covered with a blanket that would be draped over the lap of the user so the heat was contained beneath. The size of the table only really allowed for two or three people at the same time and considering it stood no higher than the knee not much was kept too warm. It was possible then to be sat at the kotatsu with nice warm feet but have freezing cold arms and hands. In many homes there would be a hole in the floor in which the legs could sit into and so therefore more of the body could be warmed beneath the table.

Our first-year room had its own kotatsu that was put to good use and we would take turns to sit at the table while the rest of us would sit nearby trying to catch a bit of extra warmth that might somehow escape from the blanket that was kept tight to the knees. Apart from the table we wore extra layers of clothing and two pairs of socks to keep us from feeling too chilly. Likewise, when we travelled to Karate training we wrapped up. But when we boarded the trains enroute we sweltered because of the over efficient heating system. Amusingly the kohais would be burdened with carrying the Nihon University baseball type jackets that were discarded by their seniors. Another comedy unfolded as the first years would offer the jackets back when we alighted from the train, for they had enough to carry with their own bags, club mitts and senior gis etcetera.

Our early morning runs at six in the morning was a cold frosty affair and it was in everyone's interest to keep moving at a moderate pace in order to stay warm unlike the hot summer days when many students would amble along lazily. I noticed too that what seemed an overnight operation every vending machine in the street that supplied cold drinks had now changed to supplying hot beverages; tea, coffee, hot chocolate, even soup. Nothing was omitted from keeping the nation warm.

Our training was now intensified because of another national championship. Armed with the knowledge that I would also be competing I was as keen as anyone to train hard. I even started to give one or two second or third years a hard time when it came to the sparring for, I knew there was little time left and my time remaining would soon pass. The focus pad training seemed to go on forever and there were few days when we didn't don our mitts and spar for the last half an hour to forty-five minutes.

It was inevitable that we all picked up a few minor knocks during these intense fighting sessions but one Thursday evening at the headquarters I crunched my right big toe on someone's elbow. It was a pain that made me feel sick. I stood to fight again when my name was called but Fumihiro Tanabe ordered me to sit back down. I fought no more that evening and Kikuta was given a direction to take me to the hospital after training. An x-ray revealed a small crack in the main knuckle of the big toe. I was downhearted to say the least. Kikuta joked that I would be having some leisure time to look forward to but I was not thinking like my friend. I could only think that my one chance to compete on Japanese soil was now jeopardised.

The next day Kobayashi sensei stopped by my room to see how I was doing. Sensing my discomfort and disappointment he told me to get ready to go. Go where I knew not but that was as much information as he would always give. We drove for about half an hour until we reached a suburb of Tokyo. I thought for a moment we had come to another of sensei's private dojos but we walked to a small house where Kobayashi opened the sliding door and called. A moment passed before a small old man appeared. He smiled widely at my instructor. I was introduced to Mr Yamashita, a judo tenth dan and a man in herbal medicine. Before long I was perched on a small couch with one sock off while the old boy chatted to Kobayashi as he busily mixed up a green substance with a pestle in a mortar. Every now and again he would add a sachet and some water and resume mixing. Finally, he approached me with the bowl in readiness to administer. Up to now I had drunk miso soup and got to like it, I had chewed wearily on Mr Tsudas manju cakes, eaten raw fish, and dabbled unsuccessfully with natto. But looking into the green mush that the little wizened man offered me only made me feel sick. One mouthful of that I thought and you will have another bowl of green stuff to clean up. No doubt seeing my worried look the medicine man laughed out loud and wheeled around to one of the cupboards where he took out what appeared a large fig leaf. He scooped out the contents of the bowl placed it in the leaf then applied it to my toe, like a cold compress. There was a relief in the coldness of the substance that enveloped my swollen foot. Mr Yamashita placed my hand on top of the wrap and gestured for me to keep it that way for a while.

Half an hour later we left the small practice and Kobayashi said I could go back in a week for further treatment if it was necessary. I stood in the corner that evening at training and punched away mindlessly as the rest trained hard. The following day was no different and I was a little depressed at the prospect of losing valuable training time. I felt like a leper for Hideo Tanabe did not speak me to during or after training. He no doubt understood the necessity to rest an injury but he could not give the time of day to those who were not training hard with the rest. He could make you feel guilty at a time you could do with a bit of encouragement. Sympathy was not an emotion that ever existed in the Nichi Dai environment and probably rightly so. But a student never sought sympathy either, however there were those times when an inspirational gesture could go a long way and finally it came from his older brother Fumihiro. That Saturday evening at the headquarters dojo the senior Tanabe sensei approached me after training and put his finger and thumb on my shoulder and said "genki?" He knew deep down I wasn't fine but it was an enquiry to my welfare that although embarrassed me warmed me.

"Hai genki desu!" I replied. Like he had done many months earlier when my feet were ripped apart with blisters and when my knee had twisted. He knew that one training session standing in the corner seemed like a week passing by. I didn't want to be there and I think he knew that and it was his way of letting me know that it was ok.

Saturday evenings since September was a regular trip for me to Uenohara and an escape from the basic university life. This Saturday was no exception. Training on a Saturday would be finished at around eight. From the dojo I would go to Suidobashi station catch a train to Shinjuku and then get on a train on the Chuo line that would take me out to Uenohara. At Uenohara station roughly ninety minutes later I would board a bus that would take me past Kobayashi's home and into the centre of the small town and right outside Mr Sakamoto's restaurant. I couldn't miss it for on the bus there was a taped message to inform passengers of the approaching stops, "Sakamoto ya" was on one of those stops.

When I walked through the door of the house at the back of the restaurant I would shout "tadaima" a stock phrase to announce "I'm home" and usually Mrs Sakamoto would reply "okaeri" to welcome me back. There would be a cooked dinner waiting for me on the dinner table and a small beer to one side. Half an hour later Mr Sakamoto would join me for his dinner and a drink plus catching up on any gossip. Often his brother and wife would stop by and join us for a glass and chat. It was all very homely and I for one was grateful for that once a week.

On Sunday I would sleep in depending on the severity of the night before and then I would sit with the kids and watch a bit of telly before helping in the restaurant should it be necessary. The afternoon I would continue with the English teaching to the same six children I had started out with in the summer. But the whole experience of spending two nights a week in Uenohara was great rest and recuperation and none more so than when I needed to recover from an injury. I would return then to the Tokyo dormitory by lunchtime on Monday ready for the week's graft.

The weekend of rest was fruitful in that the pain in my right foot had subsided enough for me to have a go at proper training. I lined up that day after the warm up with the rest and Tanemura gestured for me to stand in the corner. I declined the offer he shrugged and continued with "jun zuki hidari gamae!" I had to take things a little easier where possible and only used my left foot when it came to the front kicks on the focus pads but overall, I was glad to be back in the thick of things.

When Tanabe finally appeared, he came over and told me to stick my tongue out. He then put his hand to my forehead as if to feel for a temperature. Then he looked down at my foot that was heavily taped and lifted his leg and pretended to stamp on it. I smiled along with his little joke but he merely turned away and ordered for everyone to put on mitts. Even though I was a subject of his mirth I was pleased to be noticed again unlike the previous few days when I was an anonymous spectator. It felt like I was back on the team, although not fully fit. Six students lined up at one end of the dojo and we went into attack and counter practice for the next half an hour or so. I did what I could considering my handicap and got through another session.

At the end of training that day we sat as Tanabe gave a pep talk for five minutes then suddenly, he said "Aasa!" I jumped in my seated position as if I had done something wrong.

"Hai!" I replied. I was worried. What was the need for him to address only me?

"Shiomitsu ga Nihon e kuru yo!" I deciphered the small phrase and replied,

"Hai wakarimashita!" I replied that I had understood that Shiomitsu Sensei was coming to Japan. He didn't say when or for why but I was pleased to hear that my instructor from back home was possibly going to be in Japan at the same time as me. Or did he mean that Shiomitsu was returning to Japan, maybe to live? As I got changed that evening my head was spinning with those few words. I knew there were some ructions in the Wado Ryu organization and now I began to wonder if there were far reaching implications to the political furore that was unfolding around the Grandmaster, Hironori Ohtsuka.

That evening there was some post for me. I knew without opening the large envelope that it was a birthday card from my parents. I realized I was only a few days from my 22nd birthday. The next day or two produced some more post and it caused some mild interest from non-other than Kikuta himself whose "Nani, nani" had become almost a catchword among the first years with regards to Kikuta's nosiness.

Nani meant 'what' and from Kikuta there was always the need to know what was going on. His entrance on the day before my birthday with yet another card that was from my dear Nan in Plymouth portrayed an emotion that was simply too much to contain. I told him it was my birthday and he became excited and said that we would celebrate the next evening. The first years looked on enviously for they would not get the chance to join me for the drink, perhaps only in a capacity of serving it up and looking on. I thought then that at some point I would get a drink down the necks of my roommates before I leave for home.

The next morning, I put up my birthday cards on the low shelf that ran the length of our room. I felt close to home with the messages from my parents, my brothers, my girlfriend, and other relatives who had sent me birthday wishes. I felt even closer when I considered I had little over a month left before I returned to a life among them.

My foot continued to heal well and that evening it was put to good test with lots of fighting. I still avoided using it for kicking but I was happy moving freely on my feet so that I could compete at full speed. This was just as well for I noticed recently how much improvement the first years were making and they were using their youthfulness almost recklessly to get stuck in and mix things up. Both Enomoto and Hijikata were at me from the start with more aggression than normal. Perhaps it was their way of helping me spend my birthday.

After training that evening I travelled back with the third year contingent and we dropped into the bar near the station. There was little time left before we had to return to our rooms but true to his word Kikuta was determined for me to celebrate my birthday. Or should I should I say for us to celebrate my birthday. I sat at the table with Oshima, Fujmoto, Kenji, Kikuta, Minamidae and they duly chinked glasses with me and sincerely wished me a happy day. The guy behind the bar rushed out with some fresh meat, which we cooked on the hot plate in front of us before dipping it into soy sauce and devouring it then washing it down with even more Kirin lager that was on tap. Kikuta called from the bar to the little green phone that sat in the dining room of our abode and came back to say that Tanabe was sleeping in his room that night so we would have to return before ten. It was a brief celebration of my advancement to another year but it was appreciated nevertheless.

TWENTY-FIVE

Days off from training were few and far between but one Saturday morning I was told to be ready for a trip into town with the captain, Tanemura. I had spent very little time with this diligent young man but I was no longer ill at ease with him either. We spoke very little for an hour before we got off at our stop and walked a while. Every now and then Tanemura stopped someone to ask directions. Finally, we found our destination, a building that resembled more of a conference centre rather than a venue that would hold one of the most prestigious Karate tournaments in Japan. On this day Murase senpai was to fight in the finals of the All Japan All Style Senior Championships.

On entering the building other students from our club were already gathered. They said very little to me because of the company I was with. Nichi Dai old boys were also gathered in the corridor not wishing to miss the chance of one of their own compete at such a level. I could sense their excitement in anticipation of the contest and at the fact they were meeting old friends again. Every now and again "Chawa! Chawa!" echoed around the room as more senior old boys turned up and were welcomed by my club mates. Sometimes an old fellow would enter the building and the university boys wouldn't have a clue to his identity so they looked around at each other nervously wondering whether this person should be greeted or not. After all it could be an usher or the janitor. Then a senior would put a word in their ear and they would be off again like a clutter of chickens bowing and crowing with reverent, respectful phrases. All very amusing to the foreign bystander.

Tanemura and I moved on into a large auditorium that was as high as it was wide. A raised platform stood in the centre that was covered with one large white tatami mat measured with a perimeter and two lines that stood opposite one another only a couple of metres apart. All around the platform that stood half a metre high were a few hundred seats for spectators. A television crew was busily preparing their camera at one corner of the platform.

It wasn't long before spectators took their seats. What followed was a martial arts demonstration second to none. There was an Aikido performance that culminated with the two attackers being simultaneously held down with their arms twisted unnaturally behind their backs. Immediately after the Aikido exponents left the stage an Iaido master strode out to the middle and furiously flashed his steel sword in all directions before hacking to pieces an upright thick bamboo staff that had somehow crept up behind him. The entertainment continued with an excellent performance of some locals on drums. I don't mean from a local rock group but the ceremonial drums that need two people to carry them. There were maybe ten drummers dressed in festival attire and they dominated the acoustics of the room in which we sat. If we had wanted to speak to one another it would not have been possible. But the way the drummers attacked their instruments matched the energy and vigour of any martial artist. Therefore, the audience that was perhaps patiently waiting for a finale of top-quality fighting was indeed enthralled with this unexpected treat.

There was one more demonstration to go before Murase would take centre stage. Two fighters in karate gis and head guards squared off with one another. They wore what appeared small boxing gloves and they went at each other without reserve, without any control and with the intent of doing some damage. This was a full contact bout. But it didn't look right. The minute a good shot connected the 'scorer' would back off as if a point had scored, which kind of defeated the whole point of the full contact idea. It was just another karate match with bigger gloves. The spectators became a little restless throughout this match and seemed a little relieved when this final exhibition came to an end.

The announcement of the next match brought a sudden expectation around the auditorium as everyone craned their necks to catch sight of the competitors. First in came Seiji Nishimura the younger challenger to the national title. He had recently been training at the Tokyo Physical Centre where Murase had spent many years training and teaching. In fact, it was Murase himself who had invited Nishimura to train with him when he spotted the talent of this man, and the fact that both came from Kumamoto also contributed to the invitation. Then Murase's name was announced and I felt excited to be a part of this man's entourage as we all shouted "Murase senpai" as he approached the platform and bounded up in one leap. In my eyes as a twenty-one-year-old this senior instructor, who had so often visited our dojo and wreaked havoc with his indomitable style, was invincible. I looked at Nishimura and thought that his chances must be slim.

As is often the case when you have two skilled fighters, they can cancel each other out. There was the initial rush to get things going when 'hajime' was called but no scores were awarded and unusually there was a period of testing one another out. Both fighters stood similarly with front arm outstretched as if to get a measure of the distance that was between them. Suddenly Murase shot forward as if the lapse in action had caused his impatience. Nishimura held his nerve and countered with a trademark Nagashizuki punch that took first score even though a split second later he copped a punch in the mouth for his troubles. Murase came back quickly with a ferocious Mae geri, a front kick that found its mark low in Nishimura's abdomen. The follow up punch was not needed but hit the target anyway before the sound of the referee's 'yame' to stop the action was heard. It was all-square and there was still plenty to do for both fighters if they were to dominate this final. Nishimura, the younger fighter by a few years, started to rev up his movements to feint to create openings, however I remembered trying the same tactics against Murase without success. Murase was too unflappable to fall for such tricks. Only his outstretched front hand would move in time with the feints as if it were a radar deciphering the movements. Time was moving on however and neither side was really taking the initiative until Nishimura seized a moment of inspiration and launched a front hand punch that found its mark on the face of Hisao Murase. The score was given and then all hell let loose as Murase set about levelling the score. Nishimura swiftly sidestepped and came back in heavily with a counter punch that also found its target in the ribs of the attacker. Murase's 'haito' that stung Nishimura's ear was again too late and they were tangled up trying to upend one another before the referee parted them both. The counter punch from the younger fighter was awarded and the thirty-second bell was sounded. Still Murase pressed but the advantage was now with Nishimura for his timing and his nerve was holding well. Murase was now the one trying to feint and harry his opponent and for the first time there was a panic about Murase as he realised his dominance of the Japanese karate scene was about to come to an end unless he could come out with something special. But Nishimura had probably seen it all. Ironically, the one man who had invited him to his dojo to give him the fruits of his experience had unwittingly handed over his reign. Time was called and I sat back in my seat speechless at what I had witnessed.

As the referee raised his hand to indicate Nishimura was the All-Japan Karate Champion Murase's face remained impassive. He accepted the loss, bowed deeply to his victor, and immediately stepped back while a rostrum was brought out. There were other awards for team events that had taken place earlier in the day and once Nishimura took his trophy, we left in a hurry to get back to Hachimanyama. Returning that evening I thought back to when the Nichi Dai team bombed out of their last team contest and realized that nothing was inevitable. In fact, there is the inevitability that one day all winners shall be losers. It is how the losing is accepted that is the next phase of a champion's evolvement.

The following week's training was a further reminder that the club's next official appointment was not to be another disaster. As if Murase's loss was an inspiration of how not to perform Tanabe was attending every training session with his own inimitable style. Every time we charged up and down the dojo in relays doing our combinations, he would stand in front of one of us as if he were our opponent and pick holes in our technique, posture, and anything else he could think of. But instead of being demoralized by these antics of his we rose to his challenge; we gave him what he wanted and genuinely tried to work harder. We all wanted to be a part of a winning team and had only three weeks left to get it right. We fought daily and Tanabe often stood behind us as we fought giving his instructions from over our shoulder. I was privileged too to receive this type of coaching and I knew he was after a result from us all.

As the year was winding down so there were one or two auspicious occasions that could have been seen as distractions to our preparations but in fact proved quite the opposite in the relief from the training, not to mention the team bonding. One chilly, rainy day in early December the whole Karate club travelled by train to the Tokyo Olympic Stadium to take part in the Nihon University Sports Festival. There were members of all sporting clubs sat in a couple of sections of the huge stadium that had been the packed setting for the Olympic games back in the summer of 1964. This was the winter of 1981 however so the several hundred students and their coaching staff were huddled under umbrellas, wrapped up in warm clothing. Throughout the day there were races from the athletics club against a couple of other universities. There were young female cheerleaders frolicking on the grass in the centre of the track dancing, trying to lift the dampened spirits. Down below our seated position I saw a group of young men in university uniform wearing white gloves singing and chanting together. I asked Kikuta who they were and he explained they were 'Oendan' an official group of male cheerleaders. I found this amusing and before long the rest of Nichi Dai Karate club was laughing at my mirth. They were perhaps familiar with the idea of a club formed for the sole purpose of cheering others. In my experience boys who didn't do sport did books. Besides, I thought that was what the girls in ra ra skirts were for.

The climax of the sports day was indeed a lot of fun. A team from each sports club put forward four runners to race in a relay. However, each team would dress in its own sporting attire. There were sumo wrestlers standing at the track wearing only loincloths, boxers with gloves on, judoka not only wearing judogi but with a tatami mat strapped to their backs. I then saw our very own Kawano, Kishiyama, Iidabashi and Akii in their Karate gis trotting forward from beneath the stands to take their places on the track. What followed was a four by one hundred metre relay that appeared to be taken seriously when the starting gun sounded but which ended in a fiasco as each team struggled to get round the wet tartan track. Although the teams representing American football, baseball, and rugby went round quick with our Karate club doing its best in hot pursuit, other runners slowed to a trot under the burden of their attire. Down the back straight two gymnasts were doing flic flacs showing the animated crowd what they do best. The sumo wrestlers were not the running type either and nonchalantly walked much of the way no doubt wondering where their next meal would be coming from. All in all, an amusing afternoon's entertainment but on this day, we were hurried away from the track by Tanabe sensei who after looking at his watch saw a chance for us to get in some late training. We were on the train and back to our dormitory by four. Quickly we grabbed our karate gis and went back to the station from where we had just come. Forty minutes later we were in the dojo of the high school training rigorously as if nothing had happened that day, even though we only managed an hour and a half's practice in all.

My daily routine had not altered much throughout the week since my early sojourns to Shinjuku back in the spring. There were still long hours to wile away between the early morning run and afternoon training. This still contributed towards a yearning to be home. I longed for female company. I wanted to be able to go out for an evening without restriction on time, I wanted to be able to put my feet up on a sofa and I often wished for a decent pint of beer. Moreover, it had been a long time since I had chatted to my family and friends without having to explain three or four times what I meant. It was a thrill then when I had a visit from Shiomitsu sensei to my room one afternoon. I had been anticipating his arrival for a few days now after Tanabe sensei had mentioned it during training and he had also summoned me to his room for a late-night drink one evening, something he hadn't done in a long while. I think he not only wanted to prime me for the visit but he also wanted an impression from me of how things had gone since I had been under his tutelage.

"Hi Arthur." A familiar figure with a broad smile filled the doorway of our room. That was the first time I hadn't been called 'Aasa' in a long time and it was unexpected coming from a Japanese. I jumped up from where I was perched on the TV shelf and bowed as Shiomitsu Sensei stepped into the room and looked around him with a sense of nostalgia.

"This takes me back," he said before he stretched out his hand. A gesture too that was unfamiliar and I gushed with embarrassment as he insisted, I sit down and relax. We spoke quickly of many things but none more important than the current crisis in the Wado Kai federation. Shiomitsu had come to Japan to celebrate Ohtsuka Sensei's ninetieth birthday but there had been a recent upheaval that had caused a major decision from the Grandmaster to create his own organization. How ironic that he should leave his own group in order to remain true to his own philosophy. Shiomitsu also said that there might be a knock-on effect back in England and that he may have to branch out himself in order to stay with Ohtsuka. I assured him of my loyalty.

He then said my English was not so good and that it was a bit broken. I laughed at the irony.

TWENTY-SIX

In these last few weeks of training I tried to ascertain what might have altered in my own fighting style since I had first come to train at this club. I knew for one thing that I felt strong and that one or two techniques were now more prevalent, such as my front kick to the lower abdomen and the 'nagashi zuki' punch, both of which were the staple technique here. I remembered in the early days Tanabe trying to change my fighting stance, or kamae, from the boxer type position to an outstretched front hand type guard. I realized he had, over time, succeeded in this when I took kamae position in our dojo line up. I used to sit on my back foot too, with my rear foot turned to the side. After a few kicks in the groin my back foot turned more forwards, thus closing the gap between the legs and I felt far more protected to that area. I felt these weren't changes of a conscious issue but as of an evolvement borne out both the influence of my instructor and self-preservation.

I didn't know or I don't remember if my kata had changed in any way. To say we neglected kata in favour of fighting would be somewhere near the truth. But there were training sessions when kata training seemed to hold as much importance as the perfect ippon. I knew we had practised Kushanku probably more than any other kata and that its combination techniques were ingrained in my memory.

In our approach to the All-Japan Wado Ryu contest our fighting was naturally the main topic of training. There were one or two students though who were to be representing the club in the Kata. Okano was one and Takahashi the other. Intermittently Tanabe would ask them to perform their Kata in front of the class and then coach them. This reminded me of the first week I was here when I too was asked to perform a kata, it must have gone down well for I was never asked again. We would sometimes finish the fighting a little early and practise Seishan and Chinto, which made a change from Kushanku a dozen to fifteen times. Then one afternoon Tanabe made another one of those important announcements at the end of training. Sometimes these were short and sharp; on occasion they would be longer depending on his mood and our performance in training. Following this short speech, he stopped and then looked over us all silently. We sat in seiza still sweating and he knew we were eager to get up and back for our beer, shower and dinner in that order and no doubt that's why he held us there for the extra minute.

"Takahashi; Okano, Minamidae; Ikeda, Aasa!" Our names were spat out quickly and decisively. I felt for a moment we were in a spot of bother and couldn't think what we had done to draw any unwanted attention.

Takahashi approached me straight after training and told me we were to attend a party the next evening at a hotel in Shinjuku and we were to give a Kata demonstration. Minamidae also came over and slapped me on the back with a big toothless grin as if to say "we have got a night off training, and what's more we're going to a party!" I must admit the opportunity to get out for a night during the week was a rare one and I was honoured to be included in the team.

The next afternoon then while the rest of the club prepared their stuff to go training the five of us relaxed in front of the telly in our own rooms. What a result this was. We had an hour before we were to be picked up by minibus but I was already practicing Seishan in my room for the reality of what lay ahead that evening overshadowed the fact that we were away from training.

The party that evening was arranged to celebrate the retirement of a Nihon University senior figure. On arrival the five of us plus Hideo Tanabe and Kobayashi sensei were guided to the function suite where the typical sight of a banquet table expertly crammed with beer and food stretched out before us. We looked at one another in excitement thinking the same thing; this could be a long night. Tanabe ushered us into a room next door away from all the dignitaries where we could change, warm up and practice. To fit in with the other four I had borrowed a gi jacket from one of the third years that had the Nichi Dai motif embroidered on the left breast. When I pulled the jacket from my bag, I studied it closely before I put it on. During the months here I had never asked for this symbol to be stitched onto my own jacket considering it to be presumptive of me to be worthy of wearing it. But this one evening representing the club displaying these characters came a close second.

We stayed in this room out of the way for probably an hour working up a little sweat as we repeated the kata several times. Takahashi instructed us on some finer points ensuring we could keep the same time together. It was one thing doing this in front of the club; it was another task to perform in front of fifty or so dignitaries. While the party was under way with speeches and more songs, we stayed out of the way stretching and taking deep breaths. The tension was also showing on the faces of my club mates as they probably wished they had gone training instead. I think at that moment we would rather have gone out with our mitts on and scrapped it out with each other. This was nervousness unlike that of a pre-fight state. There was much more at stake; the guy who was retiring, both Tanabe coaches, Kobayashi, not to mention many Karate club old boys who would be looking on with a sense of nostalgia. All of whom would hope to be remembering this evening with pride and not with a sight of some poor soul embarrassing himself by losing his concentration.

A young lad with the University uniform came in to inform us to be ready. We walked swiftly out into the party and stood in our little diamond shape. My heart pounded as the room fell silent and I felt all eyes were on me as the only non-Japanese in sight. My mind swiftly went back to the demonstration I did at a contest a few months earlier. As Takahashi proudly announced "Seishan!" we moved together slowly, deliberately focussing our efforts in our block and punch sequences. Usually when performing kata there is very little to see or be distracted by but throughout the early part of this kata, I could make out unfamiliar faces staring intently at us with drinks held at chest height as if they were prohibited from sipping the beer until we had finished.

I followed closely the movements of the two figures in front of me, Takahashi, and Okano. Minamidae and Ikeda were flanking me so they were only in my peripheral sight. However, when we turned to face the opposite direction, we were away from the spectators but I was now leading the kata. The hours we had spent over the months training together, fighting and living together seemed to have given us an in- built instinct to perform this moment together. It occurred to me that Hideo Tanabe would not have put his reputation at risk if he were not confident, we could carry it off. The second phase of Seishan kata changes dramatically from slow to fast and we seemed to hit that change just right and kept it together until our final kiai signalled the finish. We bowed to a responsive, polite applause and returned to our room next door. Our relief was obvious as Takahashi punched the air as soon as the door shut behind us. We slapped each other's backs and wondered what all the fuss was about earlier. As soon as we were changed into our trousers and collared shirts Takahashi pronounced us free to enjoy the evening ahead;

"Nomimasho!" Let's drink! He said.

The five of us approached the table but Hideo Tanabe intercepted us. "Jusu dake ne!" He said curtly. That was a command not to be ignored; no beer for us, only juice. So, when the pretty serving girls approached us with more beer on offer all we could do was wave them away with a smile. With chopsticks in hand however we began to ravage the table of the food that remained. There were noodles, Chinese style beef, sushi, Sashimi, and tempura, plus tons of rice. The food at Nichi Dai was not bad but this was in a different class. My visit to the table however was interrupted by a senior dignitary who was hell bent on asking me the usual questions about where I was from and what I was doing in Japan and so on. Typically, I had to stop and stand to attention while I politely responded to the questions with a plate in one hand and chopsticks in the other, all the while trying to munch the odd mouthful. This slowed me down somewhat and out of the corner of my eye Minamidae and the rest were eating themselves silly while musing at the predicament I was in.

I felt like a naughty school kid trying not to laugh but that was in fact just how I had slotted in to this university student lifestyle in Japan. I realized the maturing of the average young Japanese fellow was slowed somewhat under the strict discipline of his educational environment. Nothing could be done without the permission of someone else.

I remember as an eleven-year-old the strict regime I had entered on the first day of grammar school. There was the uniform, the rules, the senior students, and their bullyboy attitude. But we got our heads down and made what we could of the situation. After all we were there to study. I remember a year or so later the sixth formers winning a right not to wear uniform and I felt, even as a twelve-year-old, it wasn't a good thing. Another year on and the grammar school amalgamated with another secondary school to make a fully comprehensive system and the discipline that I had been familiar with all but disappeared. Today we have kids hitting teachers when it used to be the other way round.

I was happy however to be a part of this disciplined set up. I knew if I hadn't embraced this whole concept I would have been discarded from the club in no time. As I watched Hideo Tanabe mix with the guests in his own unique arrogant style, I could see why the youngsters of the club found him intolerable. They feared him, they resented him, and they didn't understand him at all. But throughout the many months of my stay, I had witnessed dozens of visitors pay their respects to this man. Senior figures who had long since hung up their white uniforms in exchange for the blue collar but who had maintained their self-belief and determination in order to succeed in another competitive environment. Their time at Nichi Dai Karate Club had seemed an eternity and yet now they had moved on there is always an irresistible urge to go back, to reminisce.

The party ended abruptly at ten thirty and before long we were ushered into the minibus and back to the dorm. I sat in my room listening to the other lads sleeping soundly. I was a short time from saying farewell to these friends and I knew I couldn't have managed without their help. Suddenly a thought came to me. I had two bottles of wine in my suitcase that Kobayashi had given me some time ago, a souvenir of Yamanashi ken. I grabbed the two bottles and woke Hijikata who characteristically jumped to attention. We then roused the rest from their slumber. Asuka sneaked off to the kitchen while the rest of the lads sat around in a tight group. The light in the corridor was always left on so this gave enough light for us to communicate. They were all more than a little nervous about having a drink at such a time but I insisted. Asuka returned with a corkscrew and sake glasses. I then toasted a drink to them all and wished them success for their remaining time. They drank quickly their small amount so I replenished their small cups and we talked in loud whispers about my time among them. We suppressed our laughs as Hijikata did my crashing the bike impersonation. Enomoto kept banging on about leaving the club to go home but I reminded him that he had been saying that since the first night I arrived. They made jokes about the seniors and I joined in the ridicule of the guys I had befriended. These lads were naïve, timid characters with little self-esteem when I had first joined them, and in many ways not much had changed. But little by little I had noticed in each a spurt of growth in their character. They were more individual, no doubt through my knowing them better but also as a result of their time in the dojo. They were physically shaping up, and it wouldn't be long now before they too would be a senpai to new students.

As we drank in no time at all I sensed these boys around me were acting a little less restrained and then behind me Iidabashi had switched on the television. I quickly switched it off and put my finger to my lips to urge for quiet but these immature young men had a drink inside them and wanted to be drunk. To be honest they had only consumed enough to get a sparrow smashed but their total history between them of consuming alcohol probably added up to only a few minutes so they were entering a new dimension of uninhibited behaviour. This little gesture of goodwill of mine could soon backfire and I feared a mutiny. Yatabe and Tanaka, the little and large duo, were sparring with their tiny pillows in hand and Iidabashi was now dancing like Michael Jackson to his Walkman. I feared that Tanabe in the very next room would surely hear the commotion and be in at any moment. For the first time I had to act like a senior to these overgrown school kids and take responsibility.

"Oi!" My stifled command froze the activity around me and my friends looked at me in surprise. "Oyasumi" I bid them goodnight as I put the empty bottles of wine back into my case. One by one the partygoers thanked me, returned to their futons, and wished me goodnight.

TWENTY-SEVEN

The last few days of serious fighting was now in full swing as we counted down the days to the All-Japan contest. Shiomitsu sensei was now dropping in to see our final preparation and with him was Shizuo Suzuki, or Peter Suzuki as he was better known. To be honest I sensed that Tanabe didn't want to have any interruptions to our final phase but Shiomitsu enjoyed the atmosphere of the classes and trained alongside us rather than getting involved in any tuition. Now and again, he would add words of encouragement but generally left the barking to the club coach and captain. Team selection was taking place ten days before the contest and although I knew I wasn't going to be in any team I was drafted in to fight a few of the hopefuls. This made me more determined to show some aggression as well as technique and I was only too willing to open up. My injury problems were well behind me and I felt one hundred per cent fit to fight. Kishiyama and I had another set- to but this time there was not the emotion of our previous encounters; we gave, we received. Oshima and Kawano remained the dominant figures of old but they weren't the only ones to be wary of. Others were developing in confidence too and so we fought for much of the last hour of each afternoon class dragging our bodies through near exhaustion. My return date to return to England was now only two weeks away but the only thought on my mind was the championships.

The weekend before the contest I took my last trip to Uenohara. A sayonara party was thrown on my behalf in Mr Sakamoto's restaurant. All the people I had been privileged to meet came to say their farewells and gave me gifts. The children to whom I had taught English came with their parents and presented me with an ornamental pair of samurai swords. Mr Tsuda gave me a watch and there were many other smaller gifts that cost far less but were equally valuable to me. The people in Uenohara had given me the chance to see another side to Japan away from the Martial Arts and I was much the richer for it. I had left behind a close family in England but it was another close family that welcomed me so often to their home.

The morning after the party I rushed to the nearby florist and bought a bouquet of flowers for Mrs Sakamoto. For her husband I had already bought a book, during one of my trips to Shinjuku, which depicted mountains from all over the world. He sat at the breakfast table and not only was he able to identify the mountains that were pictured but showed me the ones he had personally climbed. The goodbyes that day to him, his family and even his staff were emotional but I knew that I would go back and visit this special person whose phrase "your house is my house" summed him up perfectly.

Visit him I did a few years later, more than once in fact, but tragically twenty-five years later one of those mountains would claim his life. Even nearing sixty years old the temptation to climb a mountain was still strong for Mr Sakamoto. His spirit was much like the Nichi Dai Old Boys who still don their gis and mix it with the youngsters, still wanting to taste the adventure. Some people just never grow up, but of course they wouldn't have it any other way.

On that frosty Monday morning as I took the train from Uenohara I gazed at the mountains and lakes that drifted past the windows and I took in the beauty of the Japanese countryside for the final time. I was returning to the Nihon Daigaku Karate Club for my final week's training and I thought about the months of hard training and all that went with it. Normally this trip back to the club would inject me with a feeling of anticipation and my stomach would sometimes roll at the thought of putting on those flimsy mitts. But there was no such emotion on this day. I knew there were only a few days of light training to come and a sense of regret was now beginning to creep in. Should I have tried to stay longer? Could I have maybe found a little work and paid my way to do so? Was I too willing to go home at a time when I was more settled than ever before? In fact, come February I could have taken my second dan along with the others who were next in line to grade. These were moot points now however, for my immediate destiny was already settled. I was going to fight this weekend and then go home.

The training on that Monday afternoon was light; half an hour of basic training followed by an hour of combination techniques then twenty minutes of extremely light sparring. Tuesday was the same followed by a Wednesday that was even less strenuous. I think we used up more energy getting to and from the dojo. Tanabe watched as we did our basics for the first thirty minutes but then wandered off to leave us to our own practice. Takahashi and one or two others trained in kata in preparation for their entry. There was to be no sparring so most of us did some shadow fighting in the mirror then stretched for a while before Tanemura called a halt to the evening class. We barely did an hour. But in all this we were getting mentally prepared. Physically we couldn't have felt better.

There was to be one team entered plus several individuals. I would be representing England as an outside competitor but I knew I had the support of my fellow students. Even Minamidae, my old foe, slapped me on the back after training one evening and asked if I was ready. I assured him I was.

Friday, we ran in the morning but didn't train at all in the afternoon. That evening we had steak for dinner, albeit a small steak, but it was a treat and we were excited at the royal treatment. Tanabe was buttering us up for the big day.

We slept in until seven on that Saturday. The routine that followed was the same as before; clean the place from top to bottom before breakfast. Most of the students would be going home after the contest so the place had to be ship shape. Our Nichi Dai bags were slung over our shoulders and we left enmasse to walk to the station and from there to a sports hall in Chiba prefecture.

The contest was to be held over two days. The children and then the adult preliminaries were to be contested on the first day. The finals of the individuals plus team and kata finals were to be on the Sunday. I was banking on being back to fight the next day.

Instead of watching my club mates warm up from the spectator seats I now stood in the circle that surrounded Tanemura and followed the warm up routine. Then we put on our mitts and trained our free fighting combinations with speed and vigour. I felt today had to be a success, not only for myself but also for my fellow students, and for the instructors that had allowed me into their world, a world that was often aggressive with few compliments or appraisals. But I knew overall success today would be a measure of that disciplined hard working environment.

To be fair the size of the contest was diminished somewhat due to the division of the Wado federation. But the old saying is 'that you can only beat what is put in front of you' came to mind on this day. I watched the Nichi Dai Old Boys sweep through the senior section with comparative ease. Tachizawa senior took his team, minus Murase who it was reported had joined the Wado Kai faction, to the final. These Old Boys revelled in their role of a team contest like they were on a day trip to a punch up picnic. They got hit but didn't complain, but found a thrill in dropping an opponent should he get a bit too physical. Staying within the rules was the hardest part for these university veterans; their experience of hundreds of sparring sessions gave them a distinct advantage but also their swift change of gear from calm to pure aggression was frightening, especially for the opponent. But there was no malice. They would steamroller over an opponent with a combination of punches and kicks that would often knock down an opponent simply from the momentum. But then they would stretch out their hand to help stand them back on their feet, so that they could then have another go.

While I stood watching the seniors fighting, Shiomitsu approached me with a programme in his hand and a huge grin across his face as if he knew something that I didn't. He showed me my place in the draw and explained that I had a bye in the first round. Then he pointed out who my first opponent might be should he get past his first-round fight. It was a Nihon University old boy by the name of Nishimura who I knew very well. In fact, he had taught Karate in England for a few years and had graded me to first kyu a couple of years earlier.

I remembered well that training and grading weekend in my home town at the local school gymnasium session. On the Saturday I'd had a good scrap with Nishimura as he steamed into me with the trademark Nichi Dai pressure, I had just been witnessing earlier in the senior team event. I felt at the time I had held my own a little as a nineteen-year-old brown belt but I knew I was covering up a fair bit too with the old boxing guard, and perhaps Nishimura had eased off a little when he had me under pressure. But that was then.

Shiomitsu pulled me over to a fighting area and told me to watch Nishimura fight. He said he would come forward hard and fast. I already knew that of course but my coach for the day then told me on no account was I to move back from this bull like attacking style.

"Arthur you must side step and punch his face and not think of kicking too much, above all you must beat Nishimura! After that I don't care!" Strong words from Shiomitsu but I was more than happy to have him mat side because both Tanabe and Kobayashi had more than their fair share of coaching to do. Furthermore, I felt that sense of familiarity from home backing me up.

We watched as Nishimura's first fight unfolded. My heart leapt at the sound of 'hajime' for in my mind's eye I was now standing in front of this man. Nishimura wasted no time; he closed his opponent with a few short steps then surged forward with a double punch to the face of his dithering foe. The referee's command of 'yame' was lost in the flurry of activity between the two fighters as Nishimura followed up his punches with one or two more. Just as predicted Nishimura was going to overpower this adversary with these tactics even though he would flout the rules a little along the way. Gamely his opponent tried to retaliate but he was only ever hoping to pick up the scraps that Nishimura might leave should he be careless to waste his techniques. But it was noticeable that the opponent of Nishimura did not stand his ground; and, that Nishimura was blowing a bit after the first thirty seconds. I noted these two factors but it didn't stop the adrenaline flow through my veins as I fought every move in the match in front of me.

I walked away from that area with enough information. I

thought about the hundreds of similar fights I'd had with the Nichi Dai boys over the past months and knew this was no different. I looked for Minamidae grabbed him and started to fight him as a warm up. He needed no encouragement to wind things up and for a few moments we exchanged some pretty heavy stuff. Shiomitsu asked if I was ok with Minamidae and I said it's a long story but that it was perfect for the current climate. A smile on his face meant he understood perfectly; I needed to be mentally switched on before my fight, not half way through when it could be too late.

There were one hundred and sixty competitors in my event so it was a good hour before I was finally called to the mat for the start of the second round. I was ready to go. Nishimura quickly came around the mat, shook my hand said hello and returned to his position.

"Don't be fooled by that," said my coach. "Hit his face!" Shouted Shiomitsu as I stepped forward. The referee announced "hajime" and I stepped forward with a kiai to put my nerves in order and to let my opponent know I was up for it. He stepped in for a quick attack but I was there before him; my front hand smacked him straight in the side of the head. His forward momentum kept him coming however and he tried to rough me up by grabbing me but I stood strong and punched again with my rear hand. However, the referee stopped the fight and awarded me that first punch. I had laid down the ground rules to my opponent and I was now tuned up for the next assault. I stepped forward from my line again and feinted to attack but that was a mistake for Nishimura ignored the feint and ran straight into me with a one two punch that found its mark on my mouth. The connection was solid and the referee halted the action immediately to award the point. I swallowed the blood that seeped from my lips and my emotion got the better of me I launched a low roundhouse kick that was near to the groin yet failed to score, I followed up immediately with the route one face punch that missed and now Nishimura was firing off his own punches as we were nose to nose so to speak. It got scrappy but there was plenty of fighting to be done in order to gain superiority. He grabbed me again but I was ready to take him over with a sweep but we were tangled together and both hit the floor. The referee was now diving between us to stop the fight and to bring some order to this contest.

There was perhaps a hint of desperation in both of us to succeed in this fight. There was no way I was going out of the first round in my first full scale contest in nearly twelve months, and I guess there was no way my opponent was going to be defeated by a former student, especially on home ground. As we stood opposite one another we both acknowledged the referee as we were warned for fighting after his command of 'yame'. To be honest I didn't hear him at all for all my senses were occupied with the raging bull in front of me. But now my initial nerves had settled I felt a sense of enjoyment; that I was in a hard fight and more than holding my own. But there was a lot to do.

"Hajime!" and we both bolted forward, but then I suddenly dropped back a touch and brought my opponent on to a perfect reverse punch that knocked a little wind out of him. He wanted to continue but the referee was in and awarded me the point. The next exchange saw a similar clash, both determined to be in first but neither of us hit the target so we moved away and around a little before attacking again. I tried to set up a face kick but Nishimura's experience in the UK had given him an expectation of such techniques and he stepped swiftly sideways and punched my face, I hit him back, hard, then he grabbed again before gesturing to head butt me. We were separated and he was awarded the initial face punch. Time was called and a draw was declared. That meant an extra couple of minutes with a sudden death score at stake.

I looked around at Shiomitsu who was gesturing for me to move sideways and I realised that perhaps I had been too keen to get stuck in rather that use any tactical movement. I noticed now that Nishimura was struggling to catch his breath. I had to consider these two factors. I started quickly off my line but his fatigue let him down a bit and where he expected me to be in front of him, I side stepped and he punched empty space. I sent a low roundhouse to the belly that had very little control. He weathered it well but the technique couldn't go unnoticed to anyone who watched the fight. It was the winning move and I was through to the third round.

Immediately after the fight Nishimura approached me and congratulated me. He also invited me to stay sometime at his house but I told him that I was returning home in a couple of days. Shiomitsu was pleased at the result but a little disappointed that it took me so long to get the win. "That last move you did could have been done in the first thirty seconds" he said. He was right but I felt better for the fact that I'd had a real good scrap to more than warm me up for the rest of the day.

Half an hour later and the next round was under way. When my name was called a younger fighter than Nishimura stood opposite but I was eager to start where I had left off. At the referee's command I shot forward, so too did my opponent, but I used the sidestep together with my front hand 'nagashi zuki' as the principal weapon, then followed up with my left hand to the body. This youngster was game but predictable. He tried to be first with the 'one two' to the face but I had seen it a hundred times before in the dojo of Hachimanyama so by avoiding the first punch I slotted my front hand neatly between his two. This scored a couple of times and I set him up with a roundhouse kick to the face that spoke volumes with a resounding slap to take me through again.

The fourth-round opponent was a much taller fighter, a little older than me with a bit of an attitude to go with it. There was lot of shouting and shoulder shrugging as he stepped forward and there was an air of confidence that seemed to say ‘get out of my way’. But once I smacked him in the face he stopped and looked at the referee for help. I knew then that given the point or not this guy didn’t like any rough stuff; too bad for I was not in the mood for anything dainty. I was awarded the point and went in even harder to ruffle this poor guy’s feathers. I realised that the entire attitude he displayed earlier was nothing more than a charade to intimidate me, and to cover up his own inhibitions. My attacks were strong but controlled as I continued to dominate him at close range by striking towards his face, he started to turn away and lash out a bit but his fighting spirit, or lack of it, was rumbled. The more pressure I put on him the more he faded which left him open to sweeps and head kicks. I beat him comfortably and was through to the last sixteen.

I asked Shiomitsu who my next opponent would be, for he was holding the programme and following the draw as I progressed. “Today is over” he said. “That’s it, last sixteen to come back tomorrow.” I was pleased but wanted to continue at the same time. I felt I was on a roll and wanted nothing to stop the winning momentum.

“Well done,” he said, “you beat Nishimura”. He was still buzzing from the fight a couple of hours ago but I was looking ahead to a lot more.

Not only was I through to the last sixteen but the Nihon University team had also qualified in the university section and Takahashi was into the Kata final. On top of that the Nichi Dai old boys were through in the senior team category. These championships were a minefield of various categories from kids to veterans but it was a prestigious event that was to be host to a prestigious party that Saturday evening. While my club mates returned to the dormitory Shiomitsu had made provision for me to stay at his hotel near the sports centre. This was an unexpected treat, for not only did it save a lot of journey time but it was rather more luxurious than the first-year room. There was one slight catch; I had to share my room with Peter Suzuki.

Peter Suzuki was an interesting character. Little known these days among the clubs outside of the Midlands, he was a strict disciplinarian in the dojo but I found this instructor quite jovial and not in any way condescending towards my sharing a room with him. Carrying his bag up to the room was no problem for I already had

Tanabe's and Shiomitsu' s slung over my shoulder anyway. I came back down to collect mine after. Then I had to run his bath water, "not too hot!" He requested. I did wonder what might be next but he insisted I took a beer from the fridge and put my feet up. I declined the beer and poured him one but he ordered I have at least one to share with him. The taste was good but I was determined not to have another. My senior roommate bombarded me with curious questions about my time in Japan and I eventually felt quite at ease in this man's company when I filled him in on the details as he listened intently, laughing out loud at certain places of humour or hardship.

At eight o'clock we descended the lift to meet in the lobby of the hotel and from there walked a while through the quiet streets of the surrounding district. I followed behind as the seniors in front of me chatted loudly in the chilly December evening and with their excited chatter and laughter I could see against the orange brightness of the street lamps their breath in small plumes of steam punch the cold air above their heads. Even though nobody spoke to me I was quite happy with the company I was with but then felt a tinge of regret that I wasn't back at the dormitory among my fellow students. I knew they would be reflecting on the day's events and looking forward to what might be on the final day.

I followed the small entourage into an hotel and up to another well prepared function room on the third or fourth floor. There were one or two familiar faces that I had met over the months so I mingled with a little less reserve although with the correct amount of respect. Speeches followed and guest of honour was Jiro Ohtsuka, the son of the Grandmaster, Hironori. Inevitably the Karaoke machine swung into action and one by one people took to the small stage and without embarrassment sang in front of the newly formed Wado Ryu Renmei association. I stayed well out of the way chomping on the free food and avoiding the alcohol, but it wasn't long before Peter Suzuki dragged me from my hiding place and pushed me on to the pulpit like platform where I chose to sing the Beatles' 'Yesterday' from the big book that was spread open in front of me containing all the words. Kobayashi came to me after and laughed with 'good song, good song', no doubt relieved I hadn't done what I did at the wedding party.

It wasn't long before the party came to an end. Many seniors wandered off to find other venues of entertainment that would perhaps take them well into the early hours but I was grateful when Shiomitsu signalled that we would return for a night's sleep. I had one last sip of beer with my roommate but was tucked up by midnight.

I was up early the following morning without any need for an alarm. There was no run this morning but there was an innate sense of wanting to be up and ready, maybe from the sense of anticipation or perhaps as a result of the many months of early morning training. After breakfast I ferried a few bags down to the ground floor for a few instructors then we all made our way to the sports hall where my Nihon University comrades were already limbering up. Like me a few of them were through to the last sixteen in the kumite, Takahashi was in the kata final and the team was in the last four so there was a lot in prospect for us all.

As I warmed up in earnest with my colleagues a sudden silence fell around us. We stopped and turned to see a very old figure, with the help of two assistants, one on either arm, walk very slowly across the floor. Hironori Ohtsuka made his way slowly to a place at the head table. The frail old Grandmaster of Wado Ryu was in attendance of these inaugural championships of his newly formed association. I asked a few around me if it were possible to get an autograph. They looked at me in disbelief. To think I could approach this eminent figure waving a bit of scrap paper for his signature seemed too surreal for them to comprehend.

Still, I wrestled with the idea. There was no one of more importance to me at that time than the meek looking old fellow who sat sipping green tea that someone had hurriedly placed in front of him. I had seen his face so many times in books, magazines and from within a frame hung in dojos up and down the UK. His expression always seemed to contain a sense of approval; he appeared to be everyone's grandfather with the serene look that was captured in that photograph. Yet here he was in person, much older now, but looking as every bit as content as ever I had seen him. I saw Fumihiro Tanabe speak with him and thought about nipping over when there was a chance between their conversations, maybe Tanabe would put in a word for me. But the reality of approaching the top table to ask for a signature was a bit too risky for fear of offending anyone and causing myself abject embarrassment. I turned my attentions to the task in hand in preparation for the pending next round of my contest.

I lined up at my designated area. I was the only non-Japanese remaining in the tournament, Oshima and Kishiyama were also on my area so it was likely I would face one of these should I advance through the next round. Another area of eight competitors in the same category was already under way. If I won this area I was to be in the final against the winner of the other mat.

TWENTY-EIGHT

A couple of fights went before me and then I was called forward. I felt confident and, in a way, I was glad I was facing someone unfamiliar so that I was not influenced by previous encounters. The opponent opposite me stood calmly and I knew he would be no mug for he too had come through a few rounds successfully. The referee got us under way and I bolted forward but with a modicum of reserve. I wanted to show I was up to the job without being reckless. This opponent was different than I had faced before on the previous day. He was not attacking immediately but waited patiently to see what I was up to. He seemed confident but without the attitude of superiority which can sometimes wind me up. I put together an attack that began with a front leg roundhouse to the face but my opponent simply backed away. This gave me no chance to follow up when I had anticipated him to try and jump in on me. This opponent was in no hurry and almost invited me to attack again. I began to get impatient. I could never bounce around for ever waiting for an opponent to come to me if he didn't show willing so I closed him down some more and launched a one two punch that although missed prompted a follow up front kick to the body. It found its mark and I was a point up. My opponent remained calm but I was eager to press my advantage. I expected a sudden attack but it didn't come. However, I didn't want to sit on my flimsy one-point score. I feinted to attack again and my opponent was ready and waiting, but I was confident I was the quicker. As I set up to close him down, he stepped in perfectly and caught me with a reverse punch to the body. I tried to ignore the technique and carried on to crack him one but he backed away in double quick time and the referee stopped the fight to score the point. It was still early in the fight and I knew I could pull this back but I also knew this adversary was very cagey and didn't really want to scrap. Therefore, I did not want it to go to extra time where there was little chance of forcing a point from a keen counter puncher. I pressed again, but again he waited. I feinted, I shouted, I brought up a leg to tempt him to respond but he waited. I then instinctively rushed in with another front hand attack to see what I could create and he nailed me with another body punch. He scored and I was furious. I sprinted off my line to get stuck in but he was away. I tried to corner him but he stepped out of the area. He was warned but time was now on his side. Again, he backed away at the re-start of the match and again I chased him around the area. I was desperate to get a fight out of him but it wasn't to be. Time was called and the one opponent I didn't expect in the All-Japan Championships was nothing like I had fought with all year.

I was out. I didn't even feel I had been in anything near a fight. I walked away from the area in disgust, with myself and with my opponent for running around like a member of the All Japan Track and Field Team.

I watched with little interest as Oshima cleaned up on the area and made it through to the final where he too was to come second best. Takahashi was second in the kata final but Nihon University Old Boys won the senior team event and my fellow students won the university section. For them I was pleased because they had also suffered recent setbacks but now had bounced back with this victory. I knew then that I could too. The day finished with presentations for the winners and my disappointment had faded somewhat, so I celebrated with the team their success.

There was a party for the club back at our dormitory on our return from the contest. Not the grandest of settings but a fitting one considering many of the old boys were present to toast the success of their juniors. The dining room was packed with around forty men of all ages, and the tables were filled with bottles of beer. There were one or two speeches followed by the Nichi Dai song led by young Kenji whose rendition clearly inspired those who had long ago left this humble abode. The stark surroundings of that simple kitchen diner was indeed an appropriate backdrop for the seniors who sang heartily from memory and with a sense nostalgia, relaxing their senior attitude somewhat by putting their arms around the nearest student. I looked around at Hideo Tanabe, Kobayashi, Shiomitsu, Furukawa and many other senior instructors who had from time to time graced our dojo and felt I had an invite to the best party in the world.

Over the next two days I saw many of my fellow students leave for their festive breaks. In drips and drabs, they came in to say farewell promising to write, phone and visit England one day. Some of them simply shook hands while others were a little more forthcoming with some backslapping and hugs. There remained about five students who for various reasons were staying put over the holiday period. Among them two of my closest friends, Kikuta, and Fujimoto, who both lived too far away to be going home for less than a week's break.

On Christmas Eve, the day before I departed, there was an impromptu meal and drinks for my benefit. Some hot plates were set up on the tables and more beers were brought in plus some sake. Unlike the warm environment of a few nights earlier there were only a few of us sat around the tables and only the warmth of the hot plates and the sukiyaki meal that the boys prepared kept us from freezing. There was a light-hearted, relaxed atmosphere throughout the evening, which enabled even the most junior of students to enjoy themselves, considering Tanabe and Shiomitsu were both present. I sat and soaked up the jokes and banter between the two senior instructors who delighted in ribbing each other as well as us youngsters.

This final evening as the cold beers were sunk and the hot food cooled inside us, we wrapped up in coats and tracksuits to finish off with a few photos. Tanabe, ever the photogenic, posed seriously with a katana half drawn, not realising the absurdity of his presence between old dining tables filled with dirty dishes.

It was the perfect time to thank the two people who had allowed me to fulfil an ambition that had become an obsession. Shiomitsu's faith in me had resulted in Tanabe taking me on board and I felt even then the influence of those months in Nihon University would surely remain with me for a lifetime.

Kobayashi finally turned up to have a late beer but it was only a swift one for he reminded me we had to be up early the next day. I said my goodbyes to those around me for it was well past midnight and they would probably not be around at six the next morning. Only Fujimoto said that he would be up to come to the airport.

The alarm next morning woke me from my dreams of returning home. Then the reality sunk in. It was Christmas day and considering the time difference of the two nations I figured I would be home for lunch. I was already up when Kobayashi appeared at the doorway with Fujimoto stood next to him and they both grabbed a case and a bag between them. As I passed Tanabe's room his door flung open and he came out to put his hand on my shoulder just like his brother often did, said nothing, and waved me away. As we crept quietly to the stairs there was a rush of movement from behind me and the remaining students shuffled into their slippers and pushed past us on the stairs. When I stepped out on to the street Kikuta, Ikeda, Fujimoto, and a couple of others lined up. I thought for a moment they were going to start stretching before an impromptu early morning run. They turned as I looked and they bowed, "Aasa, sayonara! Ganbatte!" 'Goodbye, good luck' they chided together. I bowed back "mata ne!" see you again, I replied.

The Japanese people revolve much of their lives around the four seasons. I had passed through those four different times in the year of '81 and I now have a memory for every emotion that comes with them. I sat as I had often done in the passenger seat of Kobayashi

Sensei's little car as we drove to the airport and I knew there was to be one more person to thank big time for allowing me not only into his way of life but into his life as a Karate instructor that had no ambition other than to see his family grow up and his students succeed.

I left behind me an institution. Twenty-five years on and the old dormitory would no longer be stood grey and ageing at the edge of the road. Nor for that matter would the same personnel be involved in the running of the brand-new complex that now stands in its place, but for me Nihon University would never be any different.

Tanabe Sensei Shiomitsu Sensei toast my return home